Modeling a New Framework for Managing Healthcare Organizations

Modeling a New Computer Framework for Managing Healthcare Organizations

Balancing and Optimizing Patient Satisfaction, Owner Satisfaction, and Medical Resources

Soraia Oueida

Routledge
Taylor & Francis Group

A PRODUCTIVITY PRESS BOOK

First published 2021
by Routledge
52 Vanderbilt Avenue, New York, NY 10017
and by Routledge
2 Park Square, Milton Park, Abingdon, Oxon, OX14 4RN

Routledge is an imprint of the Taylor & Francis Group, an informa business

© 2021 Taylor & Francis

Library of Congress Cataloging-in-Publication Data
A catalog record for this title has been requested

ISBN: 978-0-367-46268-0 (hbk)
ISBN: 978-0-367-46060-0 (pbk)
ISBN: 978-1-003-02783-6 (ebk)

Typeset in Garamond
by Deanta Global Publishing Services, Chennai, India

Contents

List of Figures

List of Tables

Objectives

The purpose of this work is to improve the management techniques of medical units and increase the overall satisfaction of the system: of patients, owners, and medical resources. Hence, the main objective is to develop a computer platform package for the management of medical organizations. The package optimizes the resource allocation of a healthcare industrial system that includes a new proposed optimization algorithm called MRA and a reward system to balance between three factors: patient satisfaction, owner satisfaction, and medical resources satisfaction. Satisfaction is defined as the state of reaching the local minima of an error concerning a certain issue. For owners, the issue is the revenue, for employees the issue is the workload versus the payment, and for patients the issue is the quality of service and the LoS. A new platform is developed for hospital management with a user-friendly interface and English-like proposed programming language along with a visual and easy way to collect and understand statistical outputs. The platform engine is based on a proposed extension of Petri net called RPN. The net is sound and guarantees the preservation of resources. It supports cooperation and scalability. It follows the optimization algorithm and reward system defined. The purpose of this work, its main and derived objectives are listed in Table 1.

Table 1 Purpose and Objectives

PURPOSE	
Improve management techniques of medical units and increase overall satisfaction	
MAIN OBJECTIVE	
Develop a computer platform package for the management of medical organizations	
DERIVED OBJECTIVES	**CHAPTERS**
Study of the healthcare system	Ch. 1
Study of the medical process and general satisfaction	Ch. 2
Simulation of the process	Ch. 3
Mathematical model and system validation	Ch. 4
Process optimization	Ch. 5
Creating the computer platform and platform testing the socio-economic benefits of the platform created	Ch. 6

Acknowledgments

As the first supporter of my research throughout the three years of my doctoral studies, I acknowledge Prof. S. Ionescu, my supervisor, for his continuous mentoring and express my sincere gratitude for his patience, motivation, immense knowledge, and valuable guidance. I would like also to thank all committee members: Prof. Gheorghe Militaru, Prof. Florin Dănălache, and Dr. Bogdan Fleacă, for their ongoing encouragement and inspiring comments. Besides my supervisor and committee members, my sincere thanks also go to Dr. Y. Kotb and Dr. S. Kadry who provided me an opportunity to benefit from their extensive knowledge and research skills which added considerably to my journey. Without their precious encouragement it would not have been possible to conduct this research. I would like to thank all the hospital emergency department members who supported me during the data collection phase and site observations. A special thanks to all who participated in the survey and who supported my work in order to get results of better quality. Finally, big thanks goes to the hospital general manager Mr. A. Assoum who showed appreciation and provided support during my project. Last but not least, I dedicate this work to my parents who I am sure are very proud of my achievement. Thank you for all the care and love you raised me on. With the strength you gave me throughout my life I could chase my dreams. To my husband and kids and some special friends and family members, thank you for your understanding and help in many, many moments of crisis and sleepless nights. This is only the beginning!

Acronyms

The list of abbreviations used in this work is listed below.
Agent Based Model (ABM)
Clinical Decision Unit (CDU)
Discrete Event Simulation (DES)
Emergency Department Information System (EDIS)
Emergency Department Over Crowding Scale (EDOCS)
Emergency Department Work Index Score (EDWIN)
Emergency Department (ED)
Electrocardiogram (ECG)
Emergency Nurse Practitioner (ENP)
Emergency Room (ER)
Emergency Radiology Unit (ERU)
General Practitioner (GP)
Health Information Technology (HIU)
Holding Unit (HU)
Information Technology (IT)
Internet of Things (IoT)
Integrated System (IS)
Key Performance Indicators (KPI)
Kolmogrov Smirnov (KS)
Length of Stay (LoS)
Maximum Reward Algorithm (MRA)
Magnetic Resonance Imaging (MRI)
Monte Carlo Simulation (MCS)
National Emergency Department Overcrowding Score (NEDOCS)
National Health Service (NHS)
Nurse Practitioner (NP)
Pediatric Emergency Department (PED)
Petri Net (PN)
Resource Preservation Net (RPN)
Registered Nurse (RN)
Radiology Unit (RU)
Real-time Emergency Analysis of Demand Indicators (READI)
System Dynamics (SD)

Definitions

Emergency Departments: The emergency department is the busiest unit in a hospital. It is considered very complex and critical. It is a 24-hour operating department, every day of the week. EDs interact with most of the other units in the hospital such as surgery, laboratory, imaging, etc.

Cooperative Systems: The cooperative system shows the difference between the cooperation of medical resources only or the cooperation of medical resources and other units (such as radiology and billing).

Non-Cooperative Systems: The non-cooperative system means that ERs are proven to be sound and working smoothly without any interaction between one another and with no cooperation between medical resources or any other unit.

Optimization: Optimization is the fact of applying enhancements on a system in order to improve the main performance measures.

Petri Net: Petri net is a mathematical concept developed in 1962 by Carl Adam Petri in order to describe a system or a process. It is designed to reflect the different states of a system. With Petri net, the dynamic behavior of these complex and concurrent systems can be easily described based on theoretical concepts and properties of such systems.

Satisfaction: Satisfaction is defined as the state of reaching the local minima of an error concerning a certain issue.

Scalability: Scalability of the framework falls under the soundness and efficiency of the general framework regardless of the number of cooperating units added to the system. It is a design quality measure of the framework.

Separability: Separability is viewing the system as a parallel system where the system is replicated as many times as the number of tokens available and every workflow instance is fully dedicated to one token.

Serializability: Serializability is viewing the system as a sequential system where tokens are executed one after another and the successful execution of one token will not cause the failure of another one.

Soundness: For a workflow to be sound, all input tokens to this workflow will eventually reach the output. In other words, there exist a minimum number of transitions that are live to guarantee that all tokens will reach the output. Therefore, the output is reachable from the input.

Workflow: Workflow is the sequence of industrial, administrative, or other processes through which a piece of work passes from initiation to completion.

Introduction

"The medical sector has been growing significantly over the past decade and healthcare services have become more complex and costly, amplified by a poor healthcare delivery system. Healthcare is a highly interconnected dynamic environment where individuals and teams contribute in order to serve patients' demands. The main focus of this work is to provide a platform to improve this revolution by taking care of the whole medical community, not just of illness but also improving patient safety, quality, and effectiveness of the healthcare system. This can be achieved by developing new methodologies in order to improve the healthcare systems available nowadays. The first area to focus on in order to develop an efficient and effective healthcare system is developing a system's perspective, where simulation modeling can be generated and a review can be achieved, thus, leading to a more effective and efficient structure. Simulation modeling can be a solution to tackle this complexity and valuable in providing predictions to forecast the outcome of a change in strategies or policies. The computer simulation is a decision-making technique that allows management to conduct experiments with models representing the real system of interest. Busy and complex healthcare systems provide big challenges to managers and decision-makers who should be able to serve the high demands under the constraints of limited budgets and the high costs of healthcare services. The highest number of patients should be cared for within a limited period of time in order to ensure patient satisfaction (reduce waiting times and increase the quality of care) and increase the hospital revenue (reduce cost). The delivery of healthcare quality can vary depending on patients' conditions, affecting the recommended care and leading, sometimes, to urgent and critical health conditions. This huge variation opens up the importance of reviewing healthcare systems' problems and improving them where some solutions are suggested" [Oueida et al. (2017a)].

This dissatisfaction with healthcare services can be a result of five major components as per the literature review presented: Timeliness of Care, Quality of Care, Errors in Care Delivery, Complexity of healthcare system, and Cost effectiveness of care [Akshay et al. (2012)]. "Industrial systems are usually composed of business processes that always compete for resources" [Zeng et al. (2012)]. "The complexity and dynamic behavior of these business processes along with the unpredictability nature require workflow systems to control the flow of work and guarantee an effective allocation of these resources" [Oueida et al. (2018a)]. A model that controls the workflow process and maintains synchronization among activities using Petri net is presented in Buckley et al. (2010). A Petri net can be used to define the flow of work and the routing possibilities. Transitions are used to model tasks. Places and arcs are used to model dependencies [Eitel et al. (2010)]. The aim of modeling a workflow using a Petri net is to solve the problem of system complexity counting on the characteristics of the Petri net: safety and soundness. These models are called workflow nets [Zeng et al. (2012)]. The majority of workflow systems suffer from some critical sections, which refers to some tasks that cannot be executed by one activity at a time. Therefore, these systems need to be handled with care in order to maintain these critical sections and guarantee the property of soundness of the system. As per the literature on workflow nets, a framework was suggested by Baldwin et al. (2004), in order to handle critical sections and evaluate the cost of executing an activity, which is a very hard and complex process due to dependencies of tasks.

A hospital, as one major and top-level healthcare system that must be examined, can be divided into different departments. These departments interact with each other and share a variety of professional resources (Doctors, Nurses, Staff, etc.). This crossover leads to a very complex and sensitive system that has to be handled with care and for which a study of all problems needs to be conducted. The emergency department (ED), being the busiest unit in a hospital, is considered very complex and critical. It is a department operating 24 hours a day, every day of the week, and should be equipped and staffed wisely in order to deal with all kind of emergencies. EDs interact with most of the other units in the hospital such as surgery, laboratory, imaging, and the like and therefore is chosen to be studied for enhancements. EDs are nowadays facing several problems that affect their daily medical service and operation. The main common issue is the overcrowding that results in long patient waiting times and long length of stay (LoS), therefore leading to patient dissatisfaction [Buckley et al. (2010)]. A possible solution to this problem can be by increasing the ED capacity and providing extra facilities/manpower. Nevertheless, this is not always an achievable solution because of the huge extra costs and budget constraints [Soremekun et al. (2011)]. Nowadays, addressing the problems of EDs relies on improving the processes of the ED, always taking into consideration the extra costs, patient safety/satisfaction, and the LoS [Holden (2011)]. Patient satisfaction can be classified under several metrics during the patient's journey through the ED [Thiedke (2007)].

In this work, the different parameters that may affect or improve patient satisfaction are presented. Moreover, a survey is conducted in the studied ED in order to discover the exact metrics affecting a patient's experience. In recent years, the efficiency of using computer simulation to express ED processes has been proven. It presents a realistic view of the system, dynamically analyzes situations, and accordingly suggests improvements to the operations [Baldwin et al. (2004)]. The main purpose of using these simulations in healthcare is to alleviate the overcrowding problem by decreasing the length of stay (LoS) and patient waiting times, to better use the available resources, and to reduce any waste or excessive costs [Alvarez and Centeno (1999)]. Discrete Event Simulation (DES) is considered the most used method and the alternative that involves less time/cost while simulating EDs [Villamizar et al. (2011)]. The purpose of this work is to study the different problems affecting the ED as presented in Chapter 1 and implement a flexible effective platform to reduce these problems, and increase patient/owner satisfaction. A SWOT analysis is presented to study the available strengths and weaknesses and analyze possible reasons for the arising problems in order to design a future plan to prevent them. Chapter 1 also includes an overview of the National Health System, emergency department problems, and simulation packages. The studied ED in this work is an emergency department located in the Middle East and is divided into two emergency rooms to serve patients coming from public and private sectors. A major challenge in healthcare is to ensure and maintain a high level of satisfaction. A survey is conducted and presented in Chapter 2 to study patient satisfaction levels and analyze available problems. This chapter also covers the literature review on healthcare, confronting problems and possible solutions. A realistic ED model is designed using the Arena Rockwell tool in Chapter 3 in order to study the patient flow and system problems. The ED is simulated during normal flow and catastrophic events where new resource allocations are suggested for better system performance. The studied ED is an emergency department having two separate emergency rooms offering public (ER A) and private services (ER B). Some specific facilities such as radiology and billing are shared between both emergency rooms. The model was built based on continuous visits to the ED and based on interviews conducted with medical staff, patients, and decision-makers. Verification and validation are then applied, where the designed model is compared and matched with the real system under study. In order to measure the level of crowding in the system and identify the bottleneck stages before starting the enhancement procedure, an indexing score called NEDOCS is used. Also in Chapter 3, the ED of the chosen hospital is simulated using a new proposed extended Petri net model. This extension model can be applied to any queuing system such as hospitals, restaurants, theaters, etc. This model is named RPN (Resource Preservation Net) where the main medical resources are non-consumable, siphons are controlled, and all resources return to their pools after accomplishing a certain task. Internal processes are simulated, such as registration, triage, examination, etc. along with external relations with other units of the hospital (such as radiology and billing).

The main objective of this study is to address the problem of long waiting times that patients face during their visits to the ED and to improve these processes, always maintaining patient satisfaction, patient safety and hospital's owner satisfaction. This proposed model is then proven to be sound mathematically. Therefore, a mathematical model is presented, and a few theorems/lemmas are defined for the first time in this work in order to prove the soundness of the Petri net model proposed, either for cooperative or non-cooperative industrial systems. The mathematical proofs and RPN model validation are presented in Chapter 4. All mathematical notations used are presented in Appendix A. The non-cooperative system means that ER A and ER B are proven to be sound and working smoothly without any interaction between each other and with no cooperation between medical resources or any other unit. The cooperative system shows the difference between the cooperation of medical resources only or the cooperation of medical resources and other units (such as radiology and billing). Scalability of the workflow is proven mathematically to remain sound, where many ERs or, more generally, any unit, can be added to the main system in order to improve the operation of the organization, while maintaining a sound cooperation among all units. These mathematical suggestions are presented using different theorems that can be applicable to any type of organization and specifically to any type of emergency department in a healthcare system. This mathematical model is then applied to healthcare in order to study the efficiency of each Emergency Room (ER A and ER B) operating separately and always maintaining the soundness of the system regardless of the contribution of the two ERs and the sharing of resources with the two external units: radiology and billing [Kotb and Baumgart (2005)]. The designed model is verified to be working properly and then validated. All performance measures are compared with the real system behavior and the model is found to be reliable.

Then, in Chapter 5 experimentation is performed where improvement is suggested. Using the Arena OptQuest tool, which is a stochastic program, simulation optimization is performed; where the optimal average LoS is analyzed as a function of the staffing level. Ten different best solutions are suggested where the optimal solution is based on an optimal staff distribution. Following this distribution, it is proven that decision-makers can efficiently enhance the system by getting a higher number of patients receiving care and a lower patient waiting time. Cost analysis is applied to all phases of experimentation in order to guarantee both patient and owner satisfaction. A participation certificate was granted from the hospital management during the phase of building the model, verifying, validating, and performing optimization on the studied ED. Improvement techniques are also presented in this chapter, such as Six Sigma and Internet of Things, which are also studied in order to propose some enhancements to the ED system, guarantee a smooth flow of patients, and eliminate wastes/bottlenecks. In Chapter 5, as part of optimization as well, the same ED is enhanced by applying a new proposed reward system and a new optimization algorithm called MRA. This reward system is generic and proposed for the first time in this work. It focuses on calculating the reward level of the ED and thus provides an insight into the problems and the bottleneck areas to be improved. It is based on balancing between three satisfaction factors: Patient, Owner, and Resources. This algorithm, called the Maximum Reward Algorithm, is also generic and is applied to the studied ED during normal flow and catastrophic events. Finally, a new platform is designed in order to provide the hospital and especially the ED with a suitable, efficient, and user-friendly software. The platform is named AMS and is presented in Chapter 6. All of the stated work above is integrated in this new platform. The software helps decision-makers with proposing the best resource allocation for the best flow of patients and improving performance metrics during normal flow and catastrophic events. Similar platforms are available in the market but do not provide, as one package, a new proposed optimization algorithm based on three satisfaction factors: patient, owner, and resources integrated with Petri net concepts where the soundness and continuity of flow are ensured. This newly proposed platform provides the user with a friendly program to load the input data collected from databases and site visits. The user-friendly interface is based on English statements and keywords only, which is a new proposed healthcare language to be used for any department in the hospital and mostly in EDs. The language primitives used in order to input data into the software are available in Appendix B. Certificates from different hospitals are granted, showing the flexibility and efficiency of the platform developed—AMS—in managing an emergency department and optimizing its activities. The socio-economic benefits of AMS are also discussed in Chapter 6 in order to prove the efficiency and reliability of this platform.

This work is organized as follows: Chapter 1 presents an introduction of healthcare systems where the objectives of choosing the emergency department as the studied industrial system along with the problems and solutions are illustrated. In Chapter 2 a literature review is presented. Chapter 3 is dedicated to defining the hospital model where simulation with Arena is presented and a new extended Petri net model is defined. Chapter 4 presents the mathematical model that proves the validity and soundness of the proposed extended Petri net model. Chapter 5 presents the optimization phase of the proposed model where a reward system and a new optimization algorithm are defined. Chapter 6 discusses the designed software and presents a guide for usage along with some simulation and optimization statistics. The social and economic benefits of the proposed platform are also illustrated in Chapter 6. Finally, Chapter 7 concludes the report and demonstrates the results and outcomes of the whole project. Appendices can be found at the end in order to support all the work done.

Chapter 1

The Healthcare System

This chapter is dedicated to describing the interaction of different units in the healthcare system and highlighting the background of the problems that hospitals and emergency departments in particular are facing nowadays, along with some possible solutions.

1.1 Structure of a Hospital

A hospital, as a major and top-level healthcare system, can be divided into different departments. These departments interact with each other and share a variety of professional resources (doctors, nurses, staff, etc.). This crossover leads to a very complex and sensitive system that has to be handled with care and for which a study of all its problems needs to be conducted. The main departments and units in the hospital are listed as follows:

- Emergency Department
- Anesthetics Unit
- Intensive Care Unit (ICU)
- General Surgery Department
- Cardiology Unit
- Radiology Unit
- ENT Department
- Genecology/Maternity Department
- Pediatric Department
- Laboratory Unit
- Hematology Unit
- Microbiology Unit
- Neonatal Unit
- Nephrology Unit
- Neurology Unit
- Oncology Unit

- Ophthalmology Unit
- Orthopedics Department
- Physiotherapy Unit
- Dentistry Unit
- Dermatology Unit
- Gastroenterology Unit
- Nutrition Department
- Pharmacy
- Admission and Discharge Department

"As a conclusion, Figure 1.1 shows the interaction between the different departments of the healthcare system. It is clear that the emergency department is the most interacting and complex unit. A patient arriving to the ED may be transferred to any other unit of the hospital depending on the diagnosis" [(Oueida et al. 2017a)]. Therefore, the most complex and interacting department of the healthcare system, the emergency department (ED) is chosen to be studied for this work.

	ED	Anesthetics	ICU	Surgery	Cardiology	Radiology	ENT	Genecology/Maternity	Pediatric	Laboratory	Hematology	Microbiology	Neonatal	Nephrology	Neurology	Oncology	Ophthalmology	Orthopedics	Physiotherapy	Dentistry	Dermatology	Gastroenterology	Nutrition	Pharmacy	Admission & Discharge
ED		x	x	x	x	x	x	x	x	x	x	x	x	x	x	x	x	x	x	x	x	x	x	x	x
Anesthetics	X		x	x																					
ICU	X	x		x						x														x	x
Surgery	X	x				x				x								x							x
Cardiology	X		x				x			x														x	x
Radiology	X																						x		
ENT	X			x		x				x														x	x
Genecology/Maternity	X									x							x							x	x
Pediatric	X									x													x		
Laboratory	X																								
Hematology	X									x													x		
Microbiology	X			x						x															
Neonatal	X					x				x														x	x
Nephrology	X			x						x														x	x
Neurology	X		x	x		x				x														x	x
Oncology	X			x		x				x														x	x
Ophthalmology	X			x																				x	x
Orthopedics	X			x															x					x	x
Physiotherapy	X			x																			x		
Dentistry	X																						x		
Dermatology	X																						x		
Gastroenterology	X					x				x															
Nutrition	X																								
Pharmacy	X																								x
Admission & Discharge	X		x																						

Figure 1.1   Interacting departments [Oueida et al. (2017a, b)].

1.2 Healthcare System Problems

Healthcare problems are very important and a priority concern that we face in our lives today. The five major components that are badly impacting the healthcare system can be highlighted as follows:

1. "Timeliness of Care: One of the dissatisfactions among patients is the waiting time which can be in some cases unpredictable, affecting the healthcare provided to these patients. This factor can hugely affect the effectiveness of healthcare delivery, where patients waiting in the queue can be in contact with other infections and environmental factors which may complicate their condition. This delay will definitely reduce the effectiveness of medical treatment. In order to avoid this kind of dissatisfaction, care providers should achieve a stable and predictable timetable workload, like at call centers, in order to avoid the waiting times and provide a consistent quality of service. Research shows that, over the last 60 years [Akshay et al. (2012)], simulation modeling has been the key factor for clinics and other medical industries to appropriately allocate resources and predict patient flow, thus maximizing utilization, providing best service and achieving patient satisfaction.

2. Quality of Care: In the health field, the quality of care falls under patient satisfaction as service and fee; thus, some complications can arise in delivering the quality of care desired. In order to represent and solve this problem, simulation modeling can be counted on, where an understandable and desirable outcome can be reached.

3. Errors in Care Delivery: Research has shown that death due to medical errors exceeds death due to real diseases or human accidents. The main problem causing these errors is the unstable structure of the healthcare service or the non-existence approach of healthcare delivery. In other words, death cannot be caused by one single medical mistake, but is the consequence of the reaction to this mistake as a complete healthcare system. Thus, fatal errors are generated by faulty systems that prevent healthcare providers from avoiding them. In order to fix these errors, systematic analysis of the major causes must be conducted; otherwise, complications may arise. To analyze the system and prevent errors, simulation modeling can play a major role nowadays, where the behavior of systems can be easily interpreted and investigated using the advanced features in different simulation languages.

4. Complexity in Healthcare Delivery: Breaking down a complex problem into several simpler steps makes it easier for it to be solved. Thus, in healthcare, using checklists to reduce the system complexity leads to efficient outcomes. These checklists can be formulated and tested using simulation.

5. Value of Healthcare Services: The value of healthcare service can be expressed by the amount of money spent by the patient versus the amount or quality of care received. But since the quality of healthcare service is variable and depends on different factors (like a patient's age, a patient's personal point of view for care), the above-mentioned formula seems ambiguous. Simulation modeling has to be integrated in the development of these processes where employees/managers get to understand the dynamics of any changes made and to put in place effective change management policies. With the increasing trend of the healthcare field adopting lean and Six Sigma culture to standardize healthcare quality, adoption of simulation modeling methodology is also going to increase [Young et al. (2004)]" [Oueida et al. (2016)].

"Healthcare Asset Allocation is the core of good management strategies. Healthcare and hospitals should stay in line with the technological developments; therefore, simulation tools are very efficient in order to stay up to date and forecast any unpredictable assumptions:

- Bed Sizing and Planning: Bed availability is the key factor affecting a healthcare system since it should be always available to serve patients' needs especially in primary care units like ICU. On the other hand, excess capacity will mean resource underutilization and extra maintenance costs, which is not a suitable solution. Therefore, simulation models should be developed and optimized to solve these problems.
- Room Sizing and Planning: Problems of room sizing and planning are related to facility design. Hospitals have to upgrade their facilities to match demand and this brings up a range of problems which can be addressed using simulation.
- Staff Sizing and Planning: For a hospital to operate effectively and efficiently, quality of service should be taken into consideration. This can be achieved by allocating the required size of resources. Simulation models should estimate and plan staff sizing in order to ensure good facility utilization.
- Health Policy Simulations: Healthcare is a variable science since it is based on different physicians' experience and concrete observations. So, one patient can go through several treatment paths under different doctors. Simulation tools should be the solution to decision-making and improving the quality of treatment. Healthcare policy simulations are also used in public health preparedness problems which deal with infectious disease outbreaks and public health response system preparation. Ambulance diversions are another class of problems investigated by healthcare simulation models. Simulation models should evaluate ambulance diversion direct impact on EDs. The criteria under evaluation are mean waiting time and percentage of ambulances diverted.
- Multi-Facility Simulation Models: Improving the functionality of one department in a hospital may increase patient dissatisfaction in another department or affect other departments' scheduling. Doctors are shared across different departments, therefore any changes performed for one department will definitely affect their work in other departments. These complex relationships existing between multiple facilities in one healthcare environment should be highly considered and highlighted, otherwise, the overall system will be affected, which is the highest reason for the low implementation of healthcare simulation models" [Oueida et al. (2016)].

"As ED is the most complex entity of the healthcare system, the most overcrowded unit and the focus of this study, Table 1.1 presents a list of some problems that may affect the ED and some proposed solutions, which researchers should approach in order to alleviate the risk. These problems/solutions will be further elaborated in Chapter 2. Note that the majority of the problems can also lead to the same patient dissatisfaction factor, i.e., long waiting times" [Oueida et al. (2017a)].

"Healthcare is one of the essential entities of a society. Through its medical services, it provides prevention, treatment, and management of illness. Nowadays, the challenges healthcare is facing are receiving much attention through the media and politics. These challenges, such as staffing shortages [Lake et al. (2010); Association et al. (2001)], aging population [Hellmich (2008)], rising costs [Bodenheimer (2005)], and inefficient hospital processes [Berwick and Hackbarth (2012)], urge the need for review and reform of healthcare practices. The Emergency Department studied in this work currently suffers from patient flow delays caused by insufficient resources (equipment and manpower), absence of computer technology, and the existence of many insurance categories

Table 1.1 Some ED Overcrowding Problems and Solutions

Problems	Bed shortage	Admission issues	Resource shortage (doctors, nurses, etc.)	Long waiting times	Admission and discharge process	Laboratory and radiology	Capacity	Different insurance coverage
Solution 1	Add extra beds	Predict stain situations	Add resources	Introduce the Triage Category System	Add discharge lounges	Add resources in these units	Hospital physical structure change	Improve payment services
Solution 2	Apply the rule of patient early discharge	Forecast disaster conditions and peak times	Change staffing schedules and shifts	Introduce the fast-track system	Add extra administrative staff	Add extra equipment for X-ray, CT Scan, MRI, etc.		Introduce tax deduction by law to push families to purchase private health insurance
Solution 3	ED re-engineering (such as adding additional units, etc.)	Increase bed capacity	Increase resource utilization	Add physicians	Hospital physical structure change	Add rooms for extra capacity for these facilities		Limitation of insurance plan to emergency situations
Solution 4	Introduce new operational rules	Consider hospital specialization	Assign part-time job resources for low-acuity patients	Assign the appropriate resource to the right patient				
Solution 5		Add observation units	Add after-hours GPs/ENPs for low severity cases	Apply the 4-hours rule				

Source: Oueida et al. (2017a,b).

Note: Table adapted from *Handbook of Research on Data Science for Effective Healthcare Practice and Administration*, p. 94 and the *International Journal of Public Health Management and Ethics.*, p. 58.

which resulted in a loss of potential revenue (patient leaving before being treated) and overcrowding (high length of stay), and affected patient's safety. These challenges are studied by collecting real data to be analyzed, conducting interviews with staff and patients in order to establish a comprehensive understanding of the ED studied. The designed model is strengthened through verification and validation using the data collected. Operations and patient flow improvement are then achieved by simulation experimentation. In order to provide a high level of service to its clients, improvement efforts on quality and safety of care are undertaken. Resource flow and allocation are identified for better performance of processes. Because of the numerous ED processes and varying acuity level of patients, the analysis of flow and the tracking of resource allocation is a challenging task. To combat these challenges, simulation modeling is used for this study.

With simulation, real-life process can be modeled and used to detect the flow of entities (resources and patients) through the system. Without interruption of the real system (ED) or any physical resource commitment, changes can be applied to any process and effects can be detected. This form of evaluation made the simulation an effective tool for many healthcare institutions. Constraints, bottlenecks, and inefficiencies can be identified and combated using the simulation model which can result in saving time and money and improving the quality of care" [Oueida et al. (2017c)]. Patient flow data is collected and analyzed along with interviews conducted with staff and patients. Then, through observations, potential improvements are identified in the ED. After understanding the flow in the real system, the model is built and tested in order to ensure it runs correctly and matches the real system. This process is performed through verification by debugging the model and checking that it runs as intended. After verification, validation is needed in order to ensure that the designed model behaves exactly as the real-life ED. After model verification and validation, experiments should be performed on the model in order to identify possible bottlenecks and constraints within the designed system. The selected performance measure of patient flow can be greatly affected by different parameters and structural assumptions. Therefore, input parameters are grouped and production runs are conducted in order to observe the effects of these groups on patient flow. The data analysis clarifies the ED's operations and helps in identifying potential areas for improvement.

Some recommendations can be proposed since patient flow varies throughout the week, such as referring to patient arrival distribution when creating staff schedules. Therefore, in order to improve patient throughput, many simulation runs are conducted, where staff levels are continuously changed in order to find the optimal input combination that maximizes patient throughput. The concept of lean, being a system of techniques used in order to study the service operation of a running system, is based on the concept of using less to do more [Miller (2013)]. It is one way in which these challenges can be addressed, where useless entities can be disregarded, non-value-adding activities can be eliminated, and business waste can be removed. In healthcare, lean thinking principles can be applied in order to improve the patient waiting time, levels of staffing, and the quality of care which can greatly impact the health community.

"The studied hospital faces common issues in the healthcare industry. The major issues fall under staffing, scheduling, and inefficient operations. Furthermore, the hospital is constituted of two different emergency rooms sharing the same facilities, such as radiology and billing, which causes patient delay and staff to be overworked (high utilization rate). Another problem is the heterogeneity of insurance coverage types in the hospital. This issue forces the billing department to deal with different types of coverage companies in order to satisfy all levels of incoming patients. This billing unit is common for all departments and is busy all day long. Due to a hiring freeze and budget constraints, this hospital's ED is understaffed, which affects the ED staff performance and their utilization, leading to patient dissatisfaction and an increase in the length of stay (LoS) especially if a radiology facility is requested" [Oueida et al. (2017c)]. In order to provide a higher quality of care, the ED of the studied hospital is chosen for this work where the objectives are as follows:

- Data collection and analysis in order to define the current state of patient flow
- Current model verification and validation using simulation in order to ensure that the designed model represents the ED's current state
- Explore potential improvements to the ED by performing experimentation and running different scenarios

To summarize, this study emphasizes on proposing a realistic simulation model of an ED using Arena. The proposed model is based on the understanding and real functioning of this ED. Therefore, a field visit is performed where real data is collected, interviews with all ED resources are conducted and a clear view of the ED operations and services are set. These steps help in constructing the model and thus making the model look more realistic. Once the model is constructed and verified to be running without any limitations, validation is performed. With validation, outputs of the model are compared with data collected from the interviews (such as patient in, patient out, resource utilization, etc.). These two should be roughly identical in order to say that the model is realistic. Only then, experimentation can be performed and different scenarios for future improvements can be proposed. The proposed model is close to the real system and can be referred to and used by decision-makers in order to improve any problem faced. Moreover, the framework proposed can be easily updated and slight appropriate changes can be performed (such as changing input data, adding/removing one unit or adding extra resources) in order to be feasible and used for other emergency departments. A SWOT analysis for this studied ED is performed below in order to identify the main problems and support decision-makers with the right recommendations for better performance expectations.

1.2.1 SWOT Analysis

Before starting a simulation, a SWOT analysis is applied on the studied emergency department in order to identify the problems, characterize them, and analyze any available alternatives in the literature [Scotti and Pietrantonio (2013)]. The SWOT analysis is a study based on problem identification and characterization: internal strengths and weaknesses are identified, and external opportunities and threats are analyzed. When the goal is achieving objectives, the strengths are referred to as factors with positives effects, while weaknesses are referred to as factors with negative effects; whereas, opportunities are indirect or external positive goals influencing the objectives to be achieved, and threats are external conditions that may affect negatively the objectives. The SWOT analysis offers decision-makers the recommendations required to alleviate the problems that arise. The analysis will follow three steps as described below:

1. Problem Identification:
    As a first step, during the problem identification phase, it is worth mentioning that through site visits, observations, meetings with staff, and based on data collected, the main problem facing the studied ED is long waiting times leading to overcrowding and bottlenecks. The problem behind this bottleneck is acknowledged as the shortage in medical resources especially during the transportation phase where a patient is meant to be transferred to another unit inside the hospital either to be admitted or to receive extra services

(lab tests, radiology facilities, etc.). Another problem affecting waiting times is the lack of technology in the hospital where patients should go through the traditional data collection and billing stages (missing computerized databases). The hospital has a plan to computerize all units and make sure to link them together so patient data will be accessible from any unit of the hospital.

2. Problem Characterization:

   Large waiting times and ED crowding are major issues currently facing the majority of hospitals. The problem arises when there is a shortage of resources such as medical staff, beds, equipment, etc. and when the number of patients arriving exceeds the number expected, leading to unreasonable waiting times. Also, the use of the ED by low-acuity patients is considered a major contributing factor in overcrowding. The studied ED follows a triage phase for controlling the flow of low-acuity patients arriving in the ED.

3. Alternative Solutions in Literature:

   Many solutions were presented in literature to alleviate the major problem facing emergency departments, i.e., overcrowding. Factors affecting these problems and possible solutions are illustrated in Table 1.1 and are further elaborated in Chapter 2.

Through the literature and the focus of this study, the main solution is based on adding resources in order to overcome long waiting times and alleviate bottlenecks; therefore, the SWOT analysis shows the strengths and weaknesses along with the opportunities and threats of applying such a solution. Figure 1.2 illustrates the template used during the initial analysis of the ED structure.

As a conclusion, based on research and the SWOT analysis performed above, it is recommended that ED decision-makers consider increasing the amount of resources, especially in the highly overcrowded areas where the amount of medical resources is insufficient to deliver the necessary care within a reasonable waiting time. By considering this solution, waiting times can be decreased, thus affecting patient satisfaction, implicitly improving a hospital's reputation.

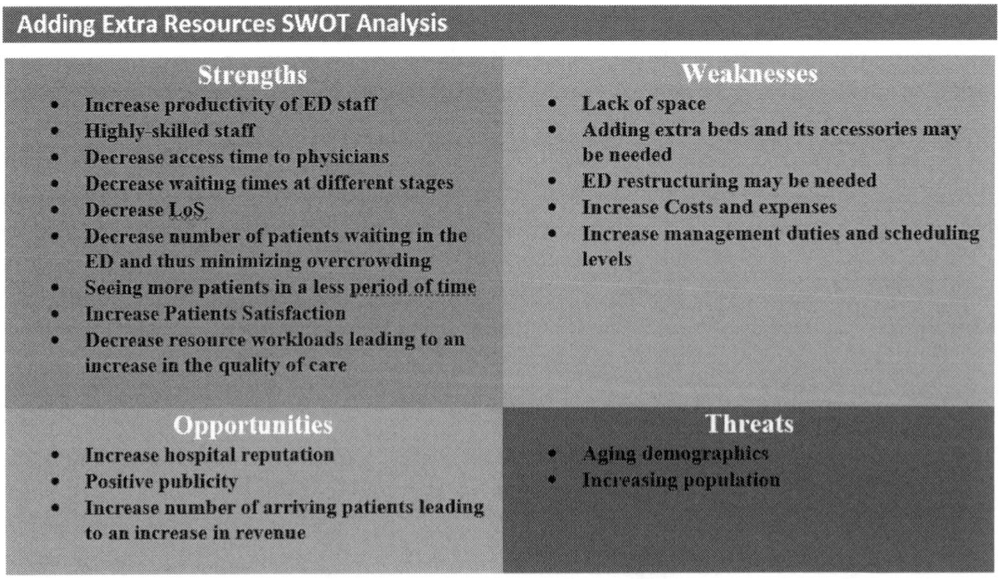

Adding Extra Resources SWOT Analysis

Strengths
- Increase productivity of ED staff
- Highly-skilled staff
- Decrease access time to physicians
- Decrease waiting times at different stages
- Decrease LoS
- Decrease number of patients waiting in the ED and thus minimizing overcrowding
- Seeing more patients in a less period of time
- Increase Patients Satisfaction
- Decrease resource workloads leading to an increase in the quality of care

Weaknesses
- Lack of space
- Adding extra beds and its accessories may be needed
- ED restructuring may be needed
- Increase Costs and expenses
- Increase management duties and scheduling levels

Opportunities
- Increase hospital reputation
- Positive publicity
- Increase number of arriving patients leading to an increase in revenue

Threats
- Aging demographics
- Increasing population

Figure 1.2   ED SWOT analysis.

1.3 Healthcare Simulation Packages

Three dynamic modeling paradigms can aid in the process of identifying complexity in a healthcare system: Discrete Event Simulation (DES), System Dynamics (SD), and Agent based model (ABM). Another simulation paradigm that serves the healthcare literature is the Monte Carlo Simulation (MCS). The main difference in the behavior of these dynamic modeling paradigms is that the first two (DES and SD) depend on the rules defined in the physical world and then the entities are modeled in the system based on these rules, while for the ABM, interaction between entities based on these defined rules is the key factor in order to develop the behavior of the system. We can classify the choice of simulation modeling paradigms based on the type of problem in the studied system. Since healthcare systems are very complex, a more developed and cost-effective simulation model should be integrated. This can be handled using object libraries and visualizations in order to handle the complexity with ease. Some popular simulation packages for healthcare systems are: Medmodel, Flexsim, Arena, and SIMIO.

Arena is a very user-friendly tool where a predictive modeling flowchart methodology can be designed in order to facilitate and quickly process a healthcare system. A common feature of Arena is the drag and drop elements and structures which allow the user to build simulations and visualize results. Moreover, model analysis is quick and easy with Arena's built-in dynamic dashboards where customized displays of the model information can be built to better understand the hospital processes and develop predictive analytics for operations. Arena users can use the basic modeling primitives included in the SIMAN blocks and elements library in order to create new modules. These modules can then be saved into templates (or libraries) and tailored to serve the project in study (i.e., healthcare modeling primitives such as doctors, nurses, beds, X-ray etc.). This mechanism provides the modeler with the ability to build a modeling system that is similar to the real system being modeled. The key factors for the success of the project are collecting accurate data and defining a realistic patient flow. From the user interface, the user can manipulate flows, delays, and patient routings. Also, the user can set resource schedules and bed capacity. Once all data inputs are set into the interface, multiple pages of output reports can be examined. For each scenario run, various key outputs can be recorded and analyzed. This analysis and comparison of scenarios lead to a thorough vision for taking correct decisions. The basic advantages of this software is: (1) process modeling for definition, documentation, and communication, (2) system simulation to understand the complex relationships and identify possible opportunities for future improvement, (3) operations visualization using the dynamic animation and graphics, (4) analyzing different scenarios to make the best decision. Models are defined in Arena to be the flowchart and data objects which define the process to be simulated. All information required to simulate a process is stored in the models. Entities are referred to as the customers being served or the patients being treated. Different type of entities can be included in one model.

Since emergency departments are unpredictable and at the frontline of healthcare service delivery, simulation is significantly needed to solve any problem that may arise. This service is time critical and death may result in the case of a non-effective system. ED departments base their challenges on resource levels and patient flow. Thus, many scenarios and experiments should be examined here in order to reduce harm and satisfy all sectors. Arena is thus an excellent simulation package used by many researchers to solve healthcare problems. The maximum capacity of the ED can be estimated, predicting patient waiting times. Based on simulation results, a study can be approached to predict the minimum number of resources required to serve maximum demand.

Chapter 2

Stages of Research on ED Management

This chapter is dedicated to highlighting the literature review on emergency department organizations and the study of satisfaction factors.

2.1 Literature Review on ED Organizations

"The healthcare is a very vast and complex system, where all departments interact with each other to offer care and service to patients. In this literature review, the ED is the focus of research, where complexity arises and prediction is highly needed. Improving EDs may lead to improving various services of the healthcare system and increasing revenue. The different problems studied by different researchers are presented along with some proposed solutions based on simulation modeling. At the end of this section Table 2.1 presents a summary on all papers studied in the literature along with the aim of the study, the results, and the simulation tool, if applicable.

An ED is the most complex unit of a hospital, where patients appear without any prior appointment, either by their own means or by ambulance. A patient suffering from an accident or a sudden injury, for example, will be directly addressed to the ED. Some of these patients may be critical cases and need immediate care, and others may need a simple treatment. Once arrived in the ED, a patient should be observed before being admitted to the hospital or referred to another unit, like imaging, laboratory, etc. This scenario leads to overcrowding at some peak times, causing a long waiting time, thus leading to dissatisfaction. There are several types of resource in an ED: staff (doctors, nurses, physicians, and technicians), static resources (triage rooms, examination rooms, x-ray room), and equipment. The process includes in general: arrival at ED, registration, triage, examination, discharge/admission/tests (tests include blood tests or imaging). EDs usually lack sufficient resources to service the unpredictable patient flow.

Most recent studies and surveys showed that EDs have a great impact on the performance of healthcare systems and on the quality of care. As EDs are linked to many other departments of the hospital, more attention should be given to them. Thus, improving healthcare generally requires the recommended improvement in EDs, where patient flow should be monitored, waiting times and length of stay (LoS) should be reduced (to satisfy patients), and revenue should be increased (to satisfy management). The most efficient way to approach these problems and find optimal solutions is to use simulation modeling" [Oueida et al. (2017c)]. "In 1995, García et al. focused their simulation modeling on the reduction of waiting times in the ED of a hospital in Miami [García et al. (1995)]. In 2003, Baesler et al. built a simulation model using Arena 4.0 in order to estimate the maximum increment rate of ED demands that a specific hospital in Chile could absorb [Baesler et al. (2003)]. The behavior of the variable "patient time" in the system was predicted and the minimum number of human resources to serve this demand was defined. Nevertheless, the system should not exceed an acceptable waiting-time level. The main focus of the hospital here was to understand the maximum extra demand their ED could absorb without facing problems, considering patient waiting time, human resources limitations, and maintaining the quality of service.

Samaha et al. studied the operation of a healthcare institution using Arena simulation modeling [Samaha et al. (2003)].

The main purpose of the model was to study the current operation and compare it to some suggested alternative scenarios that can reduce patient length of stay in the ED. Each activity in the ED during a seven-day period, 24 hours a day, was evaluated and used as input data to the constructed model. As a result, considerable time was saved without any additional costs. Alternative scenarios are suggestions proposed by the department staff in order to solve the issue of waiting times. Each scenario was implemented into the model in order to validate the output and study its efficiency. The main goal of the model was to evaluate patient waiting time, measuring patient throughput, evaluating resource utilization, and determining queue sizes; these performance measures are essential in order to assess the effectiveness of the proposed scenarios. They are collected from the output of the model where it should be analyzed, leading to a clear decision on the optimal solution for the problem. Using this simulation model, the hospital improved its service without any unnecessary expense by testing proposed solutions via the model before implementing them in the actual running system (ED) [Centeno et al. (2003); Kelton (2002)].

Some physicians refer risky and urgent patients to EDs instead of providing care in their clinics [Berenson et al. (2003)].

As a 24/7 operation without the need for appointments, the ED is the best option for medical care. Boarding or holding admitted patients until a bed is available increases the percentage of crowding as well as the waiting time to see a physician, which restrict the system's ability to respond to patient surge in the event of a disaster. Boarding patients requires monitoring, care, and critical care procedures. A study of boarding patients considers them to have a negative impact on the safety of other patients. Overcrowding can also cause ambulance diversion. When hospitals are spending time on diversion procedures, patients have to wait longer for evaluation and treatment [Chartbook (2014)].

In 2006, Jacobson et al. presented an overview of DES (Discrete Event Simulation) modeling applications for healthcare clinics [Jacobson et al. (2006)]. Kolb et al. proved that the major cause of overcrowding in an ED is the time patients spend waiting in the emergency room for in-patient assistance, which can block important ED resources [Kolb et al. (2008)]. They improved patient and staff satisfaction through their design in this study. The design consisted of a discrete event simulation model for testing buffer alternatives in the patient flow. In 2008, Park et al. proposed a forecasting model to predict patients' arrival in the ED [Park et al. (2008)]. There are papers on treatment delays for high-acuity patients [Schull et al. (2004); McCarthy et al. (2008)]; patient and staff dissatisfaction [Rowe et al. (2006); Abu-Laban (2006)]; and patients who left without being seen, reported over the years [Bullard et al. (2009)].

Moreover, studies showed that to prevent this overcrowding and access block, many strategies and solutions can be followed; it requires a system-level change by changing health policies. Access block is the delay the patient experiences between being admitted to the ED and gaining access to a dedicated bed. In 2009, Jayaprakash studied the overcrowding of EDs in Europe. Access block is one of the main reasons for ED overcrowding and the poor quality of care outcomes [Jayaprakash et al. (2009)]. Many studies from the UK, US, Canada, and Australia have proved this [Forero et al. (2010); Sun et al. (2013)].

In 2010, Gunal and Pidd presented a literature review for DES models in healthcare where a number of important conclusions were drawn about simulation modeling such as issues faced during modeling from unit-specific and facility-specific considerations [Günal and Pidd (2010)]. Paul et al. also presented a systematic review of ED simulation literature from 1970 to 2006 [Paul et al. (2010)]. As a conclusion of their study, patient perspective, environmental features, and the role of information technology should also be incorporated in future simulation efforts in order to develop solutions to ED overcrowding.

Many solutions were suggested over the years in order to alleviate the overcrowding and access block in EDs and some are presented in the sections below. Solutions were classified under three general categories: modifying a process behavior in the ED, changing staffing levels and schedules, and assessing the effect of external variables on the ED. These three categories are supported by simulation modeling techniques and optimization tools in order to find the optimal solution and guarantee the best performance of the ED" [Oueida et al. (2017a)].

2.1.1 Resource and Operational Rules Management

Reengineering and resource management of the ED consists of changing its aspect by adding specialized units responsible for specific tasks, relocating some equipment, beds, units, and changing some hospital operation rules such as introducing the early discharge of patients, etc.

2.1.1.1 ED Re-Engineering

"43% of hospital admissions originate in the ED, therefore the correlation between EDs and the several units of a hospital. Research linked America's ED overcrowding to hospital restructuring, a cause of financial pressures [Schull et al. (2001)]. Redesign or re-engineering of EDs, including unit layout changes, were presented by many researchers [Miller et al. (2004); Mould et al. (2013); Rado et al. (2014)]. Other solutions, such as opening new units, were also studied by researchers [Hannan et al. (1974)], or expanding the ED capacity [Wiinamaki and Dronzek (2003)]. In 2016, Kuo et al. proposed and analyzed the effect of relocating the ED in order to improve operation [Kuo et al. (2016)]. They used simulation with Arena to build the system and apply the suggested changes" [Oueida et al. (2017a)].

2.1.1.2 Increasing Bed Capacity

"Richmond et al. focused on the effect of bed capacity reduction on waiting times and explored the causes of these observed delays [Richmond et al. (1990)]. The complex system was simulated using a dynamic model constructed on iThink software. The model studied the effect of policies changes on the performance of the system (such as controlling the rostering of ED doctors). The shortage in bed numbers may affect elective admissions by increasing the number of cancellations" [Oueida et al. (2017b)].

"Bagust et al. used discrete-event stochastic simulation model in order to identify the dynamics of bed use in emergency admissions [Bagust et al. (1999)]. This study examined the relation between the available bed capacity and the unpredictable demand during an ED admission. The insufficient capacity for patients diagnosed for immediate admission may lead to a crisis. This fluctuation in emergency demand will affect the quality and efficiency of care in the hospital. Therefore, a deep understanding of these effects is required in order to apply the needed operational interventions and planning services for avoiding sudden problems leading to crisis. Lane et al. studied the impact of emergency demand on hourly basis, emphasizing the problem of waiting time for admissions [Lane et al. (2000)]. In this paper, an additional effect was taken into consideration, i.e., the random nature of the emergency demand admission affects the use of bed stock, which is why a discrete-event stochastic simulation modeling was used in order to investigate the complex system subject to this random effect. A relation was created between the fluctuating demand for emergency admission and the available in-patient bed capacity. The key output measures of system performance were:

1. Percentage rate of new arrivals to ED that cannot be admitted because of a lack of available beds
2. Percentage rate of number of days in a year where a critical admission could not be accommodated (crisis day arises here)
3. Bed occupancy rates

A possible intervention to alleviate the impact of rising emergency admission rates is better management of existing resources and introducing early discharges which help in raising the bed availability rate. Other interventions can be by avoiding admission if it is not necessary or finding alternatives to admission (treating a patient in a dedicated ED room, for example, without the need for hospital admission). As emergency admissions are difficult to predict, this stochastic modeling proved that spare beds are essential for emergency admissions, where efficiency and a low level of patient risk is the goal.

Lane et al.'s study focuses on the main factors behind the long waiting times for admission in an ED [Lane et al. (2000)]. Two significant insights, based on policy changes, were found: addition of resources reduces delays to patient demand, and reduction in bed numbers does not increase waiting times for emergency admissions. Bed shortage delays admission to the hospital and also causes cancellations of non-emergency admissions leading to additional future emergency cases.

One of the most significant factors affecting overcrowding is bed shortage, where patients to be admitted have to wait for the availability of a hospital bed [Derlet and Richards (2000); Miro et al. (2003)]. In the UK, this bed shortage can affect even patients who are discharged from the hospital, leading to patient dissatisfaction and bad economic events [Schneider et al. (2003)]. Derlet et al. met ED directors in order to define overcrowding and evaluate factors associated with this problem [Derlet et al. (2001)]. This study highlights the link between overcrowding problems and nurse shortages. In their perspective, crowding is related to increased patient acuity, shortage of hospital beds, insufficient space, laboratory/radiology delays, and examination delays, nursing/staff shortage, and increasing ED patient numbers. If waiting time spent by the patient in the ED exceeds the time the decision to admit is made, clinical outcomes will be badly affected [Richardson (2006); Cameron (2006)]. McCarthy et al. presented a valid performance measure for crowding which is the ED occupancy rate. This rate refers to the total number of patients divided by the total number of licensed beds [McCarthy et al. (2008)].

More studies on this subject proved that modeling methods can improve the flow of patients in an ED by defining the peak times, and the key factors causing the access block and overcrowding. These models should take into consideration input data based on daily or weekly peak times in order to be able to distribute the admissions evenly across the week and to avoid any expected congestion [Moskop et al. (2009)]" [Oueida et al. (2017a)]. "Some techniques to be considered are the patient flow systems and bed capacity management. Martin et al. found that the waiting interval time of a patient from the time of admission request until the exit from ED to be admitted is the main cause of delay in patient flow [Martin et al. (2011)]" [Oueida et al. (2017b)]. "The best logical solution to avoid access block and emergency overcrowding is to increase the bed capacity in the hospital and provide sufficient staff. When all other solutions fail, management should consider this solution of increasing the capacity of the healthcare system. In order to alleviate access block, government can also target some performance measures for the hospitals by introducing a strategy rule that must be followed by all healthcare organizations. Here, the bottleneck of the ED will be a problem to be solved through the whole organization and not just an ED issue. In this way emergency care is prioritized, which lead to a more efficient whole health care system, since the ED interacts with many other departments of the healthcare system, as discussed earlier" [Oueida et al. (2017a)].

2.1.1.3 Hospital Specialization

"The problem of ED overcrowding and patient boarding can be also alleviated by a proper assessment of the demographic needs, including population age/density, historical trauma, emergency medicine trends, and disaster preparedness. Care, another valuable factor in ED problems, should be provided based on specialization and should not depend on attracting the greatest number of patients. Therefore, hospitals should compete based on what they are able to do best. Medical outcomes were proved to be increased and cost to be reduced especially in the case of critical situations [Hillner et al. (2000)]" [Oueida et al. (2017a)].

2.1.1.4 Fast Track System

Yoon et al. suggested an efficient solution to the congestion problem by introducing the fast-track service in EDs, which is also cost-effective, safe, and satisfactory for patients [Yoon et al. (2003)]. In the UK, since 2002, "this system was deployed under the principle of 'see and treat' [Cooke et al. (2004)]. Chan et al. classified this problem into two categories: strategies addressing the ED overcrowding and strategies addressing access blocks [Chan et al. (2015)]. As per this study, solutions to these two main problems were by introducing new concepts or strategies to the healthcare system. The fast-track service discussed here can be introduced in a dedicated area of the ED with a dedicated and efficient number of staff. It was proven to play a significant role in alleviating the problem of overcrowding. This concept can decrease the overall waiting time, eliminate waste, and improve patient flow. By decreasing waiting times and shortening length of stay in EDs, congestion issues can be reduced or even solved. Some studies in this area showed that the rate of unseen patients was also reduced. The key principal for this service to succeed is to have competent and designated staff" [Oueida et al. (2017b)].

2.1.1.5 Triage System

"Another initiative for reducing patient complaints and increasing satisfaction was conducted by Cooke et al., where an arriving patient follows the process of assessment at triage stage and will be directed to the appropriate service and appropriate staff based on need [Cooke et al. (2004)]. Therefore, the triage system is also a significant way to reduce overcrowding. The triage system refers to a clinical assessment of the patient's medical status upon arrival in the ED, assessed by a primary triage nurse/physician [Robertson-Steel (2006)].

O'Shea adopted the ED crisis of America's hospitals where factors are attributed to many reasons [O'Shea (2007)]. In Maryland for example, non-urgent patients account for over 40% of ED visits. A study showed that visits to EDs increased by around 18%. One proposed solution can be by moving non-emergency patients out of emergency rooms, leaving the space for urgent patients to be treated, thus decreasing overcrowding and misuse of ED facilities" [Oueida et al. (2017a)].

"Duguay and Chetouane also adopted a simulation model using Arena in order to improve the current operation of an ED by reducing patient waiting times and improving overall service delivery and system throughput [Duguay and Chetouane (2007)]. Resource availability is directly linked to patient waiting time" [Oueida et al. (2017b)]. "Key resources such as physicians, nurses, examination rooms are considered as control variables. Some features were taken into consideration while building the model, such as the random flow of patients, seasonal illness or incident, fluctuations depending on the day of the week, and the possibility of patient arrivals increasing during a specific peak time of a given day. Triage codes are a highly considered feature for the modeling system, where an arriving patient receives a triage code based on the severity of their case after being assessed by the triage nurse. The input data collected for model design and validation are based on time durations collected at different stages of the process in the ED. Time durations can be classified under the time spent by a patient during two consecutive activities (waiting duration) and the necessary time to complete an activity (activity duration). The time from registration to available exam room was observed to be the largest waiting time in this system and is therefore considered the main focus of this study. Based on the collected data observation, several alternative resource scenarios were proposed and studied in order to choose the best option to improve this time and apply it for this unit. These scenarios were designed in a way to increase staff/room capacity and decrease the waiting time within budgetary constraints and considering what-if analysis" [Oueida et al. (2017a)].

2.1.1.6 The Four-Hours and Three-Hours Rules

"The UK NHS in 2004 introduced the four-hour rule to be applied among all hospitals. The Department of Health launched a health service plan that states a clear policy which imposes an ED not to have a patient total waiting time more than four hours. The application of this policy was not easy and many struggles were faced to achieve this target. The results of this policy was positive and created major change [Cronin and Wright (2006)]. Munro et al. achieved a reduced waiting time in his study applying this policy [Munro et al. (2006)]" [Oueida et al. (2017b)]. Banerjee et al. stated "long waits in the ED are a thing of the past in the UK" [Banerjee et al. (2008)]. "Many factors were attributed to the overcrowding of ED, all leading to the same result of adverse clinical outcomes: patient dissatisfaction. Therefore, to figure out the best scenario and best solution, first the root of the problem should be determined not to affect the entire hospital operation based on the needs of individual regions.

All patients should be observed, admitted, discharged, or transferred to another unit within four hours [Letham and Gray (2012)]. A study was performed in this area in order to look at some performance measures on emergency overcrowding, access block, and mortality rates by using, as inputs hospital data and patient data. This study showed results for pre- and post- introducing the four-hours strategy. The results proved that sometimes patient care can be compromised in order to meet the time targets [Geelhoed and de Klerk (2012)].

Another three-hours rule was suggested by some researchers in order to improve the total length of stay of the patient from arrival in the ED to departure. Discrete event simulation modeling was used and many what-if scenarios were followed in order to achieve this goal. As a result, a 30% improvement of patient LoS was proven following this approach [Oh et al. (2016)]" [Oueida et al. (2017b)].

"Due to the complexity of healthcare systems and the variation of systems from one country to another, the discussed solutions for reducing overcrowding and access block cannot be applicable in all hospitals or can be less practicable in some. Nevertheless, the strategies and management approaches discussed here were developed and applied by many hospitals for many years with evidence of efficiency and successful results. Therefore, more investigations and improvements should take these solutions into consideration depending on the place and type of system" [Oueida et al. (2017b)].

2.1.1.7 Early Discharge of In-Patients

"Avoiding ED overcrowding and access block can be achieved by early discharge of in-patients, leading to an available bed capacity for newly admitted patients. Usually, access block can increase the clinical risk of patients waiting their turn to be admitted, which is why clinicians and managers should predict, categorize the levels of risk in discharging in-patients early, and study the consequences behind this step when a sudden large bed capacity is required.

Kelen et al. described the process of discharging in-patients early by the "reverse triage," where patients should be safely selected with the lowest risk of consequences [Kelen and Scheulen (2007)]. Discharge lounges should then be dedicated for patients to wait for their discharge arrangements and some administrative paperwork, leading to a saving in bed hours and a reduced length of stay [Cowdell et al. (2002)]. This reverse triage system was fully described by an anecdotal report in 2012, evidencing the effective use of this system during an unexpected demand of beds [Satterthwaite and Atkinson (2012)]" [Oueida et al. (2017b)].

2.1.1.8 Holding Units

"The access block can be created by insufficient bed capacity, inefficient in-patient discharge, and inefficient patient flow. In the US, reviews have proven that introducing holding units can reduce access block and overcrowding by reducing the need for boarding or ambulance diversion [Institute of Medicine (2006)]. A study in Spain showed that providing a 16-bed observation unit in the ED of a 900-bed hospital improved access block [Gómez-Vaquero et al. (2009)]. Holding units can also be referred to as observation units or clinical decision units where the patient arriving in the ED can be examined and treated without the need for admission. Moreover, a special observation unit should be dedicated for patients presenting with low-acuity symptoms such as chest pain, stomach ache, etc., who may not need hospital admission. A dedicated person should be assigned to the task of admission/discharge and responding to the real-time demands of in-patients.

Other studies showed that the benefits of these holding units were not very efficient compared to other hospitals without any holding units [Schull et al. (2012)]; therefore, a careful clinical management plan and adequate support staff should be incorporated in order to achieve a successful approach. In 2015, Chan et al. also suggested these holding units allowing early discharge and increasing capacity be created using political action [Chan et al. (2015)]" [Oueida et al. (2017b)].

2.1.2 Human Resource Management

"Resource management consists of adjusting the level of resources needed and being capable of serving the maximum number of patients, assigning the appropriate resource to a certain task, and editing resource schedules, thus leading to an increase in care demand and a reduction in the patient waiting time" [Oueida et al. (2017a)].

2.1.2.1 Optimizing the GP Role

Rieffe et al. proved that bypassing the general practitioner (GP) can lead to overusing the ED for minor complaints [Rieffe et al. (1999)]. "This will decrease the service quality and increase the ED cost. Lee at al. conducted a study on ED attendees and found that 57% were only primary cases [Lee et al. (1999)]. These primary cases could consult a GP instead of using the ED and thereby causing additional patient flow. A study conducted by Van Uden et al. showed that a good way to optimize the GP role is to add after-hours services so they can be always available for primary care patients, thus reducing inappropriate referrals to the ED [Van Uden et al. (2003)]" [Oueida et al. (2017b)].

2.1.2.2 Staffing Schedules

"As discussed in many papers, researchers reached a conclusion where staff resource schedules can significantly affect the operations of the ED and have great impact on many factors causing an ED crisis. Preparing these schedules is a complex task since a large number of rules need to be taken into consideration, such as the number of consecutive shifts and weekly hours, conflicting timings, weekends, holidays, individual preferences (sick leave, special occasions).

Rosetti et al. proposed a simulation model using Arena in order to determine an optimal attending physician staffing schedules [Rossetti et al. (1999)]" [Oueida et al. (2017a)]. "Since efficient allocation of staff resources is a common problem facing EDs in any hospital, a computer simulation was suggested in order to test alternative ED attending physician staffing schedules and then analyzing the results on the patient throughput and resource utilization. The suggested simulation can even help detect any inefficiency in the actual system where patient flow, resources, layout, and staffing changes can add a noticeable effect. It is agreed that the utilization of ED nurse and physician resources has a significant impact on patient throughput and system performance; therefore, an analysis was performed in order to reduce the staff idle time and operating expenses and increase the resource utilization, taking into consideration a constant quality of patient care. This can be done by regarding the patient showing up at ED as a function of hours/day, where peak times can be determined. Four different approaches were suggested and analyzed leading to the selection of the best approach where the overall waiting time of a patient was significantly decreased on a daily/weekly basis. The approach focused on changing an existing double coverage shift of a current schedule by considering the patient arrival rates for the ED and assigning peak times during a day.

Hung presented a literature review on nurse scheduling using simulation modeling [Hung (1995)]. Other researchers proved the success of these models in nurse scheduling problems using optimization techniques [Berrada (1996); Weil et al. (1995); Jaumard et al. (1998); Komashie and Mousavi (2005)]. In 2000, Beaulieu et al. used a mathematical programming to ensure a feasible performance of this task [Beaulieu et al. (2000)]. The model constructs schedules for all staffing resources within a short period of time with less effort and proposes the best schedules, since it takes into account all possible rules. Two major objectives should be considered while modeling: maximizing personnel satisfaction and minimizing salary cost" [Oueida et al. (2017b)].

"In 2001 Carter and Lapierre and in 2007 Sinreich and Jabali adopted a simulation model in order to improve ED operations by studying scheduling policies for physicians [Carter and Lapierre (2001); Sinreich and Jabali (2007)]. Azadeh et al. applied fuzzy logic techniques in order to propose optimal nursing scheduling [Azadeh et al. (2013)]. Centeno et al. also used simulation to help ED decision-makers in their staff scheduling [Centeno et al. (2003)]. The author of this paper presented a procedure that helps in efficiently estimating required parameters for model input data in cases where assumptions are needed (i.e., where sufficient data for simulation could not be obtained). This is for the reason why, while developing the simulation model for studying and improving the operations of the ED, two challenges were faced: the significant time-varying rate of arrivals, and data paucity (shortage of data). One of the model outputs implied that by adding an extra doctor and adjusting shifts hours, the average waiting time of patient consultations can be reduced by 10%. Using different what-if scenarios, that can be simulated using this model, hospital managers can be helped in taking decisions for improving the quality of service (such as reducing waiting times) and assuring best allocation of resources. Wang et al. also focused in their study on the concept of resource allocation [Wang et al. (2009)]. Jerbi and Kamoun proposed the rescheduling of a doctor shift [Jerbi and Kamoun (2009)]" [Oueida et al. (2017a)].

Laroque et al. developed a simulation approach that analyzes how resource allocation can impact a patient's journey in an ED [Laroque et al. (2012)]. "Based on some financial restrictions, hospital management cannot assure that resources are always available to fulfill service quality. Therefore, valuable resources (such as doctors and nurses) should be fully utilized. Another factor that should be highlighted is the non-urgent patients who may visit the ED. Increase of patient flow for routine consultation may increase waiting times and thus decrease the quality of service and patient satisfaction. The authors of this paper developed a simulation model in order to evaluate the impact of staffing and resource scheduling on patient demand and to achieve insights about ED staffing policies" [Oueida et al. (2017b)].

2.1.2.3 Medical Resource is the Driver

"In most research, the focus, in order to improve the ED operation, was the patient themself. Hay et al. proved that, on the contrary, the patient should not be the driver, but the medical resource should be considered to be the main entity of study [Hay et al. (2006)]. It demonstrates the importance of assigning the appropriate doctor to a certain task (patient) along with the corresponding waiting time. Simulation modeling was used in this new approach highlighting three elements: the care paths (models including process and decision), operating priority (which is the clinical priority of the presenting case and the waiting time of patient until the process is executed); and the skill sets (where the senior doctor can perform all tasks that a junior doctor can perform but should not be called in for simple tasks). Whenever a patient joins a queue, the operating priority gradually increases relative to the waiting time. Choosing the right resource for a certain task depends on the severity of the patient's condition, the patient waiting time, and how busy the hospital is. Arena simulation was used, integrated with an Excel interface for easy configuration.

Subash et al. and Gunal and Pidd classified patients in their study under three categories: "life-threatening," "Major," and "Minor" [Subash et al. (2004); Gunal and Pidd (2006)]. They studied the effect of junior/senior doctors in consulting patient. Senior doctors are experienced consultants who can spend less time with a patient in order to reach a clinical decision thus shortening the examination time, laboratory time, assessment time, radiology, discharge time, thus, the total waiting time spent in the ED" [Oueida et al. (2017a)].

2.1.2.4 Part Time Jobs and ENPs

"Overcrowding can be related to the inappropriate usage of ED utilities by primary care attendees. In the past several years, part-time jobs were offered by some hospitals to general practitioners in order to serve ED low-acuity type of cases leading to a reduction in congestion. These general practitioners can also refer to senior doctors in the ED for advice or discussion on the treatment, which assures a high quality of care. Low-acuity patients are those having minor injuries or minor illness and they constitute the majority of the ED overcrowding. Other studies showed that using emergency nurse practitioners (ENPs) may increase efficiency since patients will be more satisfied with the quality of care delivered. Carter and Chochnov performed a systematic review of ENPs working in the ED, concentrating on the outcome measures of this approach, which is waiting time reduction, higher patient satisfaction, cost-effectiveness, and high quality of care which can be equivalent to the same care provided by a junior doctor [Carter and Chochinov (2007)]" [Oueida et al. (2017a)].

2.1.2.5 Alternative Staff Distribution

"Ahmed and Alkhamis designed a decision support system simulation combined with optimization in order to determine the optimal number of resources needed to serve an ED in Kuwait, taking into consideration management budget restrictions, maximum patient throughput, and minimum patient waiting time in the system [Ahmed and Alkhamis (2009)]. The study was made for a public hospital in Kuwait, where decision-makers should maximize utilization of resources (doctors, nurses, lab technicians) and minimize waiting times while maintaining the same level of care and a standard patient satisfaction rate. The current staff distribution was studied and resources limitation was highlighted in order to figure out an alternative staffing distribution that can improve the ED and reach the target. Patients were classified under different categories based on the severity of their cases and were transferred to the required service accordingly. This simulation/optimization model focuses on the problem of how to choose the correct distribution of resources based on the type of service and taking into consideration the constraints imposed by the limitations of the system.

Many other researchers before Ahmad et al. highlighted the same problem using the simulation and optimization techniques [Swisher et al. (2001); Blasak et al. (2003); Sinreich and Marmor (2005)]. These researchers reproduced the behavior of a healthcare system in order to evaluate its performance and analyze the outcome of different scenarios. Beaulieu et al. followed a mathematical programming approach in order to schedule doctors for an emergency room [Beaulieu et al. (2000)]. Baesler et al. adopted a simulation model based on experiments to estimate the maximum capacity for an emergency room [Baesler et al. (2003)]. Ahmed and Alkhamis' method differs from all other models since it does not deal with the mathematical model of the actual system, but combines simulation with optimization [Ahmed and Alkhamis (2009)]. A complex stochastic objective function represents the optimization model which is subject to some stochastic constraints set by the management; these values can never be analytically evaluated and need simulation intervention. The number of receptionists, doctors, nurses, and lab technicians, etc., are some of the input data required for evaluation purposes. The output of the simulation program is used for performance measures which include staff cost, system throughput, and average waiting time in the system along with detailed information about the queues formed for each type of service. Marmor discussed the complexity of the ED of a hospital and pointed at the operational managerial challenges faced [Marmor (2010)]. For this reason, a simulation framework is necessary for realistic tracking of EDs" [Oueida et al. (2017a)].

2.1.3 Considering External Factors

"External factors such as requesting extra facilities from other units of the hospital, considering different insurance coverage types, predicting strain situations, and forecasting disaster conditions affect the operation of the ED and may cause overcrowding or long waiting times. Patients arriving in the ED may be classified under different types of insurance coverage (private insurance, public health insurance, etc.). Also, some patients are uninsured and show up at the ED for free diagnosis; even if their case is not severe.

Most of the times patients arriving in the ED are referred to other units, such as imaging or laboratory, in order to undergo extra tests. These extra facilities help the doctor to come up with an accurate diagnosis and a final decision (whether a patient needs admission or not or whether they should be referred to another unit in the hospital, such as surgery, etc.). These referrals should be considered in the model for adequate results since patients may be accessing the corresponding units at the same time, thus leading to overcrowding and high waiting times in the ED. Moreover, predicting strain situations and forecasting disaster conditions are essential metrics for a successful ED operation. Thus, care demand can be predicted and the corresponding resource needs (material or human) can be forecasted for optimal operation of the ED during those peak times" [Oueida et al. (2017a)].

2.1.3.1 Considering the Lab Tests/Imaging Effect

"During the last decade, most studies, found in literature, impose an increase in the actual care process [Saunders et al. (1989); Komashie and Mousavi (2005)] or the size and operation of the ED [Samaha et al. (2003); Ruohonen et al. (2006)] in order to reach the desired service level (throughput) and reduce waiting times. Saunders et al. considered in his model, built using Siman/Cinema, several features such as lab tests, triage priorities, teaching aspects, communication delays, and physicians' collaboration [Saunders et al. (1989)]. Blood tests/results and patients were considered flowing entities in the modeling system, which means the turnaround time of these tests has a direct effect on patient throughput.

Komashie and Mousavi's main objective was to determine the effect of key resources (beds, nurses, doctors) on key performance measures (waiting times, waiting queues, and throughput) [Komashie and Mousavi (2005)]. The Arena model designed depended on variable service times that can vary according to the case of the patient. In this study several essential elements that may affect the process were not taken into consideration (lab tests, triage codes, imaging, etc.). Ruohonen et al. used Medmodel simulation software in order to evaluate, plan, and redesign healthcare systems [Ruohonen et al. (2006)]. In his study he introduced a new idea of adding a doctor with the nurse at the triage stage. Therefore, the lab tests can be ordered and medical diagnosis can be performed during the early stage of the process leading to an improvement in waiting times and system throughput. This method allows fast priority recognition and accurate treatment referral. The model adopted lab tests and resource shifts as flowing entities.

Emergency radiology has great impact on waiting time especially in the case of trauma patients. Radiology results are needed for patient assessment and discharge. Delays in radiology can lead to unnecessary use of ED beds, increase in length of stay, and an increase in patient dissatisfaction [Miele et al. (2006)]. Eskandari et al. proposed considering ED patients using other facilities in the hospital (such as MRI, CT scan etc.) as a priority over non-ED patients along with adding financial personnel and five mobile in-patient beds [Eskandari et al. (2011)]. Paul and Lin related the long waiting times in EDs to the long waits in triage, delays in tests and receiving results, waiting for a physician, or a shortage in nursing staff [Paul and Lin (2012)]" [Oueida et al. (2017a)].

2.1.3.2 Considering Uninsured Patients

"Another factor causing overcrowding can be the increase in the rate of uninsured patients since federal laws imply that an ED must take on an urgent uninsured patient who lacks access to regular primary care even if they are not able to pay the fees. Strunk and Cunningham highlighted additional factors contributing to ED rising demand such as capacity constraints for private physicians and scheduling appointments, managed-care restrictions, and some low insurance reimbursement rates [Strunk and Cunningham (2002)].

Financial constraints and hospital profit are also significant factors in ED crowding where some hospitals prefer to reserve a bed for an elective in-patient that is certain to pay the necessary fees rather than referring it to an ED patient whose payment is uncertain. One solution presented was to urge a tax deduction for health insurance allowing families and individuals to purchase personal health insurance [Butler and Owcharenko (2009)]. Private health plans limit patients showing up at the ED to those with emergency situations only, thus, improving outcomes and reducing costs" [Oueida et al. (2017a)].

2.1.3.3 Forecasting Disaster Conditions

"Factors such as managing unexpected catastrophic events (such as terrorist attacks, natural disasters, disease pandemics) should also be taken into consideration and are discussed by other researchers. The Institute of Medicine, a branch of the National Academy of Sciences, recently announced America's emergency medical system to be stretched beyond capacity and thus lacking in preparedness to accommodate disaster events [Institute of Medicine (2006)].

Disaster events are linked to abnormal conditions such as floods, volcanic eruptions, earthquakes, etc. that may disturb normal life in society. Patvivatsiri presented a computer simulation model that analyzes patient throughput, assesses resources utilization, evaluates the effect of a terrorist attack, and determines necessary staffing levels for a corresponding scenario [Patvivatsiri (2006a)]. Paul and Hariharan studied the impact of disaster events on ED capacity planning during a terrorist attack [Paul and Hariharan (2007)]. Al Kattan developed two models to represent ED operations in both normal and disaster conditions [Al-Kattan (2009a)]. ED operations in earthquake disaster events were studied [Yi et al. (2010)]. Disaster event patient arrival patterns and time durations are evaluated using Arena simulation and related to the ability of EDs to treat these patients [Joshi (2008a)]. Xiao et al. also focused on the optimization of work flow in EDs during extreme events using a DES framework [Xiao et al. (2012a)]" [Oueida et al. (2017a)].

"Gul and Guneri carried out a literature review study on simulation modeling used for EDs in both normal and disaster conditions [Gul and Guneri (2015)]. The literature in this area is vast and expanding with time and targeting ED KPIs (Key Performance Indicators) such as length of stay, resource utilization, and patient throughput. The best DES model used by many researches in this area was Arena. Immediately after a disaster, the complexity of the ED grows dramatically, therefore there is a need for simulation modeling to forecast the physical and human resources required. Using simulation modeling, many scenarios can be proposed, evaluated, and compared, and what-if analysis and optimization can be performed" [Oueida et al. (2017a)].

2.1.3.4 Considering Big Data Research

"The complexity of the ED imposes the need to share big data between different departments of the healthcare system in order to assess overcrowding. Halevy and al. showed that the more data provided as input to a simulation system the more scenarios can be conducted and predictions can be accurate, leading to decision-making for an optimal solution, improving health service quality, efficiency, and cost [Halevy et al. (2009)]. A big-data research approach is proposed in order to manage the complexity and large volume of the existing healthcare data [Diebold (2012)]. Increasing data storage capacity and diversity of data types are the main components of this research where healthcare services can be improved, depending on the multiplicity of this data. The adoption of insights gained from big-data analytics has the potential to save lives, improve the care delivery process, align payment with performance, and expand access to healthcare details [Belle et al. (2015)].

In the majority of emergency department simulations, the model is built upon incomplete data (such as missing arrival times, service times, etc.). Collecting reliable data for the system is a hard task which may often lead to invalid simulations. This problem can be solved by simulation optimization where the unavailable service time durations can be predicted through proposing new algorithms [Guo et al. (2016)]" [Oueida et al. (2017a)].

2.1.3.5 Predicting Strain Situations

"As emergency departments have become the immediate and essential medical care unit in a hospital, efficient management of patient flow and predicting resource demand is an urgent issue to focus on. Kadri et al. studied in their research, patient flow in the pediatric ED of a hospital in France using Arena simulation modeling, taking into consideration strain situations and ED states (normal, degraded, critical) which had not been defined in the literature before 2012 [Kadri et al. (2014)]. Strain situations are defined as disequilibrium in the ED where care load flow and care production capacity exceed certain thresholds. To handle this patient influx, EDs require sufficient human and material resources which are, at peak times, limited, leading to ED overcrowding and strain situations. The purpose of this study is to build a simulation-based decision support system that takes, as input, data from the hospital database and is based on interviews with healthcare staff in order to predict the strain situations. Inputs are information such as number of patient arrivals, means of arrival, arrival time, types and duration of each treatment, additional examinations, and destination after leaving the ED, as well as information regarding the strain situations. Simulation output will help hospital management to specify strain situations, examine the relationship between them, propose correction actions, and improve the service at the ED. The main strain situations observed from the data collected were the influx of patients, long waits before receiving care, shortage in nursing staff, waiting for doctors, delays in additional examinations, and the inability to transfer admitted patients. Different scenarios were proposed as solutions, such as adding a human resource (nurse/doctor) and material resources (adding an examination room with a doctor or/and a nurse). Results were examined and the best scenario was chosen after deep analysis of waiting time reduction and decrease in length of stay" [Oueida et al. (2017a)].

2.1.4 Adopting Simulation Techniques

"Due to the complexity of the ED, simulation modeling was proven over the years to be a key solution to improving operations. Optimization techniques can be also integrated with simulation and thus lead to an optimal solution for the arising and studied problems" [Oueida et al. (2017a)].

2.1.4.1 Using Queuing System Modeling

"Siddharthan et al. presented a queuing policy in order to reduce waiting times [Siddharthan et al. (1996)]. Komashie and Mousavi investigated policy and decision-making of an ED [Komashie and Mousavi (2005)], where capacity was adopted [Baesler et al. (2003)]. Lim, Nye et al. and Lim, Worster et al. used mathematical modeling techniques—queuing models, DES, SD (System Dynamics), and ABS (Agent Based Simulation)—in order to develop 29 scenarios for evaluating waiting time reduction [Lim et al. (2012a); Lim et al. (2012b)]. Abbas suggested a simulation model using different scenarios [Abbas (2014)]. This model studies the complexity of the ED in a hospital and assesses the interval between patient arrival in the ED and receiving the required care. The minimum waiting time can be reached by considering a queuing system modeling. An arriving patient enters the system through the waiting room, where they should pick a number and waits until a nurse calls their name and transfers them to the screening room to assess their case (blood pressure, fever, etc.). Based on the patient case, they will be transferred to the examination room in order to receive the necessary care. Priority discipline should be taken into consideration; patients arriving by ambulance have to receive priority and urgent care based on the severity of their case" [Oueida et al. (2017a)].

2.1.4.2 Integrating Optimization Tools with Simulation Modeling

"Recently, some studies proved that integration of other simulation methods along with the simulation modeling is optimal to find the best solution (like using OptQuest tool for optimization). Some researchers integrated simulation modeling with optimization (Opt Quest tool) in order to reach the optimal solution [Rico et al. (2007); Ahmed and Alkhamis (2009); Weng et al. (2011)]. Others integrated Balanced Scorecard (BSC) with simulation modeling in order to study the ED performance [Abo-Hamad and Arisha (2013)].

Staff scheduling was also studied in the literature in order to optimize the workload and cover patient demand [Medeiros et al. (2008); Jerbi and Kamoun (2009); Brenner et al. (2010); Kuo et al. (2012); Izady and Worthington (2012)]. Morgareidge et al. demonstrated the advantage of using SSA with DES modeling for facilitating decision-making regarding design, reducing costs, and improving the ED performance [Morgareidge et al. (2014)]" [Oueida et al. (2017a)].

Table 2.1 presents a summary of most of the papers discussed in this section, showing the aim of the study along with the software used and results achieved. The main focus is to solve the overcrowding of an ED, measuring different KPIs/factors causing this overcrowding and proposing solutions to these multiple problems using one platform.

Table 2.1 Literature Review Summary

Author	Software	Aim of Study	Results
Abbas, A. (2014)	DES	To determine the flow of patients through the emergency case and elective surgical to identify the data elements required to complete a quantitative analysis of waiting time issues	Building and validation of a simulation model using the discrete event simulation for modeling, analysis, and visualization. The basic model will be extended to simulate the effects of different operating strategies on patient waiting time in the ED
Abo-Hamad and Arisha (2013)	Extend	To present simulation with BSC and MCDM to improve patient experience in an ED	Enforcement of the national benchmark of six-hour boarding limit for EDs would have a significantly greater impact on reducing average length of stay for all ED patients than increasing medical staff or assessment cubicles
Abu-Laban (2006)	NA	To address the crisis of admitted patients in the ED of Vancouver General Hospital	Use existing hospital resources by sharing the excess workload equally throughout the hospital is a recommendation
Ahmed and Al Khamis (2009)	Simscript	To present simulation with optimization subject to budget restrictions	The optimal number of doctors, lab technicians, and nurses required to maximize patient throughput and to reduce patient time in the system was determined
Akshay et al. (2012)	SIMIO-HC	Healthcare systems are multi-facility interconnected systems. The growing complexity and medical technologies of these systems are amplified by a poor organization healthcare delivery system. Lack of flexibility and implementation in healthcare simulation software	Use a multi-paradigm simulation modeling framework in order to represent this complex interconnected system and develop an efficient and effective healthcare system. Define four dynamics of simulation success that should be followed: verification, validation, fidelity, and credibility

(Continued)

Table 2.1 (Continued) Literature Review Summary

Author	Software	Aim of Study	Results
Al Kattan and Abboud (2009)	Arena	To develop two models in order to evaluate the performance of the ED during normal and disaster operations	Using the disaster recovery plan will result in shortage of two important types of resources. To solve problems associated with shortage of resources, signing agreements with doctors and nurses from outside the hospital was suggested. Also, the ED management should plan to purchase necessary equipment, consumables, and tools required in disaster recovery
Azadeh et al. (2013)	Visual SLAM	To present an integrated fuzzy simulation on improving the quality of care in a large public hospital ED	The complete flow of patients in ED was covered and the best nursing schedule based on the minimum patient queue time was found using fuzzy logic simulation. A- cut method shows the patient waiting time in a queue in the ED is shortened, thereby raising the quality of patient care and patient satisfaction
Baesler et al. (2003)	Arena	To create a simulation model for predicting the behavior of the variable patient's time in system and estimate the maximum possible demand that the system can absorb	The set of experiments conducted were able to define the minimum number of physical and human resources required to serve this demand
Bagust et al. (1999)	Microsoft Excel 5 spreadsheet	To examine the daily bed requirements arising from the flow of emergency admissions to an acute hospital, to identify the implications of fluctuating and unpredictable demands for emergency admission for the management of hospital bed capacity, and to quantify the daily risk of insufficient capacity for patients requiring immediate admission	Spare bed capacity is essential for the effective management of emergency admissions, and its cost should be borne by purchasers as an essential element of an acute hospital service

(Continued)

Table 2.1 (Continued)   Literature Review Summary

Author	Software	Aim of Study	Results
Chan et al. (2015)	NA	To identify evidence-based strategies that can be followed in emergency departments and hospital settings to alleviate the problem of access block and emergency department overcrowding	Identified solutions are classified into the following categories: (1) strategies addressing emergency department overcrowding: co-locating primary care within the emergency department, and fast-track and emergency nurse practitioners; (2) strategies addressing access block: holding units, early discharge and patient flow, and political action (management and resource priority)
Cooke et al. (2004)	NA	To reduce attendances and waits in the ED	Good evidence exists to support the following policies: (1) fast-track systems for minor injury patients, (2) chronic disease case management, (3) home support and specialist nurse care to reduce emergency admissions. Future service delivery research should include: (1) bed management, (2) reducing delayed discharges, (3) reorganization of emergency primary care
Cronin and Wright (2006)	NA	To explore the concept of the breach-avoidance facilitator (BAF) within the Accident and Emergency (A&E) department	The A&E four-hour target was managed. The associated benefits of the role including monitoring of the four-hour target, coordination of resources, increased communication with a variety of staff members, and the completion of a real-time electronic handover form was explored
Derlet and Richards (2000)	NA	To describe the complex web of interrelated issues of overcrowding. ED overcrowding has multiple effects, including placing the patient at risk for poor outcome, prolonged pain and suffering of some patients, long patient waits, patient dissatisfaction, ambulance diversions in some cities, decreased physician productivity, increased frustration among medical staff, and violence	Solving the problem of overcrowding will not only require a major financial commitment from the federal government and local hospitals, but will also require a cooperation from managed care

(Continued)

Table 2.1 (Continued)   Literature Review Summary

Author	Software	Aim of Study	Results
Derlet et al. (2001)	NA	To describe the definition, extent, and factors associated with overcrowding in emergency departments (EDs) as perceived by ED directors	Episodic, but frequent, overcrowding is a significant problem in academic, county, and private hospital EDs in urban and rural settings. Its causes are complex and multi-factorial
Duguay and Chetouane (2007)	Arena	To reduce patient waiting times and to improve overall care delivery and system throughput	As patient waiting times are linked to resource availability, a number of alternatives were designed based on adding resource scenarios. Simulation shows that number of examination rooms had no effect on waiting time if added without a matching increase in the staff
Eskandari et al. (2011)	Arena	To find out improving scenarios for reducing waiting times of patients by using simulation and MCDM methods	The results analysis indicates that the average waiting time of non-fast-track patients by taking new policies with reasonable expenditure can be reduced by 42.3%
Forero et al. (2010)	NA	Study the access block hospital intervention from 1998 to 2008 to assess the evidence for interventions around access block and ED overcrowding. Mortality rate increased due to access block and ED overcrowding	The main causes are major increases in hospital admissions and ED presentations, with almost no increase in the capacity of hospitals to meet this demand
Garcia et al. (1995)	SIMAN	To reduce time in an ED with a fast-track lane	The simulation study revealed that indeed a fast-track lane reduces by almost 25% the time in the system for patients with low priority without negatively affecting the times of patients with higher priority

(Continued)

Table 2.1 (Continued)   Literature Review Summary

Author	Software	Aim of Study	Results
Geelhoed and de Klerk (2012)	NA	To assess whether emergency department (ED) overcrowding was reduced after the introduction of the four-hour rule in Western Australia (WA) and whether any changes in overcrowding were associated with significant changes in patient mortality rates	Introduction of the four-hour rule in WA led to a reversal of overcrowding in three tertiary hospital EDs that coincided with a significant fall in the overall mortality rate in tertiary hospital data combined and in two of the three individual hospitals. No reduction in adjusted mortality rates was shown in three secondary hospitals where the improvement in overcrowding was minimal
Gomez et al. (2009)	NA	To study and present the effect of a holding unit (HU) on access block and some medical management indicators	The opening of an HU has led to an improvement in the access block
Gul and Guneri (2015)	NA	To reveal the importance of simulation for disaster preparedness of EDs and the innovative aspects of recent ED simulation applications; it can provide an insight for researchers on ED simulation modeling in terms of showing current state and gaps to be focused on in the future	(1) Financial effects of the scenarios tested in almost all the reviewed studies related to both ED normal time and disaster time processes should be assessed. (2) Simulation modeling of an ED should consider disaster times, availability of sufficient medical staff. (3) Innovative approaches should be used in data gathering. (4) Simulation combined with other OR/MS techniques such as optimization, analytical models, MCDM, BSC, and DEA in ED should be applied
Gunal and Pidd (2006)	Micro Saint Sharp	To evaluate ED performance with the factors multi-tasking and experience level of medical staff	ED performance was predicted under different circumstances. Performance is measured as the percentage of patients who stayed in ED more than four hours

(Continued)

Table 2.1 (Continued)   Literature Review Summary

Author	Software	Aim of Study	Results
Gunal and Pidd (2010)	NA	Most reported studies are unit and facility specific which lead to a danger when building a simulation model since all units are interconnected in a hospital	Build a simulation modeling approach that links all activities of different units of the healthcare system using DES
Hannan et al. (1974)	FORTRAN IV	To evaluate potential influence of new patient demand and different administrative decision policies. The consequences of increased demand, a higher percentage of true emergency patients, installing laboratory and X-ray facilities in the emergency department, triaging patients, and scheduling non-urgency patients to smooth the demand were investigated	Total patient time in the system, times until first seen by a nurse and physician, and staff utilization percentages were used as measures of effectiveness
Hay et al. (2006)	Arena	To create models of emergency care in four UK NHS hospitals that reflect more realistically the way emergency care is actually delivered	It is best if the patient does not come first. Instead, the allocation of resource is guided by complex drivers that encompass ideas of relative suitability for the task in hand and even-handedness toward a widely varying patient demand
Izady and Worthington (2012)	NA	Setting the medical staffing levels for achieving the government target, in time-carrying demand, multiple types of patients, and resource sharing	Significant improvement on the target can be gained, even without increase in total staff hours

(Continued)

Table 2.1 (Continued)   Literature Review Summary

Author	Software	Aim of Study	Results
Jacobson et al. (2006)	NA	To provide an overview of discrete-event simulation modeling applications to healthcare clinics and integrated health care systems (e.g., hospitals, outpatient clinics, emergency departments, and pharmacies) over the past 40 years	Understand the relationship that may exist between various inputs into a health care delivery system (e.g., patient scheduling and admission rules, patient routing and flow schemes, facility and staff resources) and various output performance measures from the system (e.g., patient throughput, patient waiting times, physician utilization, staff and facility utilization)
Jaumard et al. (1998)	NA	To configure individual schedules to satisfy the demand coverage constraints while minimizing salary costs and maximizing both employee preferences and team balance	A new resource structure in the auxiliary problem is defined in order to take into account the complex collective agreement rules specific to the nurse scheduling problem
Jayaprakash et al. (2009)	NA	To study the European ED overcrowding; any potential solutions must be tailored to regional variations	Public funding directly influences potential overcrowding factors, such as number of hospital beds, community care facilities, and staffing. ED overcrowding is a universal problem with distinctly regional root causes
Jerbi and Kamoun (2009)	Arena	To suggest different alternatives according to the measures and to choose the most appropriate schedule that optimizes them	Length of stay, queuing waiting times, resources utilization and resources scheduling were evaluated as key measures of performance in order to detect the flaws that occur in the ED
Joshi and Rys (2011)	Arena	To analyze different arrival patterns on an ED capacity during a conventional terror disaster event using DES, help the emergency planners to better allocate and utilize the limited ED resources in order to treat maximum possible patients and estimate the number of additional resources that would be required in a particular scenario	Various shapes of arrival distributions were tested for different time durations. The model studied how many more resources the ED would need in order to have zero critical expire, zero Left without Being Seen (LWBS), and zero patients diverted. An addition of two full trauma resources were required in order to have zero critical expire in trauma room areas and an additional five ED beds and three nurses were required in the treatment area for patients with moderate severity to have zero LWBS and zero patients diverted

(Continued)

Table 2.1 (Continued)   Literature Review Summary

Author	Software	Aim of Study	Results
Kadri et al. (2014)	Arena	To develop a simulation-based DSS to prevent and predict strain situations in an ED in order to improve their management by the hospital system	Daily patient arrivals at the pediatric emergency department (PED) in Lille hospital, France, were studied using univariate times-series analysis. Univariate ARMA models were developed to describe daily arrivals at PED. The approach proposed and lessons learned from this study may assist other regional hospitals and their emergency departments in carrying out their own analyses to aid planning. The results have also shown the suitability of this approach in predicting the number of patient arrivals at the PED in Lille. The time series is essentially linear and therefore ARMA modeling offered robust predictions in many cases
Kelen et al. (2007)	NA	To develop a disposition classification system that categorizes inpatients according to suitability for immediate discharge on the basis of risk tolerance for a subsequent consequential medical event	The categories of a disposition classification system were defined, risk tolerance of a consequential medical event to each category assigned, critical interventions identified, and rank each (using a scale of 1–10) according to the likelihood of a resultant consequential medical event if a critical intervention is withdrawn or withheld because of discharge. The disposition classification system allowed conceptual classification of patients for suitable disposition, including those deemed safe for early discharge home during surges in demand
Kolb et al. (2008)	Arena	To study a major cause of ED crowding: holding patients waiting in the Emergency Room (ER) for inpatient unit admission where they block critical ED resources	Five patient buffer concepts which aim at relieving pressure of the ER were tested. All buffers managed to run with significantly fewer resources than the ER. Outputs have a potential impact on hospital process flow due to clear results which offer substantial improvement of hospital organization

(Continued)

Table 2.1 (Continued) Literature Review Summary

Author	Software	Aim of Study	Results
Komashie and Mousavi (2005)	Arena	To develop a model that helps the ED managers understand the behavior of the system with regard to the hidden causes of excessive waiting times	The model served in assessing the impact of major departmental resources on Key Performance Indicators, and was also used as a cost-effective method for testing various what-if scenarios for possible system improvement. The study greatly enhanced managers' understanding of the system and how patient flow is influenced by process changes and resource availability. The results also showed a possible reduction of more than 20% in patients' waiting times
Kuo et al. (2012).	Excel VBA	To model a resource allocation problem in a hospital ED by using Poisson process and parameter estimation	Different "what-if" scenarios before making any important decisions can be analyzed. This helps to enhance the quality of service that the ED is providing (e.g., reduce waiting times) since the manpower and resources can be well allocated, and more patients are expected to be treated as a consequence
Laroque et al. (2012)	NA	To analyze how the allocation decisions impact patient experience in the ED	(1) The utilization of some doctors are over 100% (requiring their scheduled breaks to be shortened); (2) adding an extra doctor to the ED and adjusting their shift hours, around 10% of average waiting time for consultation of patients was reduced; (3) 10% increase in patient numbers leads to about 20% increase in average total waiting time

(Continued)

Table 2.1 (Continued)   Literature Review Summary

Author	Software	Aim of Study	Results
Lee et al. (1999)	NA	To report the development of a comprehensive research method for identifying primary care patients attending A&E	The patients sampled were similar in sex and age distribution to A&E attendees for the whole territory. The level of GP cases was found to be 57%, with a significantly higher proportion of patients in the younger age group. The high level of use reflects the lack of a well-coordinated development of primary care services and interfacing with secondary care
Lim, Nye, et al. (2012a) and Lim, Worster, et al. (2012b)	Arena	To describe and evaluate an approach where physicians are considered 'pseudo-agents' in a DES	Utilization of nursing staff and clerks remained similar. Physician utilization rates increased by 50% in the pseudo-agent-based model. There was no change in the time from when the patient was placed in a room until the first physician visit. Time until discharge or admission increased for patients with a lower acuity. As a result, time to room for these patients also increased in addition to bed utilization. Neglecting these relationships could lead to inefficient resource allocation due to inaccurate estimates of resource utilization and waiting times
Marmor, Y. (2010)	Arena	To introduce the ED world empirically and to describe ED database. Then, a "black-box" stochastic model is fit to the number of patients in the ED. Failing to do so motivates a simulation approach	Use of simulation modeling in order to solve many problems of ED such LOS, cost, ambulance diversion etc.

(Continued)

Table 2.1 (Continued)   Literature Review Summary

Author	Software	Aim of Study	Results
Martin et al. (2011)	UML Models	To identify bottlenecks that contribute to overcrowding. The greatest source of delay in patient flow was the waiting time from a bed request to exit from the ED for hospital admission. The sources of delay in patient flow, and aspects of ED activity that could be improved were studied	Department redesign and initiative to develop a business intelligence system for predicting impending occurrence of access block were presented as a solution suggestion
McCarthy et al. (2008)	NA	To examine the validity of the emergency department (ED) occupancy rate as a measure of crowding by comparing it to the Emergency Department Work Index Score (EDWIN), a previously validated scale	The ED occupancy rate and the EDWIN classified leaving without being seen and ambulance diversion hours with moderate accuracy
Medeiros et al. (2008)	Arena	To model patient flow of an ED in an attempt to increase capacity that meets patient demand	Substantial improvements in patient care. Addition of 7,500 square feet to the existing 25,000 square foot ED. The new space, and some renovated existing space, is being designed to facilitate the improvement process of the ED
Miele, Andreoli and Grassi (2006)	NA	To study the management of the emergency radiology unit (ERU)	The ERU must be provided with due technological equipment and staff, and the processes and procedures have to be carefully organized to optimize cooperation between the radiologist and the other specialists. It is also necessary to carefully define the location of ER within the ED

(Continued)

Table 2.1 (Continued) Literature Review Summary

Author	Software	Aim of Study	Results
Miller et al. (2004)	EDsim	Alternative ED designs	(1) Removing bottlenecks means either adding more beds, adding more staff, or improving the process to move patients more quickly through the process. (2) Bottlenecks in the inpatient beds occur when the arrival volume exceeds the capacity. (3) Introduce fast-track beds for patients who only require minor treatment. (4) Focus on process improvements (bedside triage, bedside registration, reducing lab or radiology turnaround times, moving the in-patient discharge time earlier in the day, streamlining admitting activities, eliminating handoffs in the process, eliminating non-value added activities
Miro et al. (2003)	NA	To evaluate the different internal factors influencing patient flow, effectiveness, and overcrowding in the ED, as well as the effects of ED reorganization on these indicators	ED reorganization reduced the number of patients waiting to be seen from 5.8 to 2.5 and waiting time from 87 to 24 minutes. Before the reorganization, 31% and 48% of the time was considered to be overcrowded in numerical and functional terms respectively. After the reorganization, these figures were reduced to 8% and 15% respectively
Morgareidge and Hui (2014)	MedModel	To optimize patient flow and to design the space of the ED by using DES and Space Syntax Analysis (SAA) respectively	Three phases were applied: master planning, process improvement in the existing ED, and designing the new ED
Moskop et al. (2009)	NA	To identify and describe operational and financial barriers for resolving the crisis of ED crowding, along with a variety of institutional and public policy strategies proposed/ implemented to overcome those barriers	Two solutions were evaluated and designed in order to address the problem of ED crowding: (1) distribution of a warning statement to ED patients, (2) implementation of a reverse triage system for safe early discharge of hospital inpatients

(Continued)

Table 2.1 (Continued) Literature Review Summary

Author	Software	Aim of Study	Results
Mould et al. (2013)	NA	To examine the impact of the techniques, process mapping and simulation, in the redesign of ED systems	The introduction of a new staff roster, the impact on patient time in the ED were examined. The new roster was identified as a reduction in the mean patient time of 16 minutes, for the 87% of ED patients classified as minor
Munro, Mason and Nicholl (2006)	NA	To determine what measures were introduced by EDs in response to the national monitoring week in March 2003, and which, if any, of these were most effective in reducing waiting times	Departments had taken a wide range of measures to improve waiting times (such as additional senior doctor hours (39%), creation of a four-hour monitor role (37%), improved access to emergency beds (36%), additional non-clinical staff hours (33%), additional junior doctor hours (32%), additional nursing hours (29%), and triage by senior staff (28%))
Park et al. (2008)	Arena	To present a forecasting and simulation model for resource management of the ED	The near future load level of each resource was determined using the proposed simulation model. Regression models were used to estimate the daily average number of patient arrivals in 2008. The results showed that the expected daily average number of patient arrivals in 2008 would increase by 3% compared to the number of arrivals in 2007
Patvivatsiri (2006)	Flexsim	To analyze patient flow throughout the treatment process, assess the utilization of ER resources, evaluate the impact of a hypothetical bioterrorist attack, and determine the appropriate resource and staff levels for a bioterrorism scenario	The recommended staffing strategy at two bottlenecked areas of the hospital's treatment facility would allow a significant reduction in patients' total time in the ER and an improvement in the utilization of resources

(Continued)

Table 2.1 (Continued)   Literature Review Summary

Author	Software	Aim of Study	Results
Paul and Hariharan (2007)	NA	To develop a generic simulation model of hospital capacity planning during a bioterrorist attack	Developing a feedback loop to alert emergency management officials about the occurrence and type of an attack. Policy recommendations were presented
Paul et al. (2010)	NA	To highlight the contribution of simulation modeling to ED overcrowding and discuss how simulation can be better used as a tool to address this problem	Three suggestions for future research directions for simulation studies were presented: (1) Simulation models need to capture human behavior. (2) ED must be studied as part of a larger system. (3) Focus on the individual level of care and incorporate the patient perspective
Paul and Lin (2012)	ProModel	To improve a generic methodology to investigate the causes of overcrowding and solving strategies	Insufficient physicians during peak hours, the slow process of admitting patients to inpatient floors, and laboratory and radiology test turnaround times were identified as the causes of reduced ED throughput
Rado et al. (2014)	Arena	To analyze the impact of the enhancements made to the system after the relocation of the ED in Hong Kong	Current arrival rates and the actual staff schedule were evaluated as the input parameters of the model. Ten percent growth of patient arrivals leads to a big increase in the waiting times of patients for triage and for consultation. Adding an extra doctor to the midnight shift cannot benefit the walking patients but can contribute to a decrease in doctors' utilization from 88.44% to 81.64%
Richardson (2006)	NA	To quantify any relationship between emergency department (ED) overcrowding and ten-day patient mortality	Presentation during high ED occupancy was associated with increased in-hospital mortality at ten days, after controlling for seasonal, shift, and day of the week effects. The magnitude of the effect is about 13 deaths per year
Rico et al. (2007)	Arena	Nurse allocation to manage patient overflow during a pandemic influenza outbreak	Queue length did not depend on the number of nurses, but on better allocation policies

(Continued)

Table 2.1 (Continued) Literature Review Summary

Author	Software	Aim of Study	Results
Rieffe et al. (1999)	NA	To report a study designed to investigate the reasons why patients visit the ED and to determine the influence of patient characteristics on specific motives. A multi-dimensional measurement instrument was designed to identify the motives of patients who bypass their GP and visit the ED	GPs might consider improving their services in order to "entice" patients to visit them instead of an ED
Rossetti et al. (1999)	Arena	Use of computer simulation to test alternative ED attending physician staffing schedules and to analyze the corresponding impacts on patient throughput and resource utilization	The simulation model is used to help identify process inefficiencies and to evaluate the effects of staffing, layout, resource, and patient flow changes on system performance without disturbing the actual system
Rowe et al. (2006)	NA	Overcrowding is a frequent and significant occurrence across hospitals in Canada	Lack of beds may lead to overcrowding. The percentage of patients in the ED who have been admitted, but have not been transferred to a hospital ward because of a lack of bed availability, is perceived as the most important measure of overcrowding, but is infrequently collected. Electronic collection of data and contributions to a national data system should be considered. Fast-track systems can reduce overcrowding where patients with minor injuries or illnesses can reduce ED length of stay, waiting time, and the number of patients who leave without being seen. Ambulance diversion strategies, short stay units, staffing changes, and system-wide complex interventions should also be further explored
Ruohonen et al. (2006)	MedModel (Promodel)	To test different process scenarios, allocate resources and perform activity-based cost analysis	Results showed that this method improves the operation of the Emergency Department of Special Health Care substantially (over 25%)

(Continued)

Table 2.1 (Continued) Literature Review Summary

Author	Software	Aim of Study	Results
Samaha et al. (2003)	Arena	To create a model that depicts the current operations and evaluate possible alternatives to reduce LOS	The Arena model demonstrated that there are several problems in the emergency department, but also revealed that the main problem was process related, not resource dependent
Satterthwaite et al. (2012)	NA	To analyze the impact of reverse triage to rapidly assess the need for continuing in-patient care and to expedite patient discharge to create surge capacity for disaster victims	Through a combination of cancellation of all planned admissions, discharging 19 patients at least one day earlier than planned and discharging all patients earlier in the day surge capacity was made available to accommodate blast victims. Notably, reverse triage resulted in no increase in clinical risk with only one patient who was discharged early returning for further treatment
Saunders et al. (1989)	NA	To develop a model that uses multiple levels of preemptive patient priority; assigns each patient to an individual nurse and physician; incorporates all standard tests, procedures, and consultations; and allows patient service processes to proceed simultaneously, sequentially, repetitively, or a combination of these	Patient throughput time varied directly with laboratory service times and inversely with the number of physician or nurse servers. Resource utilization rates varied inversely with resource availability, and patient waiting time and patient throughput time varied indirectly with the level of patient acuity
Schneider et al. (2003)	NA	To assess the degree of crowding in hospital (EDs) and measure the degree of physical crowding and personnel shortage	This study demonstrated that EDs are severely overcrowded. Such overcrowding raises concerns about the ability of EDs to respond to mass casualty or volume surges
Schull et al. (2001)	NA	To determine the impact of systematic hospital restructuring on ED overcrowding	Restructuring should proceed slowly to allow time for monitoring of its effects and modification of the process, because the impact of incremental reductions in hospital resources may be magnified as maximum operating capacity is approached

(Continued)

Table 2.1 (Continued) Literature Review Summary

Author	Software	Aim of Study	Results
Schull et al. (2004)	NA	To estimate the effect of ED crowding on door-to-needle time for patients given intravenous thrombolysis for suspected acute myocardial infarction	ED crowding is associated with increased door-to-needle times for patients with suspected acute myocardial infarction and may represent a barrier to improving cardiac care in EDs
Schull et al. (2012)	NA	To evaluate the effect of ED clinical decision units (CDUs) on overall ED patient flow	With only 4% of ED patients admitted to CDUs, the potential for efficiency gains in these EDs was limited. The observed effects of CDU operation were in the desired direction of reduced ED LOS, reduced admission rate, and no increase in ED revisit rate
Siddharthan et al. (1996)	NA	To address the problems of EDs and adopt various strategies for operational and financial survival	The application of a priority model yields an average savings of 21 minutes or a reduction of 10% of patient time associated with waiting for the provision of medical services
Sinreich et al. (2005)	Arena	To analyze ED operations performance with a special simulation tool	The model was an effective method to assist management in evaluating different operational alternatives. The average duration of the basic elements in the patient's process were determined (to be used later in the simulation tool as default values), the basic patient streams that trigger the different processes were identified, and estimation models were developed to be used by the simulation tool

(Continued)

Table 2.1 (Continued)   Literature Review Summary

Author	Software	Aim of Study	Results
Sinreich and Jabali (2007)	S-model and SWSSA	To show that a selective downsizing process in which each resource is treated separately (increasing the work capacity of some resources is also possible), based on its unique contribution to the overall ED operational performance, can approximately maintain current ED operational measures in terms of patient LOS despite an overall reduction in staff hours	By balancing the workload of the different resources in the ED in relation to each other, SWSSA was able to achieve LOS values within 19 to 4% of the original values despite a reduction of 17.5% in the physicians' work hours and a reduction of 13% to 47% in the nurses' work hours. In order to maintain the results' cost effectiveness, SWSSA allows the sharing of resource hours between the ED and the other hospital admission departments
Subash et al. (2004)	NA	To see whether three hours of combined doctor and nurse triage would lead to earlier medical assessment and treatment and whether this benefit would carry on for the rest of the day when normal triage had resumed	Three hours of combined doctor and nurse triage significantly reduces the time to medical assessment, radiology, and to discharge during the intervention period. Waiting times at midday were shorter in the triage group. There was no significant knock-on effect for the rest of the day
Sun et al. (2013)	NA	To assess the association of ED crowding with subsequent outcomes in a general population of hospitalized patients. The primary outcome was inpatient mortality. Secondary outcomes included hospital length of stay and costs	Periods of high ED crowding were associated with increased inpatient mortality and modest increases in length of stay and costs for admitted patients
Swisher et al. (2001)	VSE	To model and analyze physician clinic operations using discrete event simulation	The simulation model presented allowed physicians to perform what-if analyses on staffing levels and facility design, as well as experiment with scheduling policies and operating hours and literally see the effects of the changes
Van Uden et al. (2003)	NA	To investigate differences in numbers and characteristics of patients using primary or emergency care because of differences in organization of out of hours care	The organization of out of hours care in Maastricht has optimized the GP's gate-keeper's function and led to fewer self-referrals at the A&E department, compared with Heerlen

(Continued)

Table 2.1 (Continued)   Literature Review Summary

Author	Software	Aim of Study	Results
Wang et al. (2009)	ARIS, Arena	To identify process bottlenecks, and adjust resources allocation or staff dimensioning without disturbing the actual system by using ARIS and ARENA software	For the purpose of reducing waiting time in EDs, doctor's efficiency improvement and quick pass process are proposed and experimented as two new solutions
Weil et al. (1995)	Ilog-Solver	To present the efficiency of Constraint Programming for solving the problem of nurse scheduling	1) It saves much time for the head nurse in the generation of schedules; 2) it helps the decision maker in decisions and negotiations; 3) it is a flexible with respect to individual requests and for overcoming unforeseen absences; 4) it is very easy to manage constraints whether, for example, to define new constraints, activating or deactivating particular constraints, or modifying an already defined constraint
Weng et al. (2011)	Simul8	Optimal Resource allocation to improve patient flow	The allocation of human resources had obvious influence on the degree of crowdedness
Wiinamaki and Dronzek (2003)	NA	To project bed requirements for an emergency care center expansion	The capacity requirements based on length of stay for each of the patient areas affected by the expansion was studied
Xiao et al. (2012)	Arena	To optimize the workflow during a patient surge of a disaster event	Reorganizing lower priority work processes and relocating the resources associated with those processes can shorten total waiting time in the ED, allowing better management of patient flows
Yi et al. (2010)	NA	To develop a generic simulation model that is capable of representing the operations of a wide range of hospitals given an earth quake disaster situation	Generalized regression equations are fitted to obtain steady-state hospital capacities. A parametric meta-model is developed to predict transient capacity for multiple hospitals in the disaster area in a timely manner, as demanded by emergency operations management for guiding the routing and treatment of injured people

(Continued)

Table 2.1 (Continued) Literature Review Summary

Author	Software	Aim of Study	Results
Yoon et al. (2003)	NA	To identify and quantify the principal ED patient care time intervals, and to measure the impact of important service processes (laboratory testing, imaging and consultation) on LOS for patients in different triage levels	The use of diagnostic imaging and laboratory tests was associated with longer LoS, varying with the specific tests ordered. Specialty consultation was also associated with prolonged LoS, and this effect was highly variable depending on the service consulted. Triage level, investigations and consultations are important independent variables that influence ED LoS. Future research is necessary to determine how these and other factors can be incorporated into a model for predicting LoS
Young et al. (2004)	NA	Improve quality, reduce waiting times, and enhance the working environment of a healthcare system	Design of industrial processes to deliver higher quality health care at lower cost. Three industrial approaches: lean thinking, theory of constraints and Six Sigma are established
Zeng et al. (2012)	Simul8	To improve ED service quality with a computer simulation. The simulation model is capable of evaluating the quality of care in terms of length of stay, waiting times, and patient flow. Sensitivity analyses have been carried out to investigate the impact of workforce and diagnosis equipment on quality performance	To ensure better clinical outcome, more nurses are needed; in addition, an additional computed tomography scanner is recommended. The model also shows that implementing team nursing policy (for two nurses) could lead to significant improvement in the emergency department's quality of care

Source: Oueida et al. (2017b).

Note: Table adapted from *Handbook of Research on Data Science for Effective Healthcare Practice and Administration*, p. 94.

2.2 The Studied Hospital Background

"The studied hospital is located in the north of Lebanon. It is a medical legacy based on more than half a century of experience and is considered as a non-profit health institution recognized as a public utility foundation since 1952. During the Lebanese Civil War (1975–1990) most public institutions were not actually functioning, which made this hospital the only shelter for the ever-increasing number of patients in need. So, in order to increase the number of beds and provide the hospital with all that it requires in terms of medical equipment, the extension of its premises became a must. Many achievements have been realized since then to expand the hospital and include new departments. A second extension was realized in 2003 when a new building was established on a lot belonging to the hospital and located across the street. It is noteworthy that these two buildings are connected through an underground tunnel where patients can be transferred safely. The hospital is composed of two buildings, as mentioned earlier. The first building is a charitable suite building which serves patients who are not taking advantage of any private medical insurance and is dedicated to patients treated at the expense of the Ministry of Health. The second is a private suite building, which is located in front of the charitable suite building, and is dedicated to patients subscribed to the cooperative government employees, insurance associations, public institutions, and patients who want to receive treatment at their own expense. Nevertheless, in case of overcrowding and high-acuity patients, the two buildings can cooperate to serve the patient in need. This hospital now has around 207 beds, distributed in different units, as shown in Table 2.2, and covers most of the medical and surgical specialties. Its ED is open 24 hours a day and serves more than 40,000 patients a year" [Oueida et al. (2017c)]. The hospital mission is to provide high-quality and safe medical services through effective leadership, best usage of resources, and continuous education to keep up with all medical change and informatics

Table 2.2   Bed Distribution in the Hospital

Unit	Bed Capacity
Number of CCU beds	7
Number of ICN beds	5
Number of ICU beds	6
Number of Renal Dialysis beds	23
Number of Oncology beds	13
Number of Pediatrics beds	24
Number of Obstetric beds	26
Number of Medical and Surgical beds	50
Number of Labour beds	7
Number of Delivery beds	36
Number of ER A beds	5
Number of ER B beds	5
Total Number of Beds	207

evolution. In this study, the ED was chosen in order to improve the hospital's service and quality and increase patient satisfaction. "The main reason to choose the ED is because it is the most interacting unit with most of the other units in the hospital; it is a 24/7 operating unit and it is open for any type of patient at any time regardless of the age, case and level of illness. This was completed by studying the problems in the two emergency rooms and proposing scenarios in order to alleviate these arising problems. The main resources available in the ED are the following:

■ Emergency Room Doctor (or ER Dr.): responsible for final diagnosis, treatment decisions, prescriptions, patient discharge or admission and the Key One person in case of a high-acuity patient.
■ Registered Nurse (RN): head of all nurses during a shift. The head nurse is responsible for the triage phase and can make decisions (like the doctor's role) only in some exceptional cases such as excessive overcrowding or disaster conditions.
■ Nurse (N): responsible for collecting blood samples, taking blood pressure/fever, giving the treatment described by the doctor or head nurse (such as a drip or any additional medication). Nurses are also responsible for collecting patient's data (such as: name, civil ID number, information about previous surgeries, information about side-effects of a certain medicine), and assisting other resources in the ED.
■ Transporter: responsible for transferring the patient from the ED to the radiology unit if needed and vice versa. Also, responsible for transferring patients to their assigned rooms in case of hospital admission.
■ Specialist: specialists are doctors available in their clinics (inside or outside the hospital). They are responsible for extra diagnosis in case the ER doctor decides that admission is a must" [Oueida et al. (2017c)].

2.3 Patient Satisfaction

"In complex systems, such as healthcare, patient satisfaction is identified as the patient experience of care and has been referred to as the indispensable outcome. The main goal of ED practitioners is patient satisfaction along with maintaining optimal outcomes. Patient satisfaction has become a very important outcome measure when assessing healthcare systems performance. Nevertheless, it is a complex and confusing concept. Some providers suggest several activities in order to enhance satisfaction without being sure if these actions really improve satisfaction or not. Also, patient satisfaction enhancement activities should not conflict with cost efficacy" [Oueida et al. (2018b)]. Several factors fall under patient satisfaction and are listed as follows:

■ Waiting time [Thomas (1998)]
■ Race and sex [Cleary and McNeil (1988); Boulding et al. (2011)]
■ Younger patients, black patients, and patients classified as at low-acuity level during triage are generally classified with low satisfaction [Toma et al. (2009); Hojat et al. (2011)]
■ Communication language among patients and providers [Caligtan et al. (2012)]
■ The treating physician's awareness of parental expectations [Shesser et al. (1986)]
■ The ED area space
■ The up-to-date equipment and technology adoption

"Interviews with physicians prove that patients have specific expectations during a clinical encounter; being aware of these expectations, the physician can then fulfill patient satisfaction [Dunn

(2010)]. Sometimes physicians may misperceive patient expectations, thus leading to poor medical practice where unnecessary care is provided. The goal of this section is to determine the contribution and effect of these factors in influencing patient satisfaction" [Oueida et al. (2018b)].

2.3.1 Background

"Patient satisfaction started to be more highlighted and discussed in the 1980s. Between 1980 and 1996 research on this topic increased significantly. The approach of considering patient satisfaction as an important measure plays an effective role in making healthcare providers accountable to their patients and thus is an important healthcare service provided by the hospital to its patient. Patient satisfaction can be referred to as a general point of view toward an experience of healthcare, may comprise an emotional facet, and relates to some desired expectations or social networks [Keegan et al. (2003)]. It is described by some authors as emergent and fluid [Meredith and Wood (1995)] or a passive form of establishing consumers' views [McIver and Carr-Hill (1989)]. A good system must address patient satisfaction as the point of care for each patient's medical care and service required before exiting the ED. Patient needs are related to healthcare resources required to accomplish a service [Sommers et al. (2007)]. To ensure patient satisfaction, each patient must be involved in the evaluation of their own experience during their visit to the facility. This will help in ensuring continuous quality and improvement. Nowadays, patient satisfaction has become a high index representing the status of a hospital/facility and a desirable outcome attracting decision-makers.

Patient experience is classified under the satisfaction or dissatisfaction in relation to a certain medical service. It is the patient's judgment on the quality of care provided during a visit. Therefore, patient satisfaction should be considered as an important factor in assessing the quality of care in hospitals [Torcson (2005)]. Other authors acknowledged in their studies that patients' reports of their health experience and their satisfaction with the quality of service are very important health measures [Bolus and Pitts (1999)]. It is obvious that focusing on the quality of care provided in health services is a priority for any healthcare system. However, the rising high cost of treatments, equipment, etc., the shortage in medical resources, and variations in clinical practice have affected the notion of quality. Thus, a quality healthcare system is one that guarantees a continuous quality of care despite all the shortages and limitations faced. The assessment of this quality is usually based on technical perspectives and the process in which the care is delivered. This assessment becomes more authentic if it is centered on patients' views, experiences, and perceptions. Thus, the system should assess these perceptions and monitor quality based on these feedbacks in order to keep operating properly [Shaikh (2005)]. Another goal of patient satisfaction research is to evaluate patients' views and associate available values with different outcomes [Van Duren (2008)].

The human connection between patients and physicians has a huge impact. The annals of medicine throughout the years stated that some excellent care delivery failed to have good patient satisfaction because of the unapproachable physician and other poor care delivery outcomes an excellent patient satisfaction because of the good relationship with the physician. Therefore, it can be said that the quality of medical care is highly influenced by the relationship between patients and physicians. Quintana et al., 2006, discussed patient satisfaction and its relation to some areas in the hospital [Quintana et al. (2006)]. They found that the shorter the length of stay, the higher the satisfaction rate was in relation to specific domains. Actually, the quality of care delivered to patients affects overall satisfaction and, indirectly, the length of stay in the hospital. Recently, a majority of hospitals have tended to reduce the length of stay in order to increase the rate of patient satisfaction [Borghans et al. (2012)].

In the 1980s, businesses approached customer satisfaction surveys in order to monitor the services they provided. Nowadays, healthcare organizations have started to adopt this concept where survey results are analyzed in order to evaluate the quality of the medical service provided. The following subsections present the survey conducted in the ED studied in this work in order to assess the main factors affecting patient satisfaction.

2.3.2 Methods and Material

This study was conducted in March 2017. The two emergency rooms (ERs) were considered for the survey: the public emergency room (ER A) and the private emergency room (ER B). Patients were selected randomly and a pre-structured survey questionnaire was provided to patients. Data was collected based on patients' experience in the ED and patient satisfaction with regard to services and management at the ED. For the purpose of obtaining accurate results, 100 patients were given the questionnaires: 50 patients from each ER. Descriptive statistical analyses are carried out on the data collected in order to evaluate patient satisfaction and are presented in the following sections.

2.3.3 Selection of Participants

The participants consisted of consecutive patients treated in the ED during March 2017 and April 2017 through different period of times (day, evening, weekdays, weekends). Some patients, such as severe cases, children, patients not willing to participate, and those unable to communicate because of language, are excluded from the survey. The survey was designed to be easy for patients to undertake. Questions are clear and straightforward in order to ensure accuracy. This will ensure that results are trustworthy and patients are not obliged to skip a question or answer anything just to finalize the survey. The design of the survey and choice of questions was based on several visits to the hospital and an overview of the problems usually faced by patients during clinical visits.

2.3.4 Data Collection and Processing

Data collection was performed before patient discharge from ED. The questions can be divided into three phases: the first phase of questions were related to the patient's impression and rating of the service and of medical care after completion of his/her demand; the second phase was related to the opinion on how to improve the operation of the emergency department and the factors affecting his/her experience during this visit. Finally, a retrospective chart review is approached. Immediately after completion of medical care and before transferring the patient to another unit or discharge, the level of satisfaction with the ED visit was determined including diagnosis, procedures followed in the ED, level of explanation of the patient's case, physicians, and other resources' skills and level of care, the time spent waiting before receiving care, the total waiting time spent in the ED, the time spent with the physician, any suspicion of unnecessary diagnosis, and whether the patient will follow the treatment/recommendations. The number of patients enrolled on this survey was 100. The last phase included reviewing the medical records after the patient left the ED in order to determine what exactly was performed with this patient. Other information collected was day of the week, shift time, the time between triage and examination, the final patient discharge, and the category of diagnosis.

2.3.5 Data Analysis

The survey was prepared using the website www.surveymonkey.com, which is an academic and student survey database for projects of all types. The main concern and outcome measure is the level of satisfaction with the ED visit. The survey was prepared using the website, then printed and provided to patients at their arrival at the ED. Another way to collect data from the survey responses was to place the link, (www.surveymonkey.com/r/XGPMF5Y), on the hospital's website where patients are requested to gain access and place their answers, as well as sharing the link on social media to grasp more general responses. The major outcome measure from this survey is to determine the level of satisfaction with the ED. We focused in this analysis on the factors that mostly affect patient satisfaction (such as long waiting times, unclear assessment of the medical case, ED layout, resources shortage, etc.) in order to figure out ways to improve based on patients' opinion and experience during their visits. Data responses were collected from the survey website and statistical analysis were performed and presented below.

2.3.6 Results and Output Statistics

From all the arriving patients to the ED, only 100 respondents took the survey and the results of each question are presented in Figures 2.1 to 2.9 (except Question 9 where answers are based on personal views and need text analysis)" [Oueida et al. (2018b)].

Output statistics are collected for each question and presented in Figures 2.10 to 2.18 (except Question 9, which needs text analysis and will be discussed separately in Section 2.3.7).

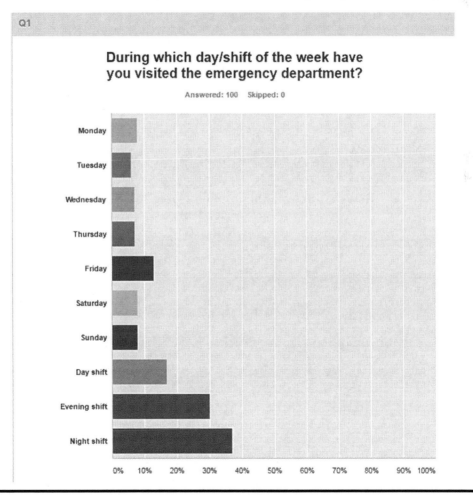

Figure 2.1   Survey Question 1: Visit day/shift—chart [Oueida et al. (2018b)].

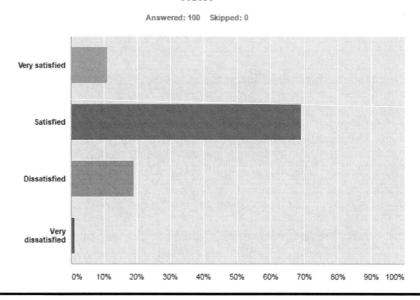

Figure 2.2   Survey Question 2: Visit experience—chart [Oueida et al. (2018b)].

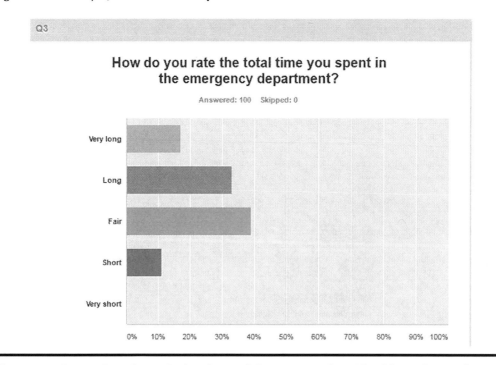

Figure 2.3   Survey Question 3: Rating the total time spent—chart [Oueida et al. (2018b)].

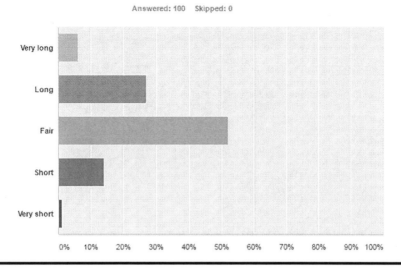

Figure 2.4 Survey Question 4: Rating time spent for initial treatment—chart [Oueida et al. (2018b)].

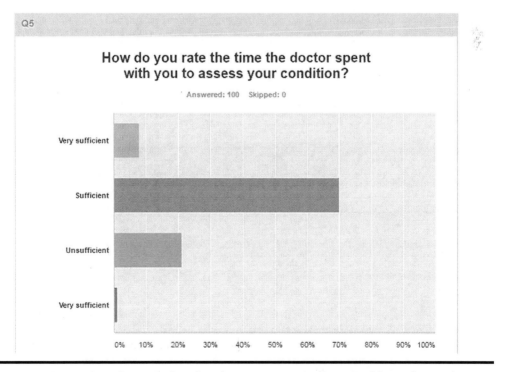

Figure 2.5 Survey Question 5: Rating time for assessment—chart [Oueida et al. (2018b)].

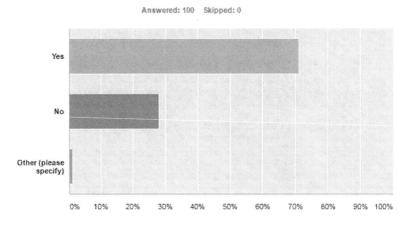

Figure 2.6 Survey Question 6: Rating quality of care—chart [Oueida et al. (2018b)].

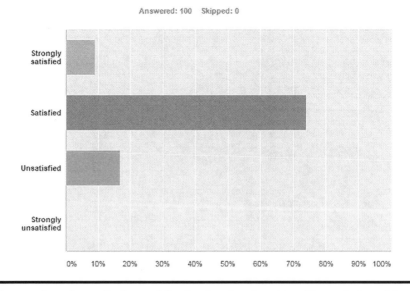

Figure 2.7 Survey Question 7: Rating satisfaction level—chart [Oueida et al. (2018b)].

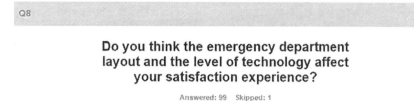

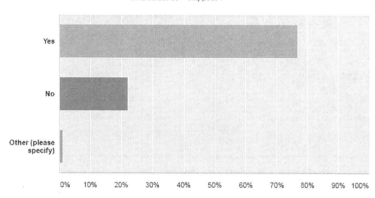

Figure 2.8   Survey Question 8: Layout and technology influence on satisfaction—chart [Oueida et al. (2018b)].

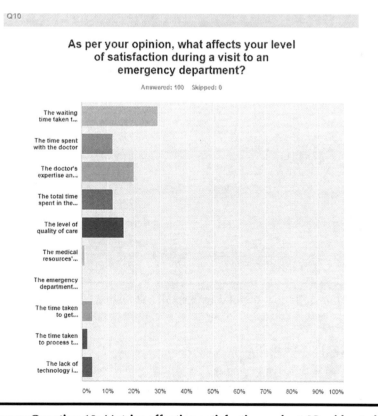

Figure 2.9   Survey Question 10: Metrics affecting satisfaction—chart [Oueida et al. (2018b)].

Answer Choices	Responses	
Monday	8.00%	8
Tuesday	6.00%	6
Wednesday	7.00%	7
Thursday	7.00%	7
Friday	13.00%	13
Saturday	8.00%	8
Sunday	8.00%	8
Day shift	17.00%	17
Evening shift	30.00%	30
Night shift	37.00%	37
Total Respondents: 100		

Figure 2.10   Question 1: Visit day/shift—statistics.

Answer Choices	Responses	
Very satisfied	11.00%	11
Satisfied	69.00%	69
Dissatisfied	19.00%	19
Very dissatisfied	1.00%	1
Total		100

Figure 2.11   Question 2: Visit experience—statistics.

Answer Choices	Responses	
Very long	17.00%	17
Long	33.00%	33
Fair	39.00%	39
Short	11.00%	11
Very short	0.00%	0
Total		100

Figure 2.12   Question 3: Rating the total time spent—statistics.

2.3.7 Discussion

"As discussed earlier, the study was performed for one month and data collection showed a sample of 100 patients that took this survey during this time period. From the records collected, the busiest day of the week was Friday, on night shifts, and this is where improvements should be most likely applied. It is clear that the main issue patients are facing during their visit to the ED is the waiting time (total of 61% of the patients); either the waiting time taken to be initially served

Answer Choices	Responses	
▼ Very long	6.00%	6
▼ Long	27.00%	27
▼ Fair	52.00%	52
▼ Short	14.00%	14
▼ Very short	1.00%	1
Total		100

Figure 2.13   Question 4: Rating time spent for initial treatment—statistics.

Answer Choices	Responses	
▼ Very sufficient	8.00%	8
▼ Sufficient	70.00%	70
▼ Unsufficient	21.00%	21
▼ Very sufficient	1.00%	1
Total		100

Figure 2.14   Question 5: Rating time for assessment—statistics.

Answer Choices		Responses	
▼ Yes		71.00%	71
▼ No		28.00%	28
▼ Other (please specify)	Responses	1.00%	1
Total			100

Figure 2.15   Question 6: Rating quality of care – statistics.

Answer Choices	Responses	
▼ Strongly satisfied	9.00%	9
▼ Satisfied	74.00%	74
▼ Unsatisfied	17.00%	17
▼ Strongly unsatisfied	0.00%	0
Total		100

Figure 2.16   Question 7: Rating satisfaction level—statistics.

(29%), the time a doctor takes to assess a patient's condition (20%), or the total time spent in the ED (12%). Another factor that should be taken into consideration while assessing patient satisfaction is the level of care the patient receives (16%). This study also shows that some patients believe that technology may affect the services in the ED and adding more expert medical staff will definitely make a difference (answers from Question 9)" [Oueida et al. (2018b)].

Answer Choices		Responses	
Yes		76.77%	76
No		22.22%	22
Other (please specify)	Responses	1.01%	1
Total			99

Figure 2.17   Question 8: Layout and technology influence on satisfaction—statistics.

Answer Choices	Responses	
The waiting time taken to be initially served	29.00%	29
The time spent with the doctor	12.00%	12
The doctor's expertise and time taken to assess your condition	20.00%	20
The total time spent in the emergency department	12.00%	12
The level of quality of care	16.00%	16
The medical resources' attitude	1.00%	1
The emergency department layout	0.00%	0
The time taken to get insurance approval	4.00%	4
The time taken to process the payment before leaving the emergency department	2.00%	2
The lack of technology in the emergency department	4.00%	4
Total		100

Figure 2.18   Question 10: Metrics affecting satisfaction—statistics.

"As a conclusion, Figure 2.19 presents a fishbone diagram for the main problem of the emergency department: patient LoS. The fishbone diagram is a cause-and-effect diagram, which presents a visualization tool for categorizing the potential causes of the problem in order to identify its root causes. These causes should be taken into consideration while studying and analyzing the system" [Oueida et al. (2017c)]. In the studied system, after conducting the site visits and interviews with different levels of staff, a clear idea about the operation of the ED, along with the types of service, are identified. Therefore, problems affecting the system and having a direct impact on the daily process of the ED are noted as: budget constraints, too many insurance companies, resource shortage, high resource utilization rates, several patient acuity levels, different patient types (age, mentality), lack of computerized documentation of information and updated equipment/software. All these problems lead to the same issue: the long waiting time. Therefore, the main concern is to find a way to alleviate this problem and reduce the total waiting time of patients in the ED.

2.3.8 Limitations

"The limitations faced during this data collection were related to the excluded patients: high-acuity cases, very old patients, or babies, and patients not willing to participate. Therefore, the outputs of this survey data collection are invalid for those groups of patients not sampled in this work from the beginning. The major reason for excluding these groups from the sampling is that they would generally report lower scores on satisfaction. Measuring patient satisfaction is a very

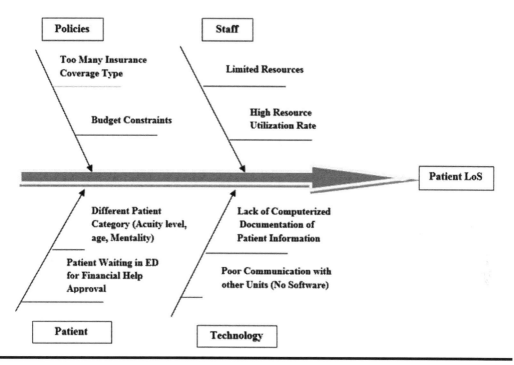

Figure 2.19 Emergency department fishbone diagram [Oueida et al. (2017c)].

complex endeavor and there is no validated 100% instrument to do it. Thus, the measure of overall satisfaction may not fully capture the real situation. Nevertheless, the surveyed outcome measures resulted in responses and output statistics similar to previous studies" [Oueida et al. (2018b)].

The information in this chapter appears in the following journals/book chapter, all authored by Soraia Oueida and reprinted by permission of the publisher:

- *International Journal of Public Health Management and Ethics*, Copyright © 2017, IGI Global, [Oueida et al. (2017a)]
- *International Review on Computers and Software* (I.RE.CO.S.), Copyright © 2017, Praise Worthy Prize, [Oueida et al. (2017c)]
- *Handbook of Research on Data Science for Effective Healthcare Practice and Administration*, Copyright © 2017, IGI Global, [Oueida et al. (2017b)]
- *Stochastic Methods for Estimating and Problem Solving in Engineering*, Copyright © 2018, IGI Global, [Oueida et al. (2018b)]

Chapter 3

Analysis of Healthcare Processes

In this chapter, the emergency department chosen to be studied is simulated using Arena Software, where the corresponding model is proposed, verified, and validated. The same emergency department is represented using a new proposed extended Petri net model, namely Resource Preservation Net (RPN). This RPN is then validated and proven to be sound mathematically through a few theorems and lemmas in Chapter 4. Arena is a good simulation tool but does not provide the mathematical validity of the model proposed. On the other hand, Petri net can. Arena, being a tool already tested in simulating healthcare systems, is considered a benchmark to rely on when proving the validity of the model proposed in this work.

3.1 The ED Patient Flow

In this section the ED patient flow is described before building the simulation model where the patient journey in the ED is illustrated from the time the patient enters the system until discharge.

3.1.1 Methodology

Emergency departments are large and complex systems where several tasks are executed with the need for different resources (human and material resources) to be available. Different types of patient (such as variety in age, type of illness, or acuity level) may be arriving into this ED, which makes the process heterogeneous and hard to handle. Thus, building, verifying, and validating the ED model is a long and difficult task. In order to efficiently understand the system, interviews with staff and on-site observations are necessary. "Patient flow delays, disruptions, and inefficiencies in the emergency department are the main purpose of this study. As a first step, defining the patient flow through the ED is essential. Next, the designed simulation model is tested in order to ensure that it accurately depicts the real ED system. Last, experimentation is applied on this

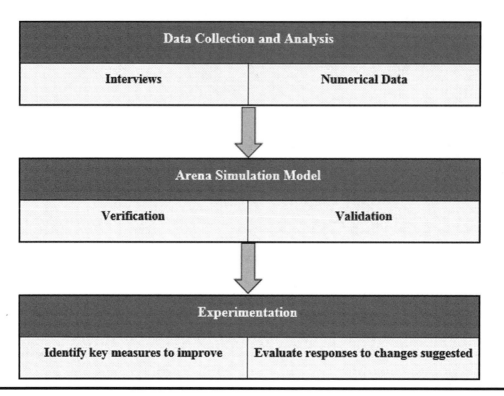

Figure 3.1 Methodology outline.

model in order to determine ways for improving patient flow. As mentioned in previous chapters and similarly to other related work (such as [Centeno et al. (2003) and Duguay and Chetouane (2007)]), the methodology is based on performing some staff changes and assessing the effect on the key performance indicators (principally the LoS). Resources are the main characteristics of the model and they are classified as human (doctors, nurses, etc.) and space (equipment, units, etc.). These resources are considered the control variables used in the future in order to perform experimentation and improvements. As agreed, because of the size and complexity of the system and the proven efficiency of simulation modeling, Discrete Event simulation (DES) is the selected tool to build the realistic model of the studied ED. The model development is made using Arena simulation software from Rockwell Automation. To establish an understanding of the ED and formulate the problem, several steps are conducted, such as site visits, data collection, research, and interviews. Then, the model is designed, verified, and validated. The Arena simulation model is built based on the current state of the ED. Finally, experimentation and analysis of this model is performed in order to improve ED operations and patient flow" [Oueida et al. (2017c)]. These steps, which form the fundamentals of a simulation study in literature [Law (2009); Baldwin et al. (2004)], are represented in Figure 3.1.

3.1.2 Emergency Department Overview

"In the studied hospital, two emergency rooms (ERs) constitute the emergency department. The first ER offers public services (ER A), whereas the second one (ER B) offers private services. Each

ER has a dedicated number of resources (doctors, nurses, etc.) but they share some facilities (radiology center, beds available for admission, insurance offices, and billing)" [Oueida et al. (2017c)].

"Six different zones can be highlighted in each ER:

- A waiting room for patients to sit and wait their turn
- A registration desk where a walk-in patient can request a service and where data about the patient is collected (name, age, previous surgeries, allergies, etc.)
- A doctor/nurse room where they can diagnose a patient's condition, consult other physicians, interpret diagnostic tests, prepare needed materials, and take treatment decisions without the need for the patient to be present
- A triage zone in case of overcrowding
- Three examination rooms
- A dedicated room for minor surgery (which can be handled inside the ER without the need for admission)" [Oueida et al. (2017c)].

In addition, the ER includes an ambulance arrival area where a nurse serves the arrived patient as a priority and moves them to the high-acuity room or surgery room; then a doctor will show up to assess the patient's case and diagnose the required treatment (such as rapid treatment/rapid surgery/admission, etc.). ED arrivals are assumed to follow a Random Exponential Process based on the data collected. Patient arrival rates (known as Tnow) are collected for 24 hours each day. The busiest days of the week are usually Friday and Saturday, which record the most arrivals, and the higher arrival rates are usually at night. "Arrivals are modeled with an average arrival rate, estimated based on a database of 48 weeks in the studied ED from August 2015 to August 2016" [Oueida et al. (2017d)]. Medical intervention is a necessity in order to improve the medical status of a patient. "Patient arrivals into the ED are of a heterogeneous type where different types of patient may appear without any prior notice whether by ambulance or any other mean of transport. Since the ED has a limited capacity of resources and it is obliged to serve all appearing patients, regardless of the type of illness or patient age, the high-acuity patients or the most serious cases should be treated immediately as a priority. Therefore, the triage stage is important in order to categorize a patient's arrival according to their condition. The triage nurse assigns a severity index to the patient based on the severity of the case. During the overall journey through the ED, a patient follows different stages, involving different type of resources (nurse, doctor, specialist, equipment, etc.). All resources should be included and specified in the model at each stage. These resources, depending on the kind of service offered and the type of patient, generate a waiting time, thus affecting the overall process. Table 3.1 presents the list of resources included in the model and their corresponding capacities" [Oueida et al. (2017c)]. The doctor represents the ER doctor responsible for diagnosis, making decisions (either admission or discharge), and writing prescriptions or ordering extra tests (such as imaging, blood test, etc.). The resources categories are: (1) the triage nurse responsible for the triage stage in order to classify patients based on their severity index; (2) the registered nurse (RN) who represents the top layer of nurses and may help the doctor in making decisions in cases of overcrowding and can assist in minor surgery taking place in the ED. In the designed model the RN is responsible for the triage stage; (3) the nurse (N) responsible for collecting information from patients, giving patients the necessary medication requested by the doctor, taking a blood sample, and preparing the patient; (4) the transporter (T) responsible for transferring the patient to another unit or to a dedicated room in cases of admission; (5) the specialist (S) that the ED doctor may rely on in order to take some critical

Table 3.1 Resources List and Capacity in the Model

Resource Type	Role	Capacity in the Model
Doctor	Diagnosis and final decision	1
RN	Classifying patients based on severity	1
Nurse	Preparing patients and assisting doctors	2
Transporter	Transporting patients to other units	1
Technician	Available for extra facilities such as in the radiology unit	3
Physician	Available in Radiology unit to check the results and provide a report	1
Receptionist	Available for registration process and opening a file	1
Accountant	Responsible for Billing	8
Facilities	Non-human resources including beds, wheel chairs, syringes, medication, etc.	5
Specialist	A senior doctor to help ED doctor in critical decisions	On Hospital Duty (not included in the model)

Source: Oueida et al. (2017c).

Note. Table adapted from *International Review on Computers and Software* (I.RE.CO.S.), p. 172.

decisions; (6) physicians (P) available in the radiology units and responsible for serving extra facilities requests such as X-rays, CT Scans, MRI, etc.

Three different ER doctors and seven different nurses are assigned for each day and during three different shifts. Specialists are on-call doctors available to the whole hospital and can be contacted if necessary. The staffing schedules are prepared by the head of the ED based on previous experience. As for the janitorial staff, they are not considered in the model since they cause negligible waiting times. In the designed model, the number of resources is the same for all shifts during one day and the corresponding processing times are also identical for all different shifts.

3.1.3 The Patient Journey in the ED

"The flow of patient in the ED varies from patient to patient depending on the case and the type of patient. Once arrived to the ED, the patient follows certain assessments before taking the appropriate decision (such as triage, waiting for consultation or directly assigned to a doctor, etc.). However, some essential steps patients must follow during the journey at the ED are: arrival, consultation, diagnosis, interpretation and decision and finally the process outcome (whether discharged or admitted to the hospital)" [Oueida et al. (2017c)]. The way patients arrive to the ED is ignored and excluded from the model design (by ambulance or any other way of transportation). All patients are treated the same once arriving to the ED and should pass by the triage stage regardless of the way of arrival. This is because patients in this area tend to use the ambulance in order to get more attention. Therefore, hospital management decided to use the triage process in order to alleviate this problem. Patient flow is illustrated in Figure 3.2

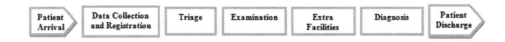

Figure 3.2   Patient journey through the ED [Oueida et al. (2017c); Oueida et al. (2018d)].

"Once a patient arrives in the ED, a nurse collects their data (name, age, service required) and then refers them to a room for an initial consultation. If the ED is crowded, triage occurs, where a triage nurse decides which patient has the highest acuity level and who should be treated first. Triage follows Canadian international standards. This triage process is very critical since it determines which patient must be seen immediately and where exactly to route the patient in order for them to be appropriately treated (such as appropriate staff resource and appropriate room). If the triage nurse is busy, patients must wait in the waiting room until the nurse is free. The triage nurse is responsible for referring high-acuity patients to a doctor for immediate examination and low-acuity patients to the waiting room until a doctor is free. After the triage process, an examination by a doctor is necessary. Severe cases are transported to an available room with the assistance of a transporter (sitting or using a stretcher or a wheelchair depending on the severity of the case). The transporter is a medical resource who helps to transfer patients throughout their journey in the hospital. Once the selected patient is in the appropriate examination room and a doctor is available, examination begins. The doctor can make a first assessment and may request additional facilities such as imaging, blood tests, the presence of a specific physician, etc. in order to finalize their diagnosis. If the patient being consulted does not need any extra services, the doctor discharges the patient with a prescription and some recommendations, if necessary. For patients who need blood tests, the blood sample is taken in the ED by an available nurse and sent with the patient to the referred floor in the event of hospital admission (such as surgery unit, maternity unit, etc.) and from there is transferred to the laboratory to be analyzed. If the patient is not to be admitted and the case is not severe, the blood sample is sent to the laboratory and the discharged patient will have to come back to the laboratory a few days later to check the test results. Otherwise, patients should wait in the waiting room until the results are ready. However, patients who need some imaging services, such as X-ray or CT scan, are transported by the medical transporter to the radiology unit.

Here, we should emphasize that patients in the public emergency room (ER A) will be transported to a different floor to undertake the necessary service; patients in the private emergency room (ER B) have to use a tunnel in order to reach the radiology unit, which may take several extra minutes. Once arrived in the radiology unit (RU), patients should wait in the waiting room until a physician is available to treat them, finalize the imaging process, and send them back to the waiting room. Here, patients should wait until the image is processed and the report is ready. Patients can then leave the RU and return to the ER where they should wait again until the appropriate doctor is available for a final diagnosis. Before the final step of checking the imaging results, patients are requested to go to the billing unit in order to pay the fees, fill out some documents, and present the type of insurance coverage they hold. In the final diagnosis step, after the test results (imaging and blood samples results) have been checked, patients can either be immediately discharged from the ED with a prescription and the necessary advice or can be admitted to the hospital. In cases of admission, patients will not be discharged from the ED until a bed is available on the appropriate floor. In some cases, the doctor may recommend minor surgery, which can be performed in the ED surgery room. In this event, an appropriate doctor for the specific kind of surgery should be called and the patient should wait in the ED until this doctor arrives. After a few hours of recovery, if needed, the patient is discharged from ED.

It is important to mention that, during the entire process of patient flow, the high-acuity patients always have priority. In critical cases, ER doctors always consult specialists, and arriving patients have priority over patients who have already been seen (these are called in-process patients [Huang et al. (2015)]) and each patient is treated by the same doctor and the same nurse throughout the process. This same-patient–same-staff rule is proven to have a significant impact on the behavior of the system [Kinsman et al. (2008)]. In some cases, the patient may be diagnosed, put on a drip in the ER, and then discharged; therefore, the patient will occupy a bed in the ER until this treatment terminates. An additional delay can be pointed out here, necessitated by the preparation and allocation of a nurse for this process. In other cases, the ER doctor may request the opinion of another specialist in order to finalize the diagnosis and decide what to do with the patient. Here, a limitation for experimentation arises since additional delays are added to the total time of the process. These additional delays affect other departments since the specialist is a part of the entire hospital system and not just the ED. The time the ED doctor takes to reach and inform the specialist, the time for the specialist to respond to this call and arrive in the ED if they are free, the discussion between the ED doctor and the specialist, are the additional delay times that occur before the specialist examines the patient and helps refine the ED doctor's diagnosis. Therefore, if an outside intervention into the ED is necessary, no improvement to the whole ED process and reduction of waiting times or overcrowding can be counted on. This delay is considered in the designed model under the doctor examination process. Diagnosis based on radiology facilities or laboratory unit requires the interaction of other resources located in other units and shared with different departments of the hospital (and being shared with two emergency rooms). Therefore, the duration fed into the model represents the total process time, including the waiting time for results and the transportation time from the ER to the RU. This presents another limitation for experimentation where reducing the waiting time in the RU cannot be a part of the improvement process. In the final stage, the patient can either be admitted to the hospital, which means being transferred to another unit in the hospital, or discharged. In the case of discharge, the patient exits the system and their place is now available for another patient. In the case of admission, the responsible ER doctor should organize the admission by phone and make sure to find an available bed in the specific referred unit of the hospital. As mentioned earlier, once the room/bed is available, the transporter will transfer the patient to the correct department" [Oueida et al. (2017c)].

3.1.4 Flowchart of the Conceptual Model

The Arena simulation tool is used to build the model. Model data inputs are collected from site observations. Although the designed model and proposed solutions for improvement are found to be reliable and consistent, it is recognized that they do not really reflect 100% the real emergency department. Some limitations are encountered while designing the model. One of these limitations is the data missing from databases and especially the service time of each process, where it was necessary to make assumptions and compare the operations of other EDs in order to predict some of the necessary data. The hospital is not fully computerized and databases for collecting and tracking the stages of patients in the ED are not available. In several interviews the owner and managing directors reflected a will to change the process in the ED and add some new software that would more reliably track patient flow. Another limitation is that patients arriving into the studied ED tend to use the ambulance as a way to track resources for high attention; thus, the case of patients arriving by ambulance is ignored and all patients are treated the same. All patients arriving into the ED should pass through the triage stage before being seen. Also, the hospital management imposes some budget constraints which only make the suggested solutions options for improvement in the future. In the designed model, only one acuity level was accounted for since data regarding how different acuity levels affected the use of resources was missing. In reality, a patient should be ranked based on the severity of their case since it affects the length of stay, the type of treatment applied, and the type of care required. The primary reason for not considering this acuity level while building this model is that the verification and validation process would have been much more complex. Finally, the most challenging part of the project is the patient arrival data. Data of patient flow in the ED is not fully observed, especially the inter-arrival rates. Therefore, some assumptions had to be made in order to design the model. "The model built for the studied emergency department, which is split into two parts—the emergency room A and the emergency room B—is presented in Figures 3.3 and 3.4. As mentioned earlier, the two emergency rooms share some facilities, such as the radiology unit and the billing department" [Oueida et al. (2017c)].

"The flow of patients during the whole process is explained as follows:

- Arrival ER: arrival of patient into the emergency department.
- Record Arrival Time: assign arrival time of patient to Tnow.
- Data Collection: the process of collecting patient information performed by a nurse once a patient arrives to the ER. Also, at this stage the patient needs to pay the consultation minimal fees at the ER desk; which is $35.
- Triage: process of defining the severity level of an arriving patient.
- Decide: the process of deciding whether the patient case is urgent or not. If the case is urgent then the patient is assigned as urgent and moved directly to the examination room. Otherwise, the patient is moved to the waiting room. In this model the routing probability here is 25% for severe cases and 75% for non-severe cases.
- Mark Urgent: process of assigning the patient to the urgent case.
- Examination: process of examination and checkup, performed by a doctor.
- Waiting Room: non-urgent patients are referred to a waiting room in order to wait for an available nurse/doctor.
- Move to Exam Room: the delay time that a patient takes in order to move to the examination room.
- Treatment by a Nurse: process of pre-checkup by a nurse until a doctor is available.
- Release Nurse: once the checkup is over, the nurse in charge should be released.
- Wait for Doctor: the delay time until a doctor is available after nurse checkup.
- Examination: process performed by a doctor in order to examine the arriving patient.
- Billing: the billing process and the registration of the file is done before getting the required treatment or prescription advised by the doctor.
- Extra Facilities: decision whether the patient needs extra facilities or not. If yes, then the patient is moved to the radiology unit. Otherwise, the patient immediately follows the process of treatment (after finalizing registration and payment). In this model, the routing probability here is 75% for patients with extra facilities and 25% for unneeded facilities.
- Radiology: represents the radiology unit where patients do X-rays, CT scan, MRI, or other types of imaging as requested by the doctor.
- Treatment: during this process the patient undergoes the required treatment as prescribed by the doctor. In the case of a radiology request, the doctor checks the imaging results before finalizing their diagnosis.
- Release Doctor: after diagnosis is finalized, the corresponding doctor is released.

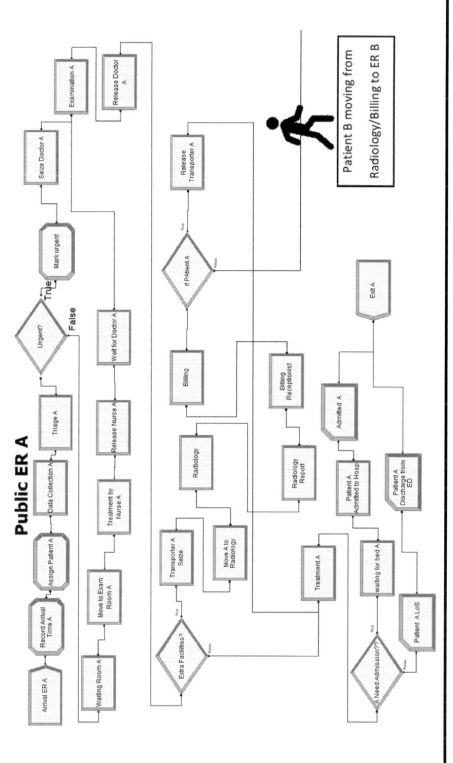

Figure 3.3 Emergency department Arena model flowchart_part a [Oueida et al. (2017e)].

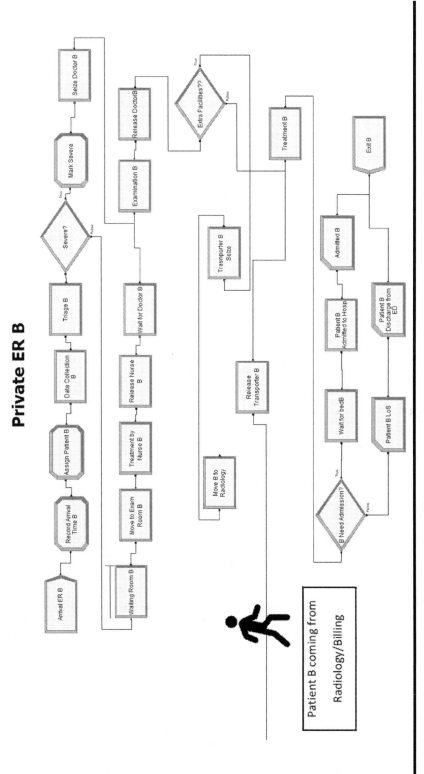

Figure 3.4 Emergency department Arena model flowchart_part b [Oueida et al. (2017e)].

- Need Admission: in this stage, and based on the doctor's diagnosis, the patient is either admitted to the hospital or discharged from the ER with a prescription.
- Waiting for Bed: in case the patient needs admission, they need to wait in the ER until a bed is available.
- Admission to Hospital: the process of admission to the hospital once a bed is available. Here the routing probability is 25% for admitted patients and 75% for patients directly discharged.
- Patient LoS: length of stay or the total time the patient spent in the system; from the time they arrived into the ER (Tnow) until discharge.
- Patient Discharge from ED: whether admitted to the hospital or not, the patient will be discharged from the ED (either to a room or home).
- Exit: the patient exits the system after finalizing all the needed tasks" [Oueida et al. (2017c)].

3.2 Simulation of Processes

Simulation is the modeling of a process or a system over a period of time. It has been a valuable and popular evaluation tool for the last 30 years. Most complex, real-world systems have stochastic or random elements which require more than analytical mathematical models in order to study their behavior. Thus, simulation modeling is an effective method to solve these problems. The main advantage of simulation is the long-term investment where testing various system scenarios is possible without the commitment of any physical resource. Arena, for example, is a very popular simulation software with a low cost that can be covered by simply implementing the solutions offered by the simulation. Another advantage is the time compression and expansion in evaluating a given system. A user can observe the behavior of the whole system, with its details, within a one-second time frame or view the data process for a time frame of a day, a month, or even a year. Regardless of the type of simulation used, the same steps should be followed when designing a model. First, a plan of study is presented to formulate the problem and clarify objectives. Here, the specific issues to be studied are also addressed. Clear vision is essential for the success of the study where people, cost, and time are wisely planned. Then data collection is needed for the second step where the model is defined. The information and data collection will be performed on the system of interest in order to determine the probability distributions and to specify the operating procedures of the random variables in the system. Now, the user is ready to build the needed model. In the process of building and validating the model, resources operating in the real system should be involved since they are familiar with the actual operations of the processes studied. In this way, the accuracy, credibility, and validity of the study are ensured. Model design can immediately begin through the use of a computer program, once enough information about the system has been gathered. Arena, a simulation modeling software, is a powerful graphical simulation offering analysis modules that can be combined with graphical templates in order to build huge and wide models [Anderson et al. (2010)]. Once model construction and verification has been done, pilot runs should be performed in order to test the sensitivity of the model's output to any small changes in the inputs. Here, if the level of change of output is high, then the user must reconsider the estimated input parameters. Once the simulation model is validated through these pilot runs, the user can design several experiments. The first step in the design process is to determine which of the made assumptions and model specifications have the greatest effect on the performance measures in order to reach the optimal performance. This analysis is used in order to decide which scenario is the best, relative to some specified performance measures. Finally, and based on this documented information, decisions can be taken and actions may be implemented in order to improve the system.

3.2.1 Data Distribution

Using the input analyzer of Arena software, the data collected for each process in the model from both ERs (public and private) are fed into the tool and the corresponding distributions are fitted. Here, it is important to highlight the fact that it is concluded from the data distribution results that both ERs follow the same rhythm of operation. They differ only when transporting the patient to the radiology unit since it is located in the building with the public ER. Patients from the private ER need to use the tunnel and thus have to travel further to reach the radiology center. The processes and other entity blocks used in the model, including the distribution summary information resulting from the input analyzer, and extra details about the performance, are classified below. The time unit used in the entire modeling process is minutes. Resource A corresponds to the public ER and resource B corresponds to the private ER.

1. Arrival into the ER: It is a create-type block following a Random Exponential distribution with a maximum arrival number of 70 patients per day (every 24 hours). This constraint comes from the hospital management. Note that only one patient can arrive at a time and there is a gap of 20 minutes between two patients. The arrival into the ER is referred to as Tnow.

2. Record Arrival Time: It is an assign-type block used to create an attribute and assign it to the patient once they have entered the ER. It assigns the arrival time (Arr time) to Tnow.

3. Assign Patient: It is an assign-type block used to create an attribute and assign it to the patient during the journey through the ED. It assigns the patient arriving into the public ER to "A" and the patient arriving into the private ER to "B."

4. Data Collection: It is a process-type block. The action to be taken is: "Seize Delay Release," where one resource (nurse) will be seized and delayed until the process is terminated. Once data collection is done, the resource will be released. This process follows a uniform distribution with a minimum of one and a maximum of three. The allocation is of type "added value," since the result from this process is the valuable information about the patient.

5. Triage: It is a process-type block. The action to be taken is: "Seize Delay Release," where one resource (RN) will be seized and delayed until the process is terminated. Once the triage is done, the RN will be released. This process follows a uniform distribution with a minimum of three and a maximum of five. The allocation is of type "added value," since the result from this process is the valuable triage decision whether the patient case is severe or not.

6. Urgent?/Severe?: It is a decision-type block. It is a two-way chance decision. The true option falls under 25% and the false under 75%. It tests the criticality of a patient case being examined by the RN. If the patient is critical then a doctor should be seized immediately. Otherwise, the patient will be referred to a waiting room where a nurse can assist until a doctor is available.

7. Seize Doctor: It is a seize-type block where one doctor is needed only as a resource. If the patient is marked as severe then a doctor should be seized immediately.

8. Waiting Room: It is a seize-type block. A patient diagnosed as not a severe case by the triage nurse will have to stay in a waiting room until a nurse is available and comes to accompany them in the examination room. Therefore, one nurse will be seized here as a resource.

9. Move to Exam Room: It is a delay-type block. The nurse assigned will transfer the patient from the waiting room to the examination room where they receive the needed pre-examination and preparation. The delay time follows a uniform distribution with a minimum of one and a maximum of two. It is a value-added allocation, since the patient is being treated.

10. Treatment by Nurse: It is a delay-type block. The nurse is still assigned as a resource. The patient marked as not severe will have to be prepared and pre-examined by a nurse until a doctor is available. The delay time follows a uniform distribution with a minimum of three and a maximum of five. It is a value-added allocation since the patient is being treated.

11. Release Nurse: It is a release-type block. The assigned nurse will be released when the treatment is over.

12. Wait for Doctor: It is a seize-type block. After being examined by the nurse, the patient needs to seize a doctor when available. Therefore, the resource type here is one doctor only and the allocation type is "wait."

13. Examination: It is a process type-block. All types of patient reach this process. If the patient is triaged as a critical case then the examination procedure takes 7 to 10 minutes, whereas the non-critical case takes 3 to 5 minutes. In order to express the dual behavior of this process, the delay time is set to the following expression: (criticality==1)*UNIF(7,10)+ (criticality==0)*UNIF(3,5). It is a value-added allocation where the patient receives the needed care.

14. Release Doctor: Once the examination process is complete, the seized doctor will be released.

15. Extra Facilities?: It is a decision type-block where 75% (true) seize a transporter to be moved to perform extra facilities and 25% (false) only move immediately to the treatment stage where no extra facilities are required. It is a two-way by-chance decision.

16. Seize Transporter: It is a seize-type block. A patient requested to be moved to the radiology unit for extra facilities such as X-ray, MRI, etc. needs to wait for a transporter in order to be transferred. Therefore, the type of resource here is transporter and the allocation is "wait."

17. Treatment: It is a process-type block. It is here where the patient receives the real diagnosis after the results from the radiology unit are examined by the doctor. The doctor may request another opinion to finalize the decision through a specialist available on call in the hospital for all departments. The action of this process is "seize delay release", where a doctor is seized and delayed until the final diagnosis is given and only then can the doctor be released. It is a value-added process where the patient will have a clear view of the situation and whether they will be treated in the ED, discharged from the ED to home, or admitted to the hospital for extra care. The delay type follows a uniform distribution with a minimum of three and a maximum of five.

18. Move to Radiology: It is a delay-type block following a uniform distribution with a minimum of 3 and a maximum of 5 in the public ER and a minimum of 10 and a maximum of 15 in the private ER. Here, the transporter seized before will be used for the transfer procedure.

19. Radiology: It is a process-type block with a "seize delay release" action. Two types of resources are seized here in order to finalize the process: a technician responsible for executing the imaging and a physician responsible for checking the results and writing the report. Once arrived in the radiology unit the patient needs to wait in a waiting room until a technician/room is available. The overall time is counted including all the delays inside the unit. The delay type follows a uniform distribution with a minimum of 10 and a maximum of 15. It is a value-added service where the patient receives the required care in order to finalize the service. Recall that the two ERs share the same radiology resources (human and machine).

20. Billing: It is a process-type block with an action of "seize delay release." In the billing unit the patient needs to open a file through a receptionist and then move to another room in order to process the payment through an accountant (whether cash or by any mean of insurance type). Therefore, two type of resources need to be seized here: the receptionist and the accountant. The delay type follows a uniform distribution with a minimum of 15 and a maximum of 45. This is the most congested unit with lots of problems, particularly because the two ERs share the same resources for billing.

21. If patient A?: It is a decide-type block with a two-way by-condition value. If the attribute named patient type is equal to "A" (true) then the patient in the billing is coming from the public ER (of type A), thus transporter A is released. If the patient is from the private ER (of type B), then transporter B is released.

22. Release Transporter: It is a release-type block. Once billing is done, the transporter is released and the patient returns to the ED with the results of the radiology unit report.

23. Need Admission?: It is a decide-type block with a two-way by-chance value. Twenty five percent of patients (true value) are admitted to the hospital and thus wait in the ED for bed availability. On the other hand, 75% of patients (false value) exit to their home.

24. Waiting for Bed: It is a process-type block with an action of "seize delay release." A nurse needs to be seized in order to assist the patient while waiting in the ED and make sure their situation is stable until a bed is available and they are transferred to the appropriate room in another department (surgery, IC, maternity, etc.). Once the bed is available, the nurse will be released. It is a value-added allocation since the patient is receiving the required care until the bed is available. The delay type follows a uniform distribution with a minimum of 15 and a maximum of 60.

25. Patient LoS: It is a record-type block. The type of this record is "time interval." It refers to the total time a patient spends in the ED during their journey from arrival to exit. It is a very important performance measure and needs to be seriously considered since it affects patient satisfaction and organization reputation. The attribute used in order to calculate this total duration is the Arr time recorded when the patient entered the ED.

26. Patient Discharged from ED: It is a record-type block. The type of this record is "count." It counts the number of patients discharged from the ED.

27. Admitted: It is a record-type block. The type of this record is "count." It counts the number of patients admitted to the hospital.

28. Patient Admitted to Hospital: It is a process-type block with an action of "seize delay release." If the patient is to be admitted to the hospital, a transporter needs to be seized for assistance. The transporter needs to transfer the patient from the ED to a specific room in another department. If a blood test has been done in the ED, the transporter also needs to transfer the sample to the patient's room. The delay type follows a uniform distribution with a minimum of two and a maximum of four.

29. Exit: It is a dispose-type block representing the exit door of the ER. There are two exit doors: Exit A and Exit B, since we have two emergency rooms representing the ED.

3.2.2 Simulation Outputs

"After building the model and fitting all data to the corresponding distributions, the model described in Section 3.1.4 is simulated in order to check the results and study the areas of interest. When running the model, ten replications are approached in order to get the average of all performance measures. The base unit used is always minutes. The model is run for one year (365 days);

ED Simulation

Replications: 10   Time Units: Minutes

Key Performance Indicators

System   Average
Number Out   49,588

Figure 3.5   Patient number out (for one year).

the number of patients out is depicted in Figure 3.5. The average total number is 49,588 patients. In order to better spot problems in the system and since the ED is complex, only one day's output is collected and analyzed. The busiest day of the week is chosen during analysis. Therefore, output data and statistics are collected and analyzed for one day. Various performance measures need to be recorded in order to verify and validate the model. These performance measures are listed as: number of patients in and number of patients out, a counter (to differentiate between completely discharged patients and admitted-to-hospital patients), patient LoS, service time spent in different queues waiting for a process to be executed, and resource utilization rates" [Oueida et al. (2017c)].

The figures below show the different results obtained from the model simulation. The number of patients in and the number of patients out resulting from the simulation of the designed system are illustrated in Figure 3.6. "The number of patients arriving into the ED is limited to an average of 138 patients per day for both emergency rooms. And the number of patients exiting the system during the 24 hours of simulation is almost 77 patients in total for both emergency rooms" [Oueida et al. (2017c)].

"The patient LoS is a user-specified attribute used to calculate and record the total time spent in the system from the time the patient arrives into the emergency room until exiting the system. These values are presented in Figure 3.7 showing a different LoS for the two different type of

NUMBER OF PATIENTS

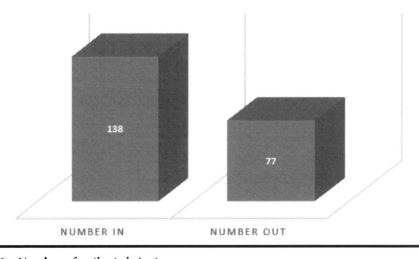

Figure 3.6   Number of patients in/out.

patient, Patient A and Patient B. The average total time spent by Patient A is around 277 minutes and for Patient B, an average of 294 minutes" [Oueida et al. (2017c)].

"The counter used to record the number of patients discharged from the system is divided into two different parts:

■ The patients discharged from the ED and admitted to the hospital (another department) in order to receive extra care. The total number is found to be almost nine patients for both ER A and ER B.
■ The patients discharged from the ED and leaving home after getting the required care inside the ED. The total number is found to be almost 30 patients for both ER A and ER B.

A chart summarizing this counter is presented in Figure 3.8" [Oueida et al. (2017c)].

"Resource utilization is presented in Figure 3.9. It is noticeable that the main problem exists with the transporters and the receptionist where the average utilization rates are 97% and 93% respectively.

The average waiting time spent in different queues in order to wait for certain processes to be executed or for certain resources to be available in order to move to execution stage is represented in Figure 3.10" [Oueida et al. (2017c)].

3.2.3 Simulation Verification and Validation

In order to represent the real system, results obtained from the simulation of the designed model should be approximately close to the current real system, otherwise, any suggestions for change and improvement may result in costly and wrong decisions [Law (2009)]. Therefore, verification and validation of the built conceptual model is necessary in order to make sure it accurately represents the real system.

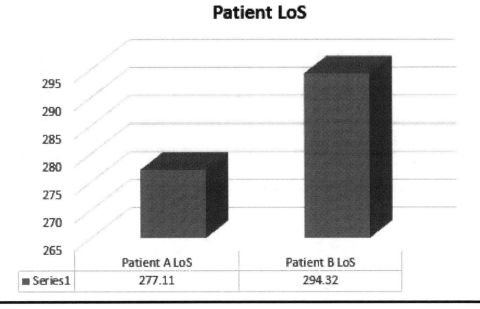

Figure 3.7 Patient LoS.

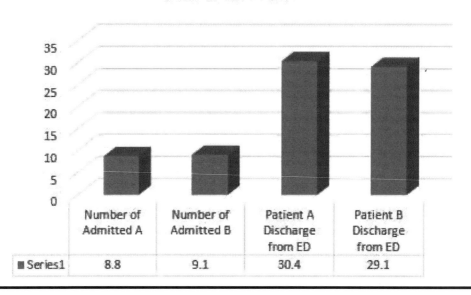

Figure 3.8   Counter details.

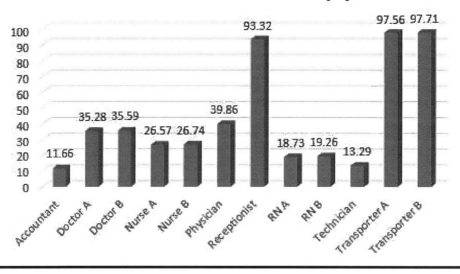

Figure 3.9   Resource utilization.

1. **Model Verification:** In the model verification stage, tests are applied to the model in order to study both desirable and undesirable situations. Several tests are applied on patient flow, arrival to and departure from the system, waiting times in queues, and service times. Conditions present in the model are evaluated and checked to be operating as intended through the run reports generated from simulating the model along with the graphs

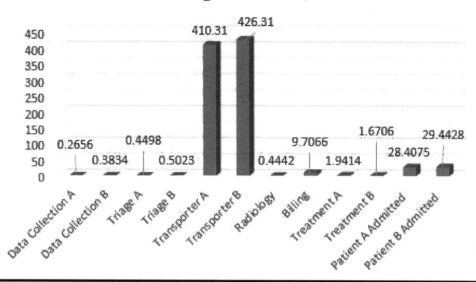

Figure 3.10 Average time in queues.

produced (such as patient-arrival-time graphs). In order to ensure the accuracy of the model, different replications are run and the average for best performance is considered.

2. **Model Validation:** "EDs are well known as complex systems; thus, it is very hard to take into consideration all its features while building the model. Studies showed that model accuracy is obtained from only 20% of the model's detail. Therefore, assumptions are necessary while building the model. In order to build this realistic and accurate model these assumptions should be carefully made and the important features that have great impact on the system's behavior should be properly chosen. In order to validate the model, the behavior of four indicators are evaluated, compared to the real system and tested to ensure identical behavior. The first indicator is the LoS (length of stay) of the patient in the system, the second is the resource workload (utilization rate), and the third refers to the duration in different stages, taking into consideration the corresponding waiting time in each stage and, finally, the number of patients exiting the system (called system number out). These indicators are used as reference for the comparison between the real system and the built model. By validating the model, some missing characteristics and available mistakes are figured out and the gaps are fixed until the system matches with reality. The output results presented in the previous section highlighted that the number of patients exiting the system is 77 on average for both ERs. In the real system, the number of patients discharged from the ED per day is on average 40 to 45 patients per emergency room, which is an average of 85 patients for both ERs. As for the LoS, the simulation output shows a value of 277 and 294 minutes for public ER and private ER respectively. Note that this slight difference between the two ERs is related to the fact that Patient B requesting an extra facility needs more time to reach the radiology unit than Patient A. These numbers match the real system where patient stay in the ED does not exceed 5 hours (300 minutes)" [Oueida et al. (2017e)]. Another matching performance measure with the real system is resource utilization, where transporters and the receptionist face major issues in order to serve all incoming patients.

In the real ED system, the transporter is responsible for transferring patients to the radiology unit or to other departments in the hospital in the event that the patient is admitted for extra care. Each ER has only one transporter, who remains busy and constantly overworked, which reflects the 97% utilization rate. The receptionist is responsible for opening the file for patients coming from both ERs and finalizing payments after the accountants finalize the process, which means that they are busy all the time, thus explaining the high utilization rate for the receptionist. This is also reflected in the large queuing average time. It is noticeable that the busiest queues are the ones waiting for Transporter A and Transporter B. This may lead to a bottleneck if the mentioned resources are on sick leave, holiday, annual leave, etc. and especially during peak times (other resources from billing unit must then fill the transporter's place, thus leading to complications in the billing department). The billing department suffers from many problems apart from lack of resources. The various types of insurance and the large amount of time that it takes for getting approvals make this unit a busy one and one with a direct effect on the ER's daily operation (increasing the average waiting time in the ED). After comparing the real system with the simulated model and finding out that the performance measures collected are almost similar, the validation is said to be complete and the model is considered reliable and thus ready for experimentation and optimization, where room for improvement can be defined.

3.3 Considering Non-Human Resources

The model described in Section 3.1.4 is simulated again after adding a new resource called "Facilities" in each ER. This resource describes everything required to deliver the needed care to patients other than human resources. This includes: beds, pillows, medication, syringes, cotton pads, wheel chairs, equipment, etc. The stages to which the new resources Facilities A and Facilities B are added are listed below: Triage A, Examination A, Treatment by Nurse A, Treatment A, Radiology A, Admission A, Triage B, Examination B, Treatment by Nurse B, Treatment B, Radiology B, Admission B. These stages include the corresponding human medical resource along with the facilities needed in order to operate and accomplish a particular service. The new halls and extra areas that are required in order to add new facilities are handled by the logistics department of the hospital and not the ED. As per the management, each resource of type "Facilities" costs, on average, $800.

3.3.1 Catastrophic Cases

In this section, catastrophic conditions are studied. A catastrophic event refers to a disaster condition due to seasonal epidemics, earthquakes, terrorist attacks, etc. After running the model again with the new resource of type "Facilities," added using Arena, for one week at a time, the system number out is found to be 489 patients exiting the system for almost 20,097 arriving patients as per Figure 3.11. It is obvious that a huge number of patients are stuck in the system because of the high surge of patients and shortage of resources (human and non-human). The number of each resource scheduled and allocated during this simulation is listed in Table 3.2.

In Figure 3.12, the utilization rate of each resource in the system is presented. From these results, it is obvious that doctors, nurses, RNs, and transporters suffer from high utilization rates (on average 99%) and thus have a very high workload. This issue, as discussed previously, may affect the level of care delivered to patients and may sometimes lead to medical errors, especially

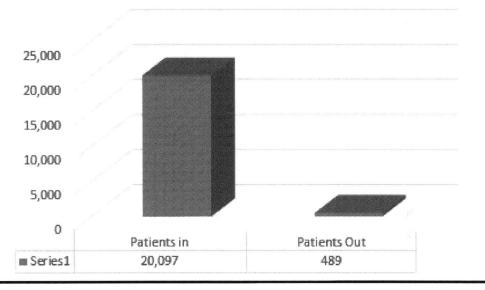

Patient In/Out During Catastrophe

	Patients in	Patients Out
■ Series1	20,097	489

Figure 3.11 System number in/out during a catastrophe.

Table 3.2 Number of Scheduled Resources

Resource Type	Number Scheduled
Accountant	8
Doctor A	1
Doctor B	1
Facilities A	5
Facilities B	5
Nurse A	2
Nurse B	2
Physician	1
Receptionist	1
RN A	1
RN B	1
Technician	3
Transporter A	1
Transporter B	1

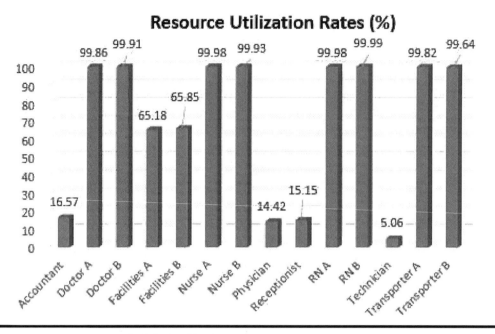

Figure 3.12   Resources scheduled utilization.

in the case of high stress and catastrophic events. It should be mentioned here that the human resources—doctors, nurses, and RNs—are linked to the non-human resource of type "Facilities" which already has a high utilization rate of almost 66%. This means that each time one medical resource is attempting to deliver a service (such as preparation for examination, examination, treatment, etc.), a resource of type "Facilities" must be available. Therefore, any suggestion of adding a new doctor, nurse, or RN in the future also implies adding additional resources of type "Facilities." During catastrophic events, the main issue is to save as many lives as possible regardless of the length of stay (LoS) of patients during their journey through the ED. Nevertheless, reducing this number (refer to Figure 3.13) may leave space for another patient to be received.

Figure 3.14 shows the average waiting time in each queue in the system. Data collection, transporter, treatment, triage, and waiting-for-doctor queues are the busiest. The medical resources responsible for serving these processes are the nurses, doctors, RNs, and transporters, and the high utilization rates discussed in Figure 3.12 support the overcrowding in these queues. The zero waiting time in the billing queue is because of a shortage in the resource of type "transporter": patients are not arriving to this stage.

3.3.2 Normal Flow Case

"The Arena model is run again for normal flow during 1 day (24 hours) after adding the new type of resource: Facilities. The base unit used is always minutes. Various performance measures are recorded such as: number of patients in and number of patients out, a counter (to differentiate between completely discharged patients and admitted to hospital patients), patient LoS, service time spent in different queues waiting for a process to be executed, and resource utilization rates. These performance measures are collected for both ER A and ER B. The figures below show the different results obtained from the model simulation. The number of resources scheduled in the

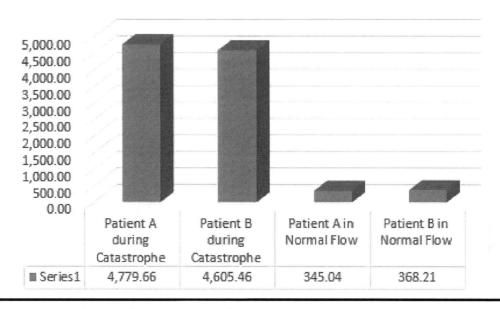

Figure 3.13 Patient LoS during a catastrophe and normal flow.

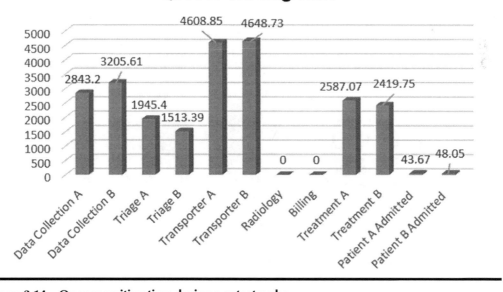

Figure 3.14 Queues waiting time during a catastrophe.

model are the current available resources in the real-life system (refer to Table 3.2). The number of patients in and the number of patients out resulting from the simulation of the designed system are illustrated in Figure 3.15. The number of patients arriving into the ED is limited to an average of 139 patients for both emergency rooms per day. And the number of patients exiting the system during the 24 hours of simulation is almost 60 patients in total for both emergency rooms.

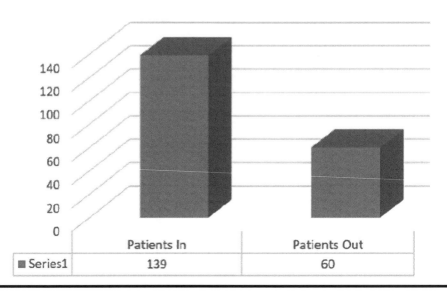

Figure 3.15 System number in/out in normal flow.

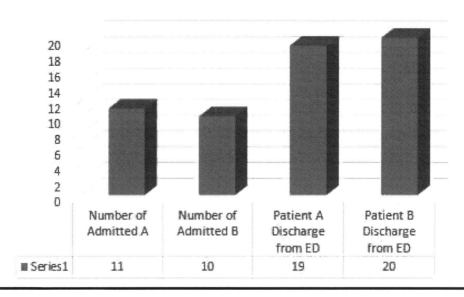

Figure 3.16 Counter details in normal flow.

The simulation shows different LoS values for the two ERs. The average total time spent by Patient A is around 345 minutes and for Patient B, an average of 368 minutes, as per Figure 3.13. A counter is used to record the number of patients discharged from the system. Patients leaving the ED may either be admitted to another unit of the hospital or discharged home. The counter details are presented in Figure 3.16.

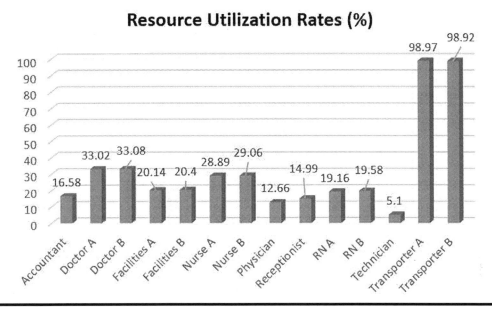

Figure 3.17 Resource utilization rates in normal flow.

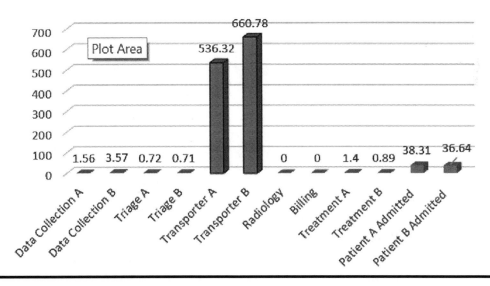

Figure 3.18 Queues details in normal flow.

The resource utilization is presented in Figure 3.17. It is obvious that the main problem exists with the transporters where the average utilization rate is almost 99% for both ERs and therefore immediate action for enhancement and better performance is needed.

The average waiting time spent in different queues in order to wait for some processes to be executed or for some resources to be available in order to move to execution stage and the number of patients waiting in each queue are represented in Figures 3.18 and 3.19. It is clear that the

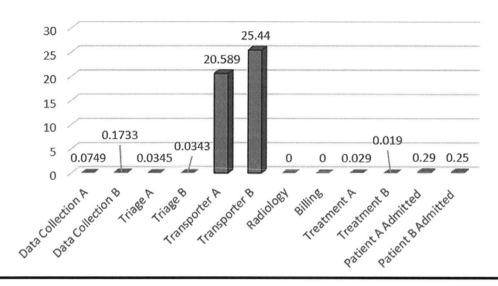

Figure 3.19 Queues waiting number in normal flow.

transporters' queues in both ER A and ER B suffer from overcrowding and this is because only one transporter serves all the patients arriving into the ED" [Oueida et al. (2017c)]. This type of resource is highly inadequate and may affect the other stages in the ED. Because of this resource shortage, some other resources may remain inactive and thus increase the waste in the system where utilization rates may be below standard. Note that patients should wait in the ED for an available transporter in case an extra facility is requested. For example, a doctor or a nurse may not proceed with their treatment and diagnosis respectively unless the transporter has accomplished their task and returned the patient to the ED after a radiology image has been requested; thus, the utilization rates of these resources may decrease but the number of patients waiting in the ED may increase, therefore increasing the LoS and decreasing the system number out. Decision-makers should make sure to look at this problem seriously. A solution to this problem will be illustrated in the optimization chapter (Chapter 5) by suggesting an optimal solution using the OptQuest tool of Arena.

3.4 Measuring Crowding Level

Overcrowding of EDs is currently a common problem in healthcare systems [Johnson and Winkelman (2011); Lowthian et al. (2011)]. Overcrowding is a factor of: number of patients arriving, number of available resources, number of available ED beds, number of available hospital beds, and waiting times at different stages. It is a problem perceived by human resources but cannot be determined quantitatively. The degree of overcrowding can be influenced by different circumstances. "This degree was measured through the literature using several quantitative scales such as: Real-time Emergency Analysis of Demand Indicators (READI), the Emergency Department Work Index (EDWIN), the National Emergency Department Overcrowding Scale (NEDOCS) and the Emergency Department Over Crowding Scale (EDOCS)" [Reeder and Garrison (2001)]. The choice of a convenient scale for a certain ED is dependent on the availability of data. Of these developed methods, the NEDOCS shows the best discriminative properties for ED overcrowding [Bernstein et al. (2003); Hoot et al. (2007); Jones et al. (2006); Anneveld et al. (2013)].

The NEDOCS tool is an efficient way of quantifying the level of crowding. When overcrowding is immediately detected, specific measures can be taken in order to guarantee efficient changes to cope with this sudden surge. This tool was developed in 2004 in order to quantitatively describe staff's sense of overcrowding. It is based on a web-calculator that converts data sets into an overcrowding score [Weiss et al. (2004)]. The NEDOCS score is chosen to be used in this study in order to calculate the level of overcrowding in the ED especially in the areas of overcrowding as detected by the simulation performed using Arena. The results are used to convince decision-makers that the ED is suffering from serious overcrowding and needs priority consideration. This overcrowding, due to the high waiting times patients experience in the ED as a result of patient surge, may affect patient satisfaction.

3.4.1 NEDOCS Variables and Definitions

The NEDOCS variables are used in order to calculate the required score. As it is a web-based tool, some variables need to be entered in order to get the score as a result. These variables are defined as below:

1. Number of ED beds: This is the total number of gurneys, chairs, and other treatment benches in use, or staffed everywhere in the ED. Unstaffed beds are excluded.
2. Number of hospital beds: This is the total number of beds in the whole hospital.
3. Total patients in the ED: This is the total number of patients in the ED and includes all patients arriving into the ED, waiting and not having been discharged.
4. ED patients on ventilator: This is the number of patients needing one-to-one nurse care. It includes: patients on ventilators, ICU admits, critical care patients, trauma patients.
5. Number of admits in the ED: This includes all admits waiting for a bed in the ED. Patients moved to other units in the hospital are excluded and considered as discharged from ED.
6. Waiting time of longest admitted patient: This is the number of the longest waiting time for an inpatient bed in the ED (in hours).
7. Waiting time of longest waiting-room patient: This is the number of the longest waiting time in the waiting room (in hours).

3.4.2 One-Shift Simulation for Normal Flow

The studied ED is simulated again using Arena during one shift (6 hours) and a normal flow of patients. The results from this simulation are used later as variables for the NEDOCS calculation. The number of patients arriving into the ED during this shift (number in) along with the number of patients leaving the ED (number out) are depicted in Figure 3.20.

The waiting time in queues are presented in Figure 3.21. It is obvious from these results that the main bottleneck is in the transporter queue where patients are waiting 122.35 minutes and 166.58 minutes respectively in ER A and ER B. Note that these values represent the queues' total waiting times and not the average waiting times. In order to get the average waiting times, these values should be divided by the number of patients waiting in the corresponding queues.

From the resource detail summary presented in Figure 3.22, the busiest type of resource is the transporter where utilization rates are on average 96% for both ERs. This is very realistic since the

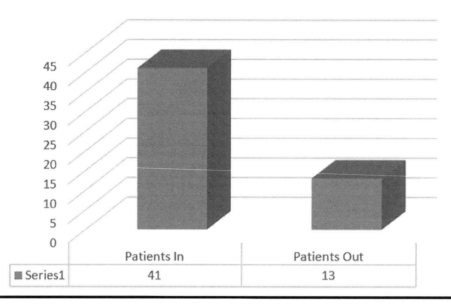

Figure 3.20   Number in/out during one shift.

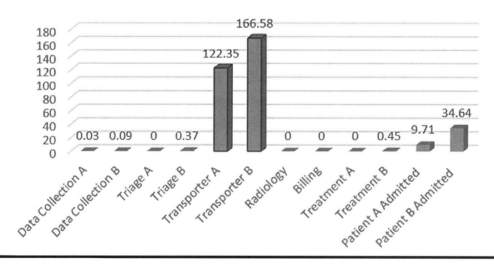

Figure 3.21   Queues waiting time during one shift.

transporter queue is the bottleneck of the system as deduced from Figure 3.21. Thus, while measuring the crowding score for this system, the measures should rely on the values of this specific queue.

The total time patients spend in the ED during this shift is represented by the LoS for ER A and ER B and is listed in Figure 3.23.

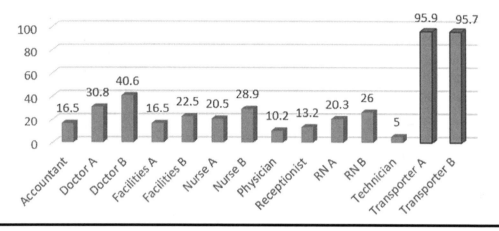

Figure 3.22   Resource utilization rates during one shift.

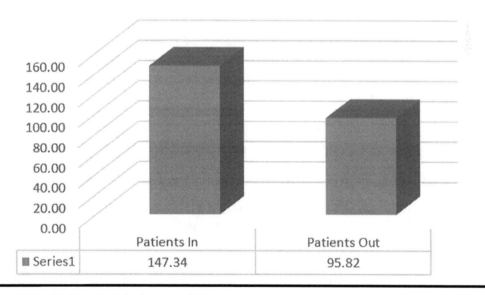

Figure 3.23   Patients LoS during one shift.

The number of patients waiting in the transporter queue for ER A and ER B is found to be on average six patients and ten patients respectively. These values are presented in Figure 3.24. This means a count of eight patients on average for the whole ED since the ED includes ER A and ER B operating at the same time and cooperating together in case of overcrowding.

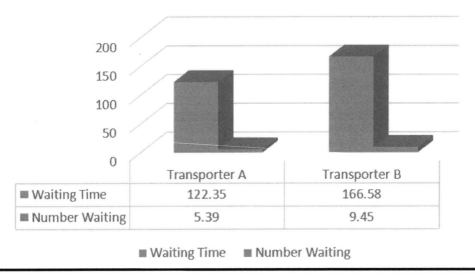

Transporter Queue
-during one shift-

	Transporter A	Transporter B
■ Waiting Time	122.35	166.58
■ Number Waiting	5.39	9.45

■ Waiting Time   ■ Number Waiting

Figure 3.24   Number of patients waiting in transporter queue during one shift.

3.4.3 Measuring the ED NEDOCS for Normal Flow

Using the results of the previous subsection, the NEDOCS score can be measured using the web-based calculator available at the below link:

www.mdcalc.com/nedocs-score-emergency-department-overcrowding

In order to update the NEDOCS score and get the required result for the crowding level, the web-based system requests that numbers be entered into seven fields. These fields are listed below:

1. Number of ED beds: five for each ER A and ER B which leads to a total of ten beds in the ED
2. Number of hospital beds: in total there are 207 beds in the whole hospital
3. Total patients in the ED: number of patients waiting in the transporter queue (which is the bottleneck stage under study). Refer to Figure 3.24
4. Number of ED patients on a ventilator: no patient is on a ventilator during the measure
5. Number of admits in the ED: total number of patients arriving into the ED (refer to Figure 3.20)
6. Waiting time of longest admitted patient (in hours): the total visit time (refer to Figure 3.23)
7. Waiting time of longest waiting-room patient (in hours): waiting time in the transporter queue under study/number of patients waiting in the transporter queue = ((122.35 + 166.58) ÷ 2) ÷ 8 minutes = 2.4 ÷ 8 hours = 0.3 hours (refer to Figure 3.21)

The numbers in these seven fields resulted from the one-shift simulation presented in the previous subsection are displayed in Table 3.3, where only the bottleneck queue is studied (transporter queue).

Table 3.3   NEDOCS Calculator Fields

Calculator Fields	Numbers
Number of ED beds	10
Number of hospital beds	207
Total patients in the ED	8
Number of ED patients on ventilator	0
Number of admits in the ED	41
Waiting time of longest admitted patient (in hours)	2
Waiting time of longest waiting room patient (in hours)	0.3

By entering these numbers into the NEDOCS calculator, the score is found to be 171 (Figure 3.25) which is determined to be a Level 5 as per the score interpretation presented in Figure 3.26. This means that the ED is severely overcrowded and thus needs urgent attention and to be considered for improvement.

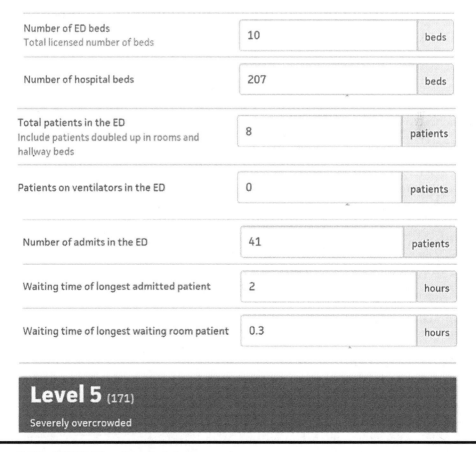

Figure 3.25   NEDOCS web-calculator.

Score interpretation:

Level	Score	Interpretation
Level 1	1-20	Not busy
Level 2	21-60	Busy
Level 3	61-100	Extremely busy but not overcrowded
Level 4	101-140	Overcrowded
Level 5	141-180	Severely overcrowded
Level 6	181-200	Dangerously overcrowded

Figure 3.26 NEDOCS score interpretation.

3.5 Control of System Flows

"Complexity, concurrency, and unpredictability of events in the majority of industrial systems impose on decision-makers the need to study the system and analyze the processes in order to find room for improvements. Industrial systems usually face one main problem: resources shortage [Zeng et al. (2012)]. Effective allocation of resources is necessary to maintain a dynamic controlled flow of operations. In this section, a new Petri net model is proposed in order to effectively control the workflow processes and maintain synchronization among activities [Buckley et al. (2010)]. Tasks and dependencies are modeled in Petri net by transitions, and places/arcs respectively [Eitel et al. (2010)]. Using Petri net modeling with industrial systems helps control and overcome the problem of complexity. Here, two main characteristics of Petri net workflows can be highlighted: safety and soundness. Ensuring the soundness of the model will definitely ensure the liveness, reachability, and efficiency of the model proposed. Moreover, model soundness guarantees a system with critical sections free and ensures framework serializability and separability. Critical sections are referred to as tasks impossible to execute by one activity at a time. A framework that handles critical sections was suggested by Baldwin et al. [Baldwin et al. (2004)].

The industrial system chosen to be studied using Petri net concepts is the same emergency department (ED) discussed in previous chapters. The main performance measures relied on during this study are patient length of stay (LoS) and the waiting times of queues. These metrics are considered the main issues currently challenging emergency departments. High waiting times may lead to overcrowding and thus affect the daily operations of the ED and may result in patient dissatisfaction [Buckley et al. (2010)]. A possible solution to these problems is to increase resource capacity. Nevertheless, adding extra resources is not always possible due to budget constraints and management limitations to providing extra facilities [Soremekun et al. (2011)].

3.5.1 Petri Net Preliminaries

Petri net is a mathematical concept developed in 1962 by Carl Adam Petri in order to describe a system or a process. It is designed to reflect the different states of a system. With the recent development of complex and concurrent systems, such as healthcare, Petri net is proven to be an efficient way to describe and analyze systems. With Petri net, the dynamic behavior of these complex and concurrent systems can be easily described based on the theoretical concepts and properties of such systems. The Petri net is a simple, flexible, and user-friendly mathematical modeling technique. The basic advantages that can be highlighted with Petri nets are the visualization of non-sequential workflows, the illustration of the system on different levels of abstraction without interrupting the actual system operation, the demonstration of dependencies and independencies in a set of events, and the modeling of real-time systems. Moreover, Petri net has the ability to apply the theory of verification of correctness of the designed framework, boundedness, reproducibility, liveness, reachability or non-reachability, invariants, and deadlocks. A Petri net graph allows you to represent your model by using nodes that either represent transitions (added as rectangles) or places (added as circles). One transition can be connected to one or more places and vice versa—one place can be connected to one or more transitions. In the case of identical types, the nodes will not be directly connected. Directed arcs are used in order to connect different types of nodes. Activities that are performed by the transitions are represented by tokens (solid circles) which reside in places. If a place (p) connected to a transition (t) is empty, the transition will not be executed. Therefore, an enabled transition exists if and only if no empty places are connected to this transition as inputs. The execution of a transition happens after it is enabled; we say the transition is fired. As a result of this firing, new tokens are created in each of the output places after removal of all tokens from each of the input places.

3.5.2 Related Work

System redesign is one approach that aims to improve the operation of a business process. Healthcare systems, being complex systems, and emergency departments, in particular, rely on simulation modeling in order to improve their operation without the real system being interrupted. Petri net was proven to be one of the efficient approaches used in order to optimize business processes and, specifically, healthcare systems. This approach makes use of redesign heuristics [Reijers (2003)]. Jansen-Vullers and Reijers (2005) presented in their study a colored PN in order to suggest a redesign approach for a mental healthcare institute. As part of system enhancement, the redesign helped in reducing the service and flow time. Moreover, the designed model was proven to be more efficient compared to the performance of previous models. Since ED overcrowding has become an important issue facing healthcare systems over the last decade, efficient flow of work and people must be optimized. Therefore, a Petri net workflow model was proposed in order to improve the structure and dynamics of an ED in the general hospital of Bari, Italy [Dotoli et al. (2010)]. The model presented a complete flow management of the patient from arrival into the ED until discharge from the ED (either discharged home or admitted to another department of the hospital). The Petri net model defined an optimization solution where system performance and optimal resource dimensions can be proposed, thus guaranteeing efficient management techniques of the ED and a maximum patient flow. Mahulea et al. proved in their study that Petri net is powerful for modeling and analysis of a healthcare system since it can efficiently represent synchronization and concurrency [Mahulea et al. (2014)]. In their study, they presented a methodology using Petri net that can be applied on a primary healthcare system where patients follow a certain route in order to be diagnosed and cured. This route can be represented using Petri net models and different resources can be assigned depending on the type of activity required. Based on the designed Petri net, the healthcare operation can be studied and different indices can be estimated accordingly. Another approach was proposed by Augusto and Xie (2014). The authors designed a new methodology called MedPRO in order to address problems faced by the healthcare system and integrated it with simulation in order to address a specific healthcare case study. The special class of Petri net used is called Health Care Petri net (HCPN). HCPN models serve also for scheduling and planning healthcare activities and were proved to be efficient [Augusto and Xie (2014)]. A common way used by some healthcare organizations to solve the overcrowding problem in EDs is early discharge and introducing the home care option as an alternative. The paper, approaching this alternative procedure, suggests the design of an integrated system (IS) using Petri net which will be devoted only for home care management. The IS can monitor the daily life of the home patient, detect possible problems, and ensure communication among families, doctors, nurses, and emergency call centers [Fanti et al. (2014)].

Several related works presented a Petri net workflow to study the flow of a system and control resource allocation [Park (2000)]. Verification and simulation of business processes/workflows are also presented in [Van der Aalst (1998); Van Der Aalst (2000); Van der Aalst (2003); Piera et al. (2004)]. Problems facing ED systems have been the main subject in literature when it comes to healthcare management. Improving ED processes is the key to patient satisfaction, always taking into consideration the cost/revenue [Holden (2011)]. Computer simulation was proven to be the best way to present effectively the flow in a real-time system without any interruption of daily operations. Using simulation, the system can be analyzed and enhancement can be suggested [Baldwin et al. (2004)]. To alleviate the overcrowding problem and prevent bottleneck, waiting times and patient LoS should be reduced. Also, better resource allocation of available resources may reduce waste and undesirable cost [Reijers (2003)]. Business processes can be enhanced using simulation, where the real system continues its normal flow of operation without any real interruption in its activities. The system is redesigned and represented by a model to describe all its processes. Emergency departments being complex and concurrent systems rely on simulation in order to improve their operation. Accordingly, Petri net was proven to be one of the efficient approaches used in order to optimize this type of systems [Reijers (2003)]. Jansen and Reijers [Jansen-Vullers and Reijers (2005)] used colored Petri net in order to model a mental healthcare institute. Service time and flow time were reduced as part of system improvement. As per the literature, overcrowding of emergency departments is the major problem facing healthcare systems, which imposes the need to optimize its flow of work and resource capacity levels.

3.5.3 New Proposed Petri Net Framework

The new proposed Petri net is named Resource Preservation Net (RPN) [Oueida and Ionescu (2017)]. A few theorems and lemmas of soundness are proposed to support the new extended proposed Petri net model and are discussed in detail in Chapter 4, where the theory behind it and the mathematical model are presented. This new type of Petri net (PN) is very useful for systems with sensitive resources. Resources flowing into the system are not consumable; rather, they are preserved. Resources include customers or any human resources used to serve the customer through the flow. All these resources should return to their corresponding pools when a task is accomplished. This means that when a resource is injected into a transition it will always get out. All siphons are controlled; in other words, it is guaranteed that when certain siphons lose their marking they will eventually get it back after a certain period of time. This RPN can be applied to any queuing system such as healthcare, restaurants, banks, etc. RPN is an extended version of the general PN existing in the literature with some changes that depict the resource-aware structure. This proposed RPN is applied to a real-life problem in Section 3.5.4 in order to model and optimize the studied ED in this work. A comparison between the general Petri net (PN) and the proposed valid RPN is presented in Figure 3.27.

In Figure 3.27 (Part a), as seen in the RPN (left-hand side), for every place type in the set of input places of a certain transition, that type has to exist as an output place. The number of input

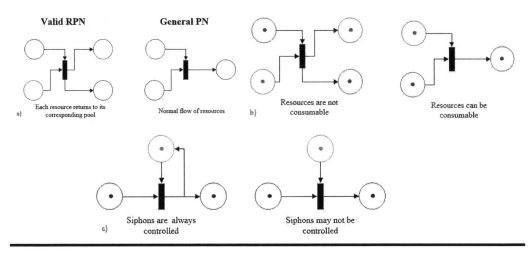

Figure 3.27   A comparison between RPN architecture and regular Petri net [Oueida et al. (2018d); Oueida and Ionescu (2017); Oueida et al. (2018c)].

places and output places does not have to be the same; it is the existence of place types that has to match one-to-one between input set and output set. In Figure 3.27 (Part a), the general PN (right hand side) does not have such constraint, which means that certain types might be suppressed during transition execution. Figure 3.27 (Part b) shows the property of resource preservation. In the left-hand side, the RPN preserves the resource; in other words, the number of input tokens is equal to the number of output tokens; whereas in the right-hand side, tokens could be consumed as a general PN. In Figure 3.27 (Part c), the left-hand side shows the RPN with the property of controlling siphons, which is a basic property that has to be satisfied in any RPN. The right-hand side of Figure 3.27 (Part c) shows a general PN where siphons do not have to be controlled.

3.5.4 Application of RPN in Healthcare

The proposed RPN is used to describe the chosen ED operation and illustrate the flow of patients. The Petri net framework is modeled by two RPNs in order to describe the two emergency rooms that constitute the ED: ER A and ER B. The entities described in the model are the same for both ERs and some are common (such as for radiology and billing). The customer refers to the patient and the resources to the medical resources who serve this patient. In this RPN, the transitions represent each stage of the model. The places represent the entity pools, such as patients or medical resources and the transfer between stages. These places and transitions are connected with directed arcs called connections. Each entity in the model has a defined number of resources or tokens, which is called marking.

Figures 3.28 and 3.29 represent the flow in each ER and the common units between the two ERs, respectively. The stages in Figure 3.28 are similar for ER A and ER B. The common units which are represented in Figure 3.29 are radiology and billing. On the other hand, Figure 3.30 describes the cooperation of the two ERs. In Figure 3.30, patients leaving the radiology/billing stage will follow the checking attribute stage.

This patient will continue their flow by moving to Treatment A if coming from ER A and to Treatment B if coming from ER B. It should be mentioned here that in Figure 3.30, the patient, whether A or B, should follow the remaining flow after reaching the treatment stage.

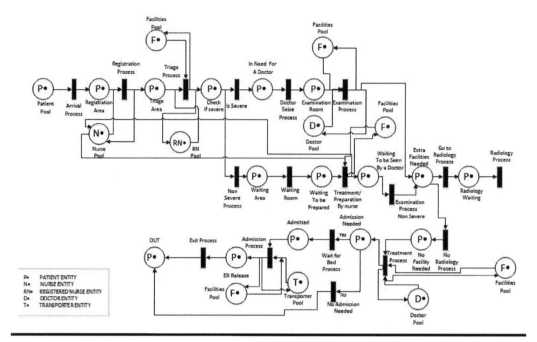

Figure 3.28   Emergency room stages [Oueida et al. (2018d); Oueida and Ionescu (2017); Oueida et al. (2018c)].

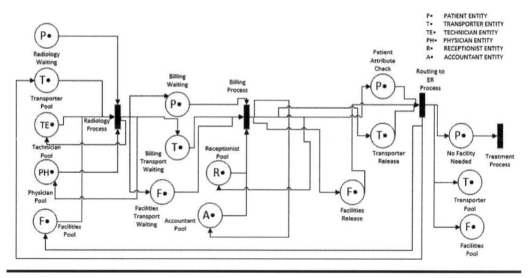

Figure 3.29   Petri net radiology/billing [Oueida et al. (2018d); Oueida and Ionescu (2017); Oueida et al. (2018c)].

The medical resource pools are named as follows: Doctor Pool, RN Pool, Nurse Pool, Transporter Pool, Accountant Pool, Receptionist Pool, Physician Pool, and Technician Pool, Facilities Pool. In order to control the critical sections in the model and avoid siphons, these resources should always return to their corresponding pools after accomplishing a certain task. We say here that the model is sound [Mahulea et al. (2014)]. The only entity that flows from the beginning till the end of the system is the patient. All these resources are non-consumable.

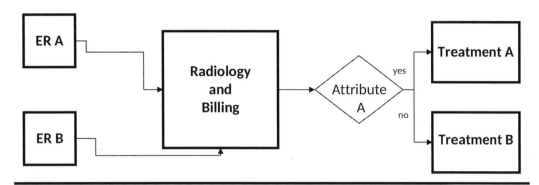

Figure 3.30 Petri net model flowchart [Oueida et al. (2018d); Oueida and Ionescu (2017); Oueida et al. (2018c)].

As for the patient, this is an entity that flows from the beginning till the end of the system and is not consumable. The flow of patients in the system is described from arrival into the ER until exit either to another unit (admitted to hospital) or home. Some transitions need more than the patient entity as entry place in order to be enabled.

3.6 Simulation and Results

The proposed model RPN is simulated and the results are shown in Figure 3.31. The results show that the billing unit suffers from a bottleneck, which is normal since this unit is shared by the two emergency rooms, ER A and ER B. Thus, the highest utilization rate is for the corresponding resources: accountant and receptionist. These resources, being the busiest in the system, must be considered for future optimization.

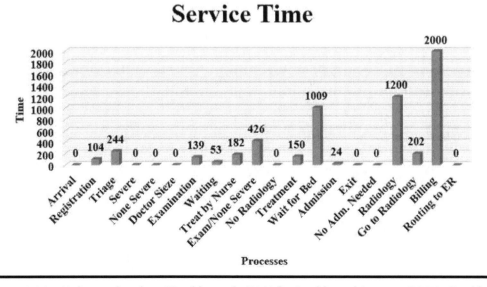

Figure 3.31 Units service time [Oueida et al. (2018d); Oueida and Ionescu (2017); Oueida et al. (2018c)].

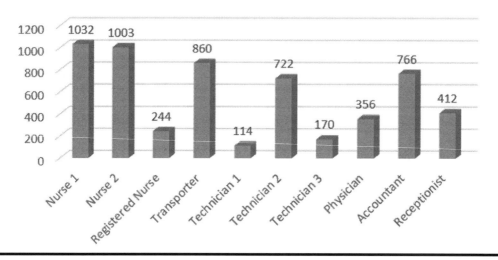

Figure 3.32   Resources workload [Oueida et al. (2018d); Oueida and Ionescu (2017); Oueida et al. (2018c)].

Also, the radiology unit should be considered for future improvement as per the simulation results. The workload of each resource is depicted in Figure 3.32.

It is obvious from the results that nurses are very busy and also need to be considered during future optimization stages, along with technicians and accountants. Since transporters wait for patients to finish a certain activity in another unit and then forward them to the emergency department and vice versa, they suffer from a high workload and busy service times. The future optimization phase should include different allocation of these resources or adding more medical resources. By suggesting new resource dimensions, the average waiting time of patients may be decreased, always maintaining the same level of care and a reduced resource workload. In Section 3.2, the same ED was simulated using Arena software and the results obtained are similar to the RPN simulation. This similarity in results validates the RPN simulation outputs and thus the model is considered reliable and ready for future experimentation" [Oueida and Ionescu (2017)].

The information in this chapter appears in the following journals/conference papers, all authored by Soraia Oueida and reprinted by permission of the publisher:

- *International Journal of User-Driven Healthcare*, Copyright © 2017, IGI Global, [Oueida et al. (2017e)]
- *International Review on Computers and Software* (I.RE.CO.S.), Copyright © 2017, Praise Worthy Prize, [Oueida et al. (2017c)]
- *Multimedia Tools and Applications*, Copyright © 2019, Springer, [Oueida et al. (2018a)]
- *International Conference on Management and Industrial Engineering*, Copyright © 2017, Niculescu Publishing House, [Oueida et al. (2017d)]

Chapter 4

Mathematical Model and System Validation

In this chapter "the proposed Petri net model, RPN is validated using discrete mathematics. All mathematical notations are presented in Appendix A. The validation is performed through proposing a theorem of soundness and a few lemmas. The model is validated for non-cooperative and cooperative systems" [Oueida et al. (2018c)].

4.1 Model Definition

"An RPN is a undecuple that is defined as:

$$RPN = \left\langle P_p, P, T, R, \lambda, \Lambda, F, i, o, M, \Theta(P_p, R) \right\rangle \quad (4.1)$$

Where,

- P_p is the pool of preserved resources
- P is the set of places
- T is the set of transitions
- λ is the set of requests for service
- Λ is the set of capabilities
- $\Theta(P_p, R)$ is the mapping function that assigns resources to pools
- R is the set of resources
- $F = P_p \times T \cup T \times P_p \cup P \times T \cup T \times P$ which is the topology of the workflow. Note that the places here are classified into regular places and pools. Pools are places that have the initial marking of resources and all pools are controlled siphons. Siphons are places that, if not properly controlled, might not be marked again once they lose their markings
- M is the marking of the RPN
- i is the input place of the RPN
- o is the output place of the RPN

A transition can be fired only if the required number of tokens at the input place is met. Different types of resources are defined in the system, each responsible for a certain task in order to accomplish the activity. A Petri net is a RPN if and only if the two conditions below are met:

1. $\forall \Theta(P_j) \mid P_j \in \bullet T_s$, $\exists P_k \mid P_k \in T_s \bullet$ and $\Theta(P_j) = \Theta(P_k)$. In other words, the first condition implies that for every type of place such that this place is the input to a transition T, there exists another place that is the output to this transition and where each type of place at the input is equal to the corresponding type of place at the output. This is because resources should always return to their pools once the activity is accomplished. Where, Ts is any transition belonging to the set of transitions T.

2. $\forall P_j \in \bullet T_s$, $\sum_{k=1}^{n}(a_k) \in P_j$ where a_k represents the token in a place. In other words, for every place that belongs to the input of a transition T, the sum of tokens a that are in this particular place and required to fire this transition will be equal to the sum of tokens that are generated in the output place of this transition after T is fired.

where $0 \leq j \leq \|P\|$ and $0 \leq s \leq \|T\|$

Then, after T is fired:

$$\sum_{k=1}^{n}(a_k) = \sum_{j=1}^{m}(a_j) \Bigg| a_j \in T \bullet \text{ and } a_k \in \bullet T$$

This means that the tokens are not consumable and at the end of the model all the input tokens will exit the system" [Oueida et al. (2018c)].

4.2 RPN as a Non-Cooperative System

"In this section a theorem is proposed in order to prove that the RPN is sound and is called the theorem of soundness [Centeno et al. (2003)]. This RPN consists of one unit and is proved for now to be sound, operating separately from any other unit in the system or vice versa. The proof will be done in both ways and will be presented as part (a): the result of assuming that RPN is sound and part (b): proving that RPN is sound assuming a certain flow of customers in the model.

For a workflow to be sound, all input tokens to this workflow will eventually reach the output. In other words, there exist a minimum number of transitions that are live to guarantee that all tokens will reach the output. Therefore, the output is reachable from the input.

Theorem 1 *RPN is sound if and only if:*

1. $\forall P_p \times T \neq \emptyset$, $\exists T \times P_p \neq \emptyset$, $\exists i \in P \mid \bullet i = \emptyset$, $\exists o \in P \mid o\bullet = \emptyset$, $M(i)\tau_1 \equiv M(o)\tau_2$, *where* $\tau_2 \geq \tau_1$

2. $\sum_{j=1}^{n}((M(P_j)) \mid P_j \equiv \bullet T_s = \sum_{k=1}^{m}((M(P_k)) \mid P_k \equiv T_s \bullet$

3. $\forall P_j$, $P_j \in P_p$, $\exists \tau, T_\tau \mid M_\tau(P_j) = M_0(P_j)$ and $P_j \in T_\tau \bullet$ and $\bullet T_\tau \in P_j$

4. $\Lambda \subseteq T$

Where,

- $P_j \in \{P\}$
- $M(P_j)$ is the marking of a certain place P with index j
- $\bullet i$ is the set of input transitions to place i
- $o \bullet$ is the set of output transitions from place o
- n is the total number of input tokens to a transition
- m is the total number of output tokens to a transition
- $T_j \in \{T\}$
- $\tau \geq 0$
- $M_\tau(P_j)$ is the marking of a certain place at time τ
- $M_0(P_j)$ is the marking of a certain place at initial time

It is worth noting that pools are considered as siphons and therefore they have to be properly controlled. In other words, the marking of pools at the input transition should be equal to the marking of pools at the output transition. Resources should return to their pools after accomplishing a service. Moreover, customers entering the system should leave the system after receiving the required service. When a customer requests a service from the set of requests, λ, the resource responsible to accomplish this task should have the capabilities to serve this customer. These capabilities are referred to as a set Λ.

RPN is assumed to be sound if and only if the four set of equations from Theorem 1 are met. The first equation identifies the correct topology of the RPN. Transitions that are consuming tokens from resource pools have to end up producing the same tokens into the same pools. This ensures that siphons are controlled. RPN is sound if for every existing connection between the place P_p and a transition T, there exists another connection between that specific T and that same place; where P_p is the set of pools. Therefore, $\forall P_p \times T \neq \emptyset$, $\exists T \times P_p \neq \emptyset$. Also, the first place in the workflow noted by the input i and the last place noted by the output o have no connected places where i means a transition connected to the input of i and o means a transition connected to the output of o. Therefore, $\exists i \in P | \bullet i = \emptyset$ and $\exists o \in P | o \bullet = \emptyset$. Since the RPN is sound, then the marking of the inputs should be equal to the marking of the outputs in order to ensure a stable flow of customers in the system; where the marking is the number of needed tokens in order to fire a certain transition T that will be then executed. This means that each customer entering the system has to leave it after a certain period of time when all the needed care is attained. Therefore, M $(i) \equiv$ M (o). In the second condition of the theorem, the total sum of markings of a certain place P_j should be equal to the total sum of markings of another place P_k; where P_j is the input place of a certain transition T_s and P_k is the output place to this transition in order to ensure the soundness of the workflow RPN. This states that the preserved resources denoted by P_j, P_k are not consumable and should return to their corresponding pools once the transition is executed. Therefore,

$$\sum_{j=1}^{n}(M(P_j)) | P_j \equiv \bullet T_s = \sum_{k=1}^{m}(M(P_k)) | P_k \equiv T_s \bullet$$

RPN is guaranteed to be sound if siphons are controlled as per the third condition of the theorem; where siphons are a set of places P such that any token taken out from the siphon must return back to that siphon. So, if siphons are not properly controlled, they might lose their marking and therefore affect the soundness of the system. So, for every place P_j that belongs to the pool of resources P_p, there exists a time τ where these resources return to their corresponding pools; which means that the marking of this P_j at that time τ is equal to the initial marking of that place P_j. It is worth noting here that a resource can move along with customers through many consecutive transitions, if needed, in order to accomplish a certain task and then go back to its pool when all the needed care is already given. Therefore, $\forall P_j$, $P_j \in \bullet P_p$, $\exists \tau$, $T_\tau \mid M_\tau(P_j) = M_0(P_j)$ and $P_j \in T_\tau \bullet$ and $\bullet T_\tau \in P_j$.

Finally, Condition 4 of Theorem 1 guarantees that each resource serving a particular customer in order to execute a certain transition should have the capability to handle and serve this customer otherwise that customer will be lost in the system and will not follow a certain flow in order to reach the output; where the set of capabilities needed, Λ, should belong to that transition T that is being executed. Therefore, $\Lambda \subseteq T$.

To conclude, Theorem 1 guarantees that for a sound RPN:

1. The system is structurally valid
2. Resources are not consumable
3. Siphons are controlled
4. Resources have the capability to serve customers

Proof 1 (Proof of Theorem 1 – Part A) *Since RPN is sound, then*

1. $o \in [i\rangle$, *therefore,*
2. $\forall T_j \in T$, $T_j \in [i\rangle$, *therefore,*
3. $\exists P_p \times T \neq \varnothing$ *and* $M(P_p)_{t1} = M(P_p)_{t2}$ *where* $_{t2} \geq _{t1}$, *therefore,*
4. *since* $\exists P_p \times T \neq \varnothing$ *then,* $\exists T \times P_p \neq \varnothing$, *therefore,*
5. $\forall M_t \in [M(i)\rangle$ *where* $t > 0$, *therefore,*
6. $\exists \tau \mid M_\tau = M(o)$ *for* $t > \tau$, *where* τ *is the time taken from input to output, therefore,*
7. $\forall M \in M(i)$, $M \in M(o)$, *then* $M(o) = M(i)$ *Where,*
   - $M(i) = M - M(P_p)$
   - $M(i)$ *is the input marking of the workflow (customer)*
   - $M(P_p)$ *is the marking of the pools (resources). These pools are siphons*
   - $M(o)$ *is the output marking*
   - M *is the total marking*
      Since RPN is a sound workflow therefore by the definition of the workflow:
8. $\exists i \in P \mid \bullet i = \varnothing$ *and* $\exists o \in P \mid o \bullet = \varnothing$
      Since $M(o) = M(i)$, *therefore,*
9. $\forall T \in M_{\tau-1}(\bullet T) = M_\tau(T\bullet)$, *where transition T fires out on time* τ *and* $\bullet T = T \bullet = P_p$, *therefore,*
10. $\displaystyle\sum_{j=1}^{n} (P_j) \mid P_j \equiv \bullet T = \sum_{k=1}^{m} (P_k) \mid P_k \equiv T \bullet$, *therefore,*
11. $\forall P_j$, $P_j \in P_p$, $\exists \tau$, $T_j \mid M_\tau(P_j) = M_o$ *and* $P_j \in T_\tau \bullet$ *and* $\bullet T_\tau \in P_j$
12. *Since RPN is sound and since* $\forall M(o) \in [M(i)\rangle$, *therefore,*
13. $\forall \lambda \in \Lambda$, $\exists T_j \in T \mid T_j \equiv \lambda$ $\Lambda \subseteq T$

In other words, since RPN is assumed to be sound, then the output is reachable from the input $(o \in [i\rangle)$ and therefore for every transition T_j that belongs to the set of transitions T, this specific transition T_j belongs also to the reachability of the input i $(\forall T_j \in T, T_j \in [i\rangle)$ and thus there exists a connection between a specific place P_p with a transition T and the marking of this place at a time t_1 is equal to the marking of this place at a time t_2 ($\exists P_p \times T \neq \emptyset$ and $M(P_p)_{t1} = M(P_p)_{t2}$); where t_1 and t_2 are two different times during the flow of customers in the system. Then, there exists also a connection from this transition T to the place P_p ($\exists P_p \times T \neq \emptyset$ then, $\exists T \times P_p \neq \emptyset$). This describes the topology of the net, specifically, the connections between siphons (P_p) and the set of transitions (T). We can then say that for every marking at time t that belongs to the reachability marking of the input i ($\forall M_t \in [M(i)\rangle$, the marking at time t is equal to the marking of the output; where τ is the total time from input to output ($\exists \tau | M_\tau = M(o)$). Therefore, the marking of arriving customers $M(i)$ is equal to the marking of the output $M(o)$ since the customer is reaching the output ($\forall M \in M(i)$, $M \in M(o)$, then $M(o) = M(i)$). This means that the RPN is structurally stable. $\exists i \in P | \bullet i = \emptyset$ and $\exists o \in P | o \bullet = \emptyset$): this equation describes the behavior of the input and output places of a sound workflow. This means that for any workflow, the input place is not preceded by any node and the output place is not followed by any node.

($\forall T \in M_{\tau-1} (\bullet T) = M_\tau (T \bullet)$): this equation states that the marking of the input of a transition T at a time $\tau - 1$ is equal to the marking of the output of the transition T at a time τ after this transition is being executed. Here, siphons are being controlled; which means every resource that is entering a transition to fire it and execute it should also leave this transition after a certain time. Therefore, resources are not consumable and should return to their corresponding pools where the total sum of marking of a specific place P_j belonging to this pool and connected to the input of the transition T is equal to the total marking of place P_k that is connected to the output of the transition T. A conclusion can be reached here, that for every P_j belonging to the pool of resources P_p, the marking of place P_j at a certain time τ is equal to the output marking of P_j; where P_j is connected to the input of the transition T_j at time τ and also connected to the output of the transition T_τ at time τ ($\forall P_j, P_j \in P_p, \exists \tau, T_j | M_\tau (P_j) = M_o$ and $P_j \in T_\tau \bullet$ and $\bullet T_\tau \in P_j$). Therefore, siphons are controlled.

Since RPN is sound and all customers entering the system reach the output and leave the system ($\forall M(o) \in [M(i)\rangle$), therefore, for every set of requests λ that belongs to a pool of capabilities, there exists a transition T_j that belongs to the set of transitions to be executed to accomplish a certain flow of the customer in the system, such that this T_j is equal to λ since the transition to be executed needs a resource that has the required capabilities. Therefore, the set of capabilities Λ belongs to the set of transitions otherwise the customer cannot flow to the output and reach the end of the workflow net ($\forall \lambda \in \Lambda, \exists T_j \in T | T_j \equiv \lambda, \Lambda \subseteq T$).

Proof 2 (Proof of Theorem 1 – Part B)

1. *if* $\exists P_p \times T \neq \emptyset, \exists T \times P_p \neq \emptyset, \exists i \in P | \bullet i = \emptyset, \exists o \in P | o \bullet = \emptyset,$ *and* $M(i) \equiv M(o)$ *therefore,*

2. $\forall P_j, P_j \in P_p, \exists \tau | M_\tau (P_j) = M_0 (P_j)$ and $P_j \in |T_\tau\rangle$ and $T_\tau \in |P_j\rangle$

1. *Since* $\forall P_j, P_j \in P_p, \exists \tau, T | M_\tau (P_j) = M_0 (P_j)$ and $P_j \in |T_\tau\rangle$ and $T_\tau \in |P_j\rangle$, *therefore,*

3. $\sum_{j=1}^{n} (M(P_j)) | P_j \equiv \bullet T = \sum_{k=1}^{m} (M(P_k)) | P_k \equiv T \bullet$

   Since $\sum_{j=1}^{n} (M(P_j)) | P_j \equiv \bullet T = \sum_{k=1}^{m} (M(P_k)) | P_k \equiv T \bullet$ *and* $\forall P_j, P_j \in P_p, \exists \tau,$

   $T | M_\tau (P_j) = M_o (P_j)$ and $P_j \in |T_\tau\rangle$ and $T_\tau \in |P_j\rangle$, *therefore,*

4. $\forall a | a \in M_0 (i), a \in M_t (o)$

where, $t \geq 0$ and $M_0(i)$ is the marking of the input at time 0 and $M_t(o)$ is the marking of the output at time t. Therefore, RPN is sound.

In other words, the RPN is proven to be sound if the four characteristics of Theorem 1 are satisfied. If the workflow is structurally valid, which means there exists a connection between the set of places P_p and the set of transition T and no nodes are preceding the input of the workflow and no nodes are following the output, plus the marking of the input is equal to the marking of the output ($\exists P_p \times T \neq \emptyset$, $\exists T \times P_p \neq \emptyset$ and $\exists i \in P | \bullet i = \emptyset$, $\exists o \in P | o \bullet = \emptyset$, and $M(i) \equiv M(o)$), therefore, for every place P_j that belongs to the set of places P_p, there exist a transition T at a time τ where the marking of the place P_j at time τ is equal to the initial marking of P_j and P_j belongs to the reachability of T and T belongs to the reachability of P_j at time τ ($\forall P_p$, $P_j \in P_p$, $\exists \tau | M_\tau(P_j) = M_0(P_j)$ and $P_j \in [T_\tau\rangle$ and $T_\tau \in [P_\tau\rangle$); this means the workflow resources that belong to the set of places P_p are not consumable and they return to their corresponding pools after serving a certain transition T $\left(\sum_{j=1}^{n} (M(P_j)) | P_j \equiv \bullet T = \sum_{k=1}^{m} (M(P_k)) | P_k \equiv T \bullet \right)$. Since resources return to their corresponding pools, this means siphons are controllable; where for every token a, such that a belongs to the initial marking of the input, a belongs as well to the marking of the output at a time t, where t is the time taken for the customer to move from input to output ($\forall a | a \in M_0(i)$, $a \in M_t(o)$). Combining all these characteristics will ensure that tokens will eventually reach the output and therefore RPN is sound.

To conclude Theorem 1, four lemmas are proposed and they are based on previous proofs of the theorem.

Lemma 1 (For Theorem 1) *For every RPN such that RPN is sound, this RPN is structurally valid.*

Proof 3 (Proof of Lemma 1) $\forall$ *RPN | RPN is sound,* $\exists P_p \times T \neq \emptyset$ *and* $\exists T \times P_p \neq \emptyset | P_p$, $T \in \{RPN\}$ *and* $\exists i \in P | \bullet\ i = \emptyset$ *and* $\exists o \in P | o \bullet = \emptyset$, *therefore,* $M(i) \equiv M(o)$.

In this proof, the characteristics of the net are mentioned as a start. The first two equations $\exists P_p \times T \neq \emptyset$ and $\exists T \times P_p \neq \emptyset$ describe the topology of the net and how siphons are connected to transitions. The equations show that if a pool is an input to a set of transitions, this set of transitions will bring tokens back to the same pool. This way the siphon is controlled. For the equations: $\exists i \in P | \bullet i = \emptyset$ and $\exists o \in P | o \bullet = \emptyset$, they describe the basic feature of a workflow, that is, there is one place that is considered as an input and it is not preceded by any other node and there is one output place that is not followed by any other node. Therefore, tokens that are injected to the input will eventually end up being in the output ($M(i) \equiv M(o)$).

Lemma 2 (For Theorem 1) *For every RPN such that RPN is sound, the resources are not consumable and return to their corresponding pools. A resource can move with a customer into different consecutive stages, if needed, before returning to its pool.*

Proof 4 (Proof of Lemma 2) $\forall$ *RPN | RPN is sound,* $\exists P_j \equiv \bullet T$ *and* $\exists P_k \equiv T \bullet$ $| \sum_{j=1}^{n} (M(P_j)) = \sum_{k=1}^{m} (M(P_k))$. *Then,* $\Sigma M_0(P) = \Sigma M_\tau(P)$. *Therefore, resources are not consumable.*

The equations $\exists P_j \equiv \bullet T$ and $\exists P_k \equiv T \bullet$ show again the topology of the net where siphons are reachable from the sequence of transitions that consume from those siphons. For any transition, the number of input tokens equals the number of output tokens ($\sum_{j=1}^{n} (M(P_j)) = \sum_{k=1}^{m} (M(P_k))$). Therefore, the sum of all markings in the net will not change by time and therefore there are no consumable resources ($\Sigma M_0(P) = \Sigma M_\tau(P)$).

Lemma 3 (For Theorem 1) *For every RPN such that RPN is sound, the siphons are controllable.*

Proof 5 (Proof of Lemma 3) $\forall$ *RPN* | *RPN is sound,* $P_j \in P_p$, $\exists \tau$, $T | M_0(P_j) = M_\tau(P_j)$ *and* $P_j \in \left[T_\tau \bullet \right\rangle$ *and* $\bullet T_\tau \in \left[P_j \right\rangle$

Since RPN is sound then the initial marking of a place P_j is equal to the marking of that place at a certain time τ after the resource has moved into the required stages in order to accomplish a required service ($M_0(P_j) = M_\tau(P_j)$). Therefore, the place P_j is reachable from the output of transition T and the transition T is reachable from that place P_j ($P_j \in \left[T_\tau \bullet \right\rangle$ and $\bullet T_\tau \in \left[P_j \right\rangle$). Then, all siphons are controllable.

Lemma 4 (For Theorem 1) *For every RPN such that RPN is sound, the system's resources have the capability to serve a certain customer and to execute a certain transition.*

Proof 6 (Proof of Lemma 4) *Having* Λ *to be the set of capabilities of resources,* $\forall \lambda \in \Lambda$, $\exists T_j \in T | \lambda \equiv T_j$. *Therefore,* $\forall RPN | RPN$ is sound, $\exists \Lambda \subseteq T | T \in RPN$.

In this proof, the equations describe the mapping between resource capabilities and transitions that belong to the workflow. In other words, for the transition to fire certain resource capabilities have to be available" [Oueida et al. (2018c)].

4.3 RPN as a Cooperative System

"The theorems suggested here are to prove the soundness of the system including the cooperation between the two RPN_A and RPN_B. RPN_A refers to the RPN of UNIT A and RPN_B refers to the RPN of UNIT B. The main reason for cooperation between the two RPNs is the blockage at one UNIT and therefore the need for sharing resources. RPN_A can share resources (staff or customer) with RPN_B if needed and vice-versa. This can result in guaranteeing a load balance between the two RPNs of an organization and covering an RPN that is not capable of accomplishing a task. The theorem will be proved based on the suggestion that each RPN, separately, is already sound. The only limitation here is that resources being shared, if any, should be capable of serving this task coverage needed. The cooperative system is defined as follows:

$$\begin{aligned} RPN_c &= \left\langle \text{Stages, Resources, Patients} \right\rangle \\ RPN_c &= RPN_A \otimes RPN_B \end{aligned} \tag{4.2}$$

where, the operator $\otimes$ is used to represent the cooperation framework. This operator joins two cooperative sound frameworks RPN_A and RPN_B leading to a collective framework as a result and which will be proven to be sound as well. The resources, being shared, are defined as the set of pools: $P_p = \{P_{p1}, P_{p2}, \ldots, P_{pn}\}$.

There are two cases here, either sharing only staff resources (see Theorem 2) or sharing staff resources and customers along with other units, such as radiology, billing, etc. (see Theorem 3).

The following theorems demonstrate the soundness of the cooperative framework. We assume that all resources are defined and initially, resources are not shared. Mathematically, $RPN_A \cup RPN_B \subseteq$ Resources and $RPN_A \cap RPN_B = \{\varnothing\}$.

The cooperation is studied in two different cases, namely loosely coupled and tightly coupled. A loosely coupled case is when only resources are shared between different RPNs. On the other hand, a tightly coupled case is when resources and customers are shared and can move among the RPNs.

Theorem 2 is described by the following, where RPN_A and RPN_B share only resources.

Theorem 2 $RPN_c = RPN_A \otimes RPN_B$ *is sound if:*

1. RPN_A *is a sound RPN*
2. RPN_B *is a sound RPN*
3. $\forall P_{pj} \in P_{pA},\ P_{pj} \in [P_{pB})\ and\ \forall P_{pk} \in P_{pB},\ P_{pk} \in [P_{pA})$
4. $\forall P_{pj} \in P_{pA},\ P_{pj} \in \bullet T_B\ and\ P_{pj} \in [T_B \bullet),\ and$
5. $\forall P_{pk} \in P_{pB},\ P_{pk} \in \bullet T_A\ and\ P_{pk} \in [T_A \bullet),$
6. $\exists \tau\ where\ M_\tau(P_{pA}) = M_0(P_{pA})\ and\ M_\tau(P_{pB}) = M_0(P_{pB}),$
7. $\exists \Lambda_A,\ \Lambda_A \in T_A | \Lambda_A \subseteq T_B\ and\ \exists \Lambda_B,\ \Lambda_B \in T_B | \Lambda_B \subseteq T_A,$

Proof 7 (Proof of Loosely Coupled Case) *Since RPN_A is sound and RPN_B is sound as proved in Theorem 1, therefore, $M_\tau(P_{pA}) = M_0(P_{pA})$ and $M_\tau(P_{pB}) = M_0(P_{pB})$. Since $\forall P_{pj} \in P_{pA},\ P_{pj} \in [P_{pB})$ and $\forall P_{pk} \in P_{pB},\ P_{pk} \in [P_{pA})$, therefore $P_{pj} \in P_{pB}$ and $P_{pk} \in P_{pA}$. Since $T_B \in [P_{pA})$ and $T_A \in [P_{pB})$, therefore, $P_{pj} \in [T_A)$ and $P_{pk} \in [T_B)$. From Theorem 1, $P_{pA} \in [T_A)$ and $P_{pB} \in [T_B)$, therefore the cooperative framework is sound.*

In other words, this theorem shows the life cycle of the resource from the minute it is sent to a different RPN until it goes back to its initial RPN. The resource leaves the pool to join transitions in a different RPN. Since the RPN in the destination is also sound, it will end up being assigned to its resource pools, which in turn will direct the token to its initial RPN that will put that resource into its initial pool.

Theorem 3 is described by the following where RPN_A and RPN_B share resources and customers.

Theorem 3 $RPN_c = RPN_A \otimes RPN_B$ *is sound and tightly coupled if:*

1. $\exists\ RPN_A$ *and RPN_B | RPN_A is sound and RPN_B is sound and $RPN_A \otimes RPN_B$ is sound and loosely coupled.*
2. $\exists T_A \times P_B \cup P_A \times T_B | \forall a_A \in RPN_A,\ a_A \in [RPN_B)\ and\ \forall a_B \in RPN_B,\ a_B \in [RPN_A).$

Proof 8 (Proof of Tightly Coupled Case)

1. *since $\exists\ RPN_c = RPN_A \otimes RPN_B$ | RPN_c is sound loosely coupled from Theorem 2. Therefore, all siphons are controlled.*
2. *since $\exists T_A \times P_B \cup T_B \times P_A$ therefore, $a \in M(P_A \cup P_B)$.*
3. *since $P_A \in [P_B)$ therefore, $a_A \in$ output of RPN_A and $a_B \in$ output of RPN_B therefore, RPN_c is a sound tightly coupled framework.*

In other words, the framework is proven from Theorem 2 to be a sound loosely coupled framework. In this theorem we prove that it is also a sound tightly coupled framework, where for every patient a that will be transferred from one ER to another, this patient will return back to the original department to finalize the process and exit the system. a_A refers to a patient that starts in RPN_A and a_B refers to a patient that starts in RPN_B.

As a conclusion for Theorems 2 and 3, in the loosely coupled case, all pools are shared between the two RPNs. As for the tightly coupled case, all pools and patients are shared.

Lemma 5 (For Theorem 2) *For every cooperative system RPN_c, if this workflow is sound then, each contained workflow RPN_A and RPN_B are also sound.*

$\forall\ RPN_c = RPN_A \otimes RPN_B$, *if RPN_c is sound then RPN_A is sound and RPN_B is sound.*

Proof 9 (Proof of Lemma 5) *If RPN_c is sound therefore,*

1. $M_\tau(RPN_c) \equiv M_0(RPN_c)$ *therefore,*
2. $\forall P_{pj} \in P_{pA}$ *and* $\forall P_{pk} \in P_{pB}$, $P_{pj} \in \bullet T_B$ *and* $P_{pj} \in T_A \bullet$ *and* $P_{pk} \in \bullet T_A$ *and* $P_{pk} \in T_B \bullet$ *therefore,*
3. $\displaystyle\sum_{i=1}^{n} M_\tau(RPN_A) \equiv \sum_{j=1}^{m} M_0(RPN_A)$ *and* $\displaystyle\sum_{i=1}^{n} M_\tau(RPN_B) \equiv \sum_{j=1}^{m} M_0(RPN_B)$
4. $M_0(i_A) = M_\tau(o_A)$ *and* $M_0(i_B) = M_\tau(o_B)$ *where $M_0(i)$ is the marking of the input at initial time and $M_\tau o$ is the marking of the output at time τ. therefore, RPN_A is sound and RPN_B is sound.*

In other words, if the cooperative system RPN_c is sound then, there exists a time τ where the marking of this workflow is equal to the initial marking. Therefore, since resources are being shared between RPN_A and RPN_B, then, for every resource P_{pj} belonging to the pool of resources of RPN_A, noted here as P_{pA}, this resource belongs to the input of the transition T_B serving RPN_B and to the output of the transition T_A since the resource should return to its original RPN_A. Also, for every resource P_{pk} belonging to the pool of resources of RPN_B, noted here as P_{pB}, this resource belongs to the input of the transition T_A serving RPN_A and to the output of the transition T_B since the resource should also return to its original RPN_B. Therefore, the sum of markings at a time τ of RPN_A is equal to the initial marking of RPN_A and the sum of markings at a time τ of all resources in RPN_B is equal to the initial marking of RPN_B. Also, the initial marking of the input place of RPN_A will be equal to the marking of the output place of RPN_A at a certain time τ and the initial marking of the input place of RPN_B will be equal to the marking of the output place of RPN_B at a certain time τ.

This means that all resources in a certain RPN_A or RPN_B are reaching the output from the corresponding input. Therefore, RPN_A is sound and RPN_B is sound.

Lemma 6 (For Theorem 2) $\forall$ *sound tightly coupled RPN, $\exists RPN_i \in RPN \,|\, RPN_i$ is loosely coupled and RPN_i is sound.*

Proof 10 (Proof of Lemma 6) *Since RPN_A is sound and RPN_B is sound, therefore*

1. $M_0(i_A) = M_\tau(o_A)$ *and* $M_0(i_B) = M_\tau(o_B)$ *and*
2. $M_0(P_{pA}) \equiv M_\tau(P_{pA})$ *and* $M_0(P_{pB}) \equiv M_\tau(P_{pB})$ *therefore,*
3. $P_{pA} \in \bullet T_A$ *and* $P_{pB} \in \bullet T_B$ *and* $P_{pA} \in T_A \bullet$ *and* $P_{pB} \in T_B \bullet$, *therefore,*
4. $\forall P_{pj} \in P_p, \exists P_{pj} \in P_{pA} | P_{pj} \in \bullet T_A$ *and* $P_{pj} \in T_A \bullet$ *and*
5. $\exists P_{pk} \in P_{pB} | P_{pk} \in \bullet T_B$ *and* $P_{pk} \in T_B \bullet$, *therefore,*
6. $M_0(P_{pj}) \equiv M_\tau(P_{pj})$ *and* $M_0(P_{pk}) \equiv M_\tau(P_{pk})$, *therefore, $\forall RPN_i \in RPN$, RPN is sound and RPN_i is sound and loosely coupled.*

In other words, since RPN_A and RPN_B are two sound frameworks that are cooperating together, then, the initial marking of the input place of RPN_A is equal to the marking of the output place of RPN_A at a time τ and the initial marking of the input place of RPN_B is equal to the marking of the output place of RPN_B at a time τ. Also, the initial marking of resources pool in RPN_A is equal to the marking of this pool at a time τ and the initial marking of resources pool in RPN_B is equal to the marking of this pool at a time τ. Moreover, the pool of resources of RPN_A, P_{pA}, belongs to the input of the transition of RPN_A, $\bullet T_A$, and then belongs to the output of the transition after being served, $T_A\bullet$; similarly, the pool of resources of RPN_B, P_{pB}, belongs to the input of the transition of RPN_B, $\bullet T_B$, and then belongs to the output of the transition after being served, $T_B\bullet$. Therefore, for every resource P_{pj} belonging to the pool of resources P_p, either for RPN_A or RPN_B, there exists a resource P_{pj} that belongs to the pool of resources of RPN_A, P_{pA}, where P_{pj} is serving a transition in RPN_A and there exists a resource P_{pK} belonging to the pool of resources of RPN_B, P_{pB}, where P_{pk} is serving a transition in RPN_B. Therefore, the initial marking of the pool P_{pj} is equal to the marking of this pool at a time τ and the initial marking of the pool P_{pk} is equal to the marking of this pool at a time τ. Thus, for every RPN_i that belongs to a workflow RPN, RPN is sound and RPN_i is sound and loosely coupled" [Oueida et al. (2018c)].

4.4 Framework Scalability

"Scalability of the framework falls under the soundness and efficiency of the general framework regardless of the number of cooperating RPN added to the system. It is a design quality measure of the framework. RPN_c is guaranteed to be scalable and remain sound as demonstrated below using mathematical induction [Sipser (2006)].

Proof of Scalability:
    Mathematical induction technique is used in order to prove the scalability of the framework. Mathematical induction is a mathematical proof technique that allows the proof of a statement following three steps:

1. The base case where in this case the framework is proven to be sound for one RPN_c, where $RPN_c = RPN_1 \otimes RPN_2$
2. The second step is the inductive hypothesis where the framework is assumed to be sound for (k) RPN_c where $RPN_c = \{RPN_1 \otimes RPN_2 \otimes \ldots \otimes RPN_k\}$
3. The final step which is the inductive step where the framework is proven to remain sound for (k+1) RPN_c, $RPN_c = \{RPN_1 \otimes RPN_2 \otimes \ldots \otimes RPN_k \otimes RPN_{k+1}\}$

Theorem 4 $\forall RPN_c | RPN_c = \{RPN_1 \otimes RPN_2 \otimes \ldots \otimes RPN_n\}$, *if RPN_1, RPN_2, …, RPN_n are sound RPNs therefore RPN_c is sound.*

Proof by Induction:
    The three steps mentioned earlier are represented as follows:
    Base case: $\exists RPN_c = RPN_1 \otimes RPN_2 | RPN_c$ is sound. RPN_c is a cooperative sound system as proven before in Theorem 2.
    Inductive Hypothesis: Given (K) RPN, it is assumed that $\exists RPN_c = \{RPN_1 \otimes RPN_2 \otimes \ldots \otimes RPN_k\} | RPN_c$ is a sound cooperative framework.
    Inductive Step: It is required to prove that $RPN_c = \{RPN_1 \otimes RPN_2 \otimes \ldots \otimes RPN_k \otimes RPN_{(k+1)}\}$ is a sound cooperative framework.
    Proof 11 *Assuming $RPN_A = \{RPN_1 \otimes RPN_2 \otimes \ldots \otimes RPN_k\}$ and $RPN_B = RPN_{k+1}$ then if RPN_A is sound from the inductive hypothesis and RPN_B is sound from Theorem 1, therefore the cooperation $\otimes$ between them is still sound from Theorem 2, then $RPN_c = \{RPN_1 \otimes RPN_2 \otimes \ldots \otimes RPN_k \otimes RPN_{(k+1)}\}$ is still sound. Therefore, the framework is scalable.*

Lemma 7 (For Theorem 4) *For every cooperative system RPN_c that is sound, if a new sound workflow, RPN_p cooperates with RPN_c, the total workflow remains sound. Given (n) RPN | RPN_c = {RPN$_1$ ⊗ RPN$_2$ ⊗ … ⊗ RPN$_n$}, $\forall RPN_i$ ⊗RPN_c|RPN_i is sound, then RPN_c remains sound"* [Oueida et al. (2018c)].

4.5 Framework Separability and Serializability

"A workflow is said to be separable if and only if the execution of the multiple tokens in the input will not affect each other. In other words, if the execution of a token A will cause token B not to reach the output, then the workflow is not separable. Separability is viewing the system as a parallel system where the system is replicated as many times as the number of tokens available and every workflow instance is fully dedicated to one token [Kotb and Baumgart (2005)].

Serializability is viewing the system as a sequential system where tokens are executed one after another and the successful execution of one token will not cause the failure of another one. Since siphons are controlled, then resources are always available in their pools at a certain time.

4.5.1 Non-Cooperative Systems

In this subsection, three theorems are presented in order to proof the separability and serializability of the proposed RPN model with no cooperation among systems.

Theorem 5 *if RPN_Θ is sound, then RPN_Θ is separable.*

Two-way proof:

☐ If RPN_Θ is sound, then RPN_Θ is separable.

Proof 12 (Proof a of Theorem 5) *Since RPN_Θ is sound, therefore $\forall m \in i, o \in [m\rangle$, where $m \in P_p$ and P_p represents the patient pool. Therefore, $\forall a \in P_R$, $M_{t+\tau}(P_R) \in [M_t(P_R)\rangle$.*

Where, $P_R = P_G - P_p$, P_G is the total pools and a represents tokens available in places P. Therefore, $\forall a \in P_p$, $\exists \tau | M_{t+\tau}(P_R)$ is sufficient for output o to be reachable by token a. Therefore, RPN_Θ is separable.

In other words, since the RPN is sound, it means the output is reachable from the input at a certain time τ and critical sections are controlled. Therefore, resources return to their pools and are available for another patient. Thus, the activity of a certain patient at time t does not affect another activity of another arriving patient at time $t + \tau$.

☐ If RPN_Θ is separable, then RPN_Θ is sound.

Proof 13 (Proof b of Theorem 5) *Since RPN_Θ is separable then, $\forall M_{t+\tau}(P_R) \in [M_t(P_R)\rangle$. Therefore, $\forall a \in i(t)$, $a \in o(t + k\tau)$. Therefore, RPN_Θ is sound.*

In other words, if RPN is separable, that means tokens are not affecting each other and therefore, the marking of resources at a certain time $t + \tau$ belongs to the reachability of the marking of this pool at a certain time and therefore a certain patient/token belonging to the input i at time t will definitely belong to the output o at time $t + k\tau$. Thus, critical sections are controlled and therefore the system is sound.

Theorem 6 *if RPN_Θ is sound, then RPN_Θ is serializable.*

Two-way proof:

 ☐ If RPN_Θ is sound, then RPN_Θ is serializable.

Proof 14 (Proof a of Theorem 6) *Since RPN_Θ is sound, then $\forall M_t \in i$, $M_{t+\tau} \in o$ and since $M(P_p) > M(P_R)$, therefore $\exists \tau | M(P_R) = 0$ and since $o \in \left[M(i) \right\rangle$. Therefore, $\exists \tau | P_R(\tau) \neq 0$.*
Therefore, $\forall a_i, a_j, \tau(a_i) > \tau(a_j)$, therefore RPN_Θ is serializable.

In other words, if RPN is sound then for every marking belonging to the input *i* at a time *t*, the marking belongs also to the output *o* at a time *t+τ*. Since the number of patients is always greater than the number of resources available then, the marking of patient's pool is greater than the marking of resource's pool; which means that at a certain time τ, the marking of resources pool can be equal to 0 where no resources are available. Also, since the output *o* is reachable from the input *i* then, there always exist a certain time τ where a resource returns to its corresponding pool and therefore $P_R(\tau) \neq 0$. This leads to having two tokens a_i and a_j where the time of execution of one token is greater than the time of execution of the other token and therefore both tokens are not being executed at the same time. Therefore, RPN is serializable.

 ☐ If RPN_Θ is serializable, then RPN_Θ is sound

Proof 15 (Proof b of Theorem 6) *Since RPN_Θ is serializable, then, $M_\tau(P_R) \geq 1$ and $\forall \tau$, $M_\tau(i) \neq 0$. Therefore, $O \in \left[M(i) \right\rangle$. Therefore, RPN_Θ is sound.*

In other words, since RPN is serializable then the marking of the resource pool is definitely greater than or equal to 1; which means there is always an available resource in the corresponding pool as long as there is an available token at a certain time τ. Therefore, the output is always reachable. Since the output is always reachable from the input, therefore RPN is sound.

 Theorem 7 *if RPN_Θ is serializable, then RPN_Θ is separable.*

Two-way proof:

 ☐ If RPN_Θ is serializable, then RPN_Θ is separable.

Proof 16 (Proof a of Theorem 7) *From Theorem 6, if RPN_Θ is serializable then RPN_Θ is sound. From Theorem 5, if RPN_Θ is sound then RPN_Θ is separable. Therefore, if RPN_Θ is serializable then RPN_Θ is separable.*

 ☐ If RPN_Θ is separable, then RPN_Θ is serializable.

Proof 17 (Proof b of Theorem 7) *From Theorem 6, if RPN_Θ is sound then RPN_Θ is serializable. From Theorem 5, if RPN_Θ is separable then RPN_Θ is sound. Therefore, if RPN_Θ is separable then RPN_Θ is serializable"* [Oueida et al. (2018c)].

4.5.2 Cooperative Systems

"In this subsection, three theorems are presented in order to proof the separability and serializability of the proposed RPN model with cooperation among systems.

Theorem 8 *RPN$_e$ is separable if RPN$_c$ is sound.*

<u>Two-way proof:</u>

☐ If RPN$_c$ is sound, then RPN$_e$ is separable.

Proof 18 (Proof a of Theorem 8) *From Theorem 4, since RPN$_e$ is sound and from Theorem 5, if RPN$_e$ is sound then RPN$_e$ is separable, therefore, RPN$_e$ is separable.*

☐ If RPN$_e$ is separable, then RPN$_c$ is sound.

Proof 19 (Proof b of Theorem 8) *From Theorem 4, RPN$_e$ is sound and from Theorem 3, RPN$_e$ is scalable. Then, RPN$_e$ is a valid RPN. Therefore, from Theorem 5, iff RPN is sound then RPN is separable. Therefore, RPN$_e$ is separable.*

Theorem 9 *RPN$_e$ is serializable iff RPN$_c$ is sound.*

Proof 20 (Proof of Theorem 9) *From Theorem 4, RPN$_e$ is sound. From Theorem 3, RPN$_e$ is scalable. Then, RPN$_e$ is a valid RPN, therefore, from Theorem 6, iff RPN is sound then RPN is serializable. Therefore, RPN$_e$ is serializable.*

Theorem 10 *RPN$_e$ is serializable if RPN$_c$ is separable.*

Proof 21 (Proof of Theorem 10) *From Theorem 4, RPN$_e$ is sound. From Theorem 3, RPN$_e$ is scalable. Then, RPN$_e$ is a valid RPN. Therefore, from Theorem 7, iff RPN is serializable then RPN is separable. Therefore, RPN$_e$ is serializable iff RPN$_e$ is separable"* [Oueida et al. (2018c)].

4.6 RPN Application to Automation

"This section is dedicated to applying the proposed model, RPN, to robot automation in order to demonstrate the generality of the proposed framework. Figure 4.1 shows the environment and the setup of the proposed problem. It is an industrial environment where moving objects from Zone A to Zone B is required. Zone A has the objects stacked. It is required to move those objects into the stack in Zone B. The assumption is that two types of heterogeneous robots are there. The first type robots are the pickers and the second type robots are the movers.

The process is assumed to be as follows:

1. Two pickers pick an object if available from Stack A then hand it over to a mover.
2. The pickers go back to their home area (Pool) to be ready for another pick if available.
3. The mover moves the object from Zone A to Zone B.

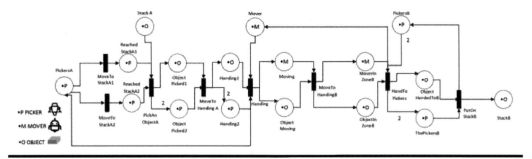

Figure 4.1 Two different types of mobile robots cooperating to move a stack of objects from Zone A to Zone B [Oueida et al. (2018d)].

4. The mover hands the object to two pickers in Zone B.
5. The mover goes back to home zone (Pool) to move another object when ready.
6. The pickers of Zone B pick the object and stack it on Stack B.
7. The pickers go back to their home zone to be ready to pick another object from movers.

Figure 4.1 shows a proposed RPN structure for the problem described. According to the mathematical description defined previously in Section 4.1, the problem is presented as follows:

- $Pp_{=1P}Mover_{,P}Picker_1$
- P = {$Stack_A$, $Stack_B$, $ReachedStack_{A2}$, $ReachedStack_{A1}$, $Object Picked_1$, $Object Picked_2$, $Handing_1$, $Handing_2$, $Moving$, $ObjectMoving$, $MoverInZoneB$, $ObjectInZoneB$, $Picke B$, $ObjectHandedToB$}
- T = {$MoveToStack A_1$, $MoveToStack A_2$, $PickAnObject_A$, $MoveToHanding_A$, $Hand$, $MoveToHanding_B$, $HandToPickers$, $PutOnStackB$}
- R = {$Picker_1$, $Picker_2$, ..., $Picker_8$, $Mover_1$, $Mover_2$, $Mover_3$}
- Λ = {$Picking$, $Moving$, $Handing$}
- $λ$ is the request of pickers for movers or movers for pickers
- is the topology of the RPN shown in Figure 4.2
- i is $Stack_A$
- o is $Stack_B$
- M = [10, 4, 0, 0, 0, 0, 0, 0, 3, 0, 0, 0, 0, 4, 0, 0, 0]
- $Θ(P_p, R)$ is the mapping function that assigns resources to pools

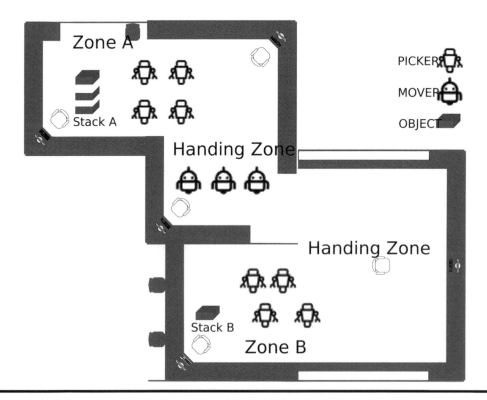

Figure 4.2   RPN structure of the robot automation process proposed [Oueida et al. (2018d)].

λ here is a request that is being sent from movers to pickers or from pickers to movers. If the mover wants to hand objects to a picker, it sends it as a request λ and if the picker wants to take an object from a mover it sends λ.

For M, we assume that we start with *Stack $_A$* as 10 objects. *Stack $_B$* is initially empty. We have 4 Pickers in zone A, 4 pickers in zone B and we have 3 movers. M refers here to the initial marking of the Petri net. The first value refers to the number of objects in the system which is 10. The second value refers to the number of pickers in Zone A which is 4. The third value refers to the number of movers which is 3 and the last value refers to the number of pickers in Zone B which is 3. All other values are set to zero since places have no tokens and transitions did not fire yet. The robots are non-consumable resources that belong to their pools. The pools are controlled siphons by the definition of the RPN. The soundness of the model is given by the Theorems and their proofs. Note that this proposed design is not targeting the solution of cooperative robotics. Cooperative robotics set up is only to show the modeling capability of the proposed RPN. The robots are considered non-consumable resources as stated earlier" [Oueida et al. (2018d)].

The information in this chapter appears in the following journals, all authored by Soraia Oueida and reprinted by permission of the publisher.

- *Complexity*, Copyright © 2018, Hindawi, [Oueida et al. (2018c)]
- *Sensors*, Copyright © 2018, MDPI, [Oueida et al. (2018d)]

Chapter 5

Optimizing the Structure of the ED

In this chapter, the emergency department chosen to be studied is optimized using the OptQuest tool in Arena, where room for enhancements is proposed. Performance measures such as LoS, Resource Workload, and System Number in/out are studied. The same model is optimized mathematically by proposing a new reward system. This reward system, namely Resource Preservation Net (RPN), takes into consideration the enhancement of three factors: customers, owners, and employees to improve the ED system. Moreover, different improvement techniques are proposed such as using Six Sigma and introducing Internet of Things (IoT) in order to ensure continuity of patient flow and overcome bottlenecks.

5.1 Continuity of ED Flows

Hospital emergency departments are large, complex communities with different business environments and operational constraints. In order to solve process problems and perform organizational improvements to these systems, a data-oriented and process-focused business approach is required. Process improvements should focus on the process problem and not on people problems. The flow of patient must be continuous and fluent in order to ensure that all patients receive the required care and exit the system in a minimum period of time, leaving room for other patients to come through. Medical errors can always occur regardless of the quality of resources. Dealing with these is the goal of the Six Sigma technique. Mistake-proof processes should be developed and quantitative measurement skills should be applied in order to ensure a world-class-quality-level, effective, and adaptable healthcare industry [Johnson et al. (2004)]. Six Sigma technique is presented in Section 5.1.1 and is applied on the studied ED using the Minitab tool. Moreover, technology is a very efficient way to enhance a healthcare system, provide continuous patient flow, and ensure satisfaction, which will be elaborated in Section 5.1.3. These improvement techniques overcome bottlenecks and ensure soundness of the healthcare system, where each patient arriving into the ED will exit after a period of time, receiving all the medical care required, and under an acceptable satisfaction level.

5.1.1 Lean Thinking and Six Sigma

The total waiting time (referred to as LoS) a patient spends in the emergency department and the waiting time spent in queues are some global concerns since the long wait for delivery of care may result in low patient outcomes and thus affect system satisfaction. The simulation model designed previously to depict the real-life system of the ED is verified and validated using the hospital's databases, interviews conducted with patients, staff, and management, along with surveys and observations. These data can be used in order to assess the current status of the ED, the levels of crowding and satisfaction, and opens up the possibility of proposing solutions and ways for improvements by eliminating waste and providing continuity of patient flow. Many authors in past literature proposed some simulation models in order to study emergency departments using Six Sigma techniques focusing on the improvement of two measures: waiting time and LoS. Mandahawi et al. (2017), proposed a model that resulted in reducing the waiting time by 61%, the LoS by 34%, and thus improved the Sigma level from 0.66 to 5.18 and from 0.58 to 3.09 for waiting time and LoS, respectively [Mandahawi et al. (2017)]. In this subsection, the concept of Lean Six Sigma is applied where Minitab tool is used in order to analyze the data.

Six sigma is a problem-solving method and quality improvement project that provides businesses in general and healthcare in particular with the suitable tools to improve the performance of a product or service [Coleman (2012); Westgard and Westgard (2017)]. When it comes to increasing the process performance and minimizing waste in order to reach high customer expectation, Six Sigma is the best technique to be conducted. It aims to study the system and eliminate process variation and process defects and make sure that patients flow smoothly through the system. Therefore, efficiency and profitability can be guaranteed. This technique focuses on five phases: Define, Measure, Analyse, Improve, and Control [Pyzdek and Keller (2014)]. For example, in healthcare processes, the Sigma level is used as a performance indicator to indicate the defects in the system [Devore et al. (2013)]. Six Sigma is widely used in the healthcare sector. Nurses' perceptions and evaluations of healthcare development was described and analyzed using Lean and Six Sigma concepts [Eriksson (2017)]. Another author applied Lean Six Sigma method to the medical records department of a hospital [Bhat et al. (2016)]. Moreover, a simulation-based Six Sigma approach was successfully used to determine the optimal number of consultation rooms, investigating room capacities, determining longer appointment time in the outpatient departments, and improving ED waiting times [Chia and Lin (2016); Barrios and Jiménez (2016); Habidin et al. (2015)].

5.1.2 Six Sigma Application to ED using Minitab

As discussed previously, Six Sigma is a set of quality management techniques and tools used for improving business processes. It is known as the DMAIC method (Defining the process, Measuring parameters, Analyzing the problem, Improving the process, and Controlling the progress made). In order to apply Six Sigma to the studied ED, Minitab tool is used. Minitab is a popular tool that allows various statistical calculations to be performed, such as normality test, process capability analysis, and so on. It is a user-friendly interface providing quick and effective solutions for any Six Sigma project analysis.

The case study: This is the define process stage. Management has requested an increase in revenue after a decrease noticed for the past year mainly caused by the emergency department. The main goal is to determine what caused this sudden decline in patient preference and revenue.

Steps: As a first step, causes must be identified. For this reason, surveys, interviews, and observations were conducted in the emergency department. These are the stages of measuring parameters and analyzing the problem. Discussions were held with patients and medical staff such as doctors, nurses, etc. The problem was identified by the number of patients being seen and thus a scientific approach is adopted in order to identify the causes. Six Sigma was the tool used to identify these causes using Minitab statistical analysis. Data was gathered from a survey designed in Section 2.3 and is fed into a Minitab worksheet and subjected to analysis. At first, the collected data is classified into nominal and ordinal categories. Nominal data is categorized according to descriptive or quantitative information, and this indicates the relative importance of parameters under consideration. In this case, the number of complaints is the nominal data against the services offered by the hospital. Figure 5.1 shows the data added to the worksheet.

Generating Graphs: A bar chart is first generated to interpret the data entered and to define the cause of this problem. Figure 5.2 represents this bar chart and defines the main three causes of the problem faced by the emergency department under study: poor technology, high LoS, and high waiting time in queues.

To further examine the number of complaints in percentage or proportional data, a pie chart is used. It shows the relative contribution that different categories contribute to total. It is useful to have the relative importance of the parameters under study. Figure 5.3 defines this proportion; where 30.8% of patients complained of poor technology, 20.2% complained of high LoS, and 13.4% complained of high waiting times. These percentages imply the need for management to consider enhancing the technology level in the ED. Moreover, high LoS, caused as well by high waiting time in queues, is another cause of the studied problem and needs to be improved.

Being still under the defining phase and finding the problem, a Pareto analysis is used to better select the problems and initiate the improvement needed. Pareto charts practice the 80/20 theory where the problems of quality improvement can be solved. For example, 80% of effect is caused by 20% of causes. Figure 5.4 shows the Pareto chart with the cumulative values of complaints against poor technology, high LoS, and high waiting time are high at 64.4%, while other complaints are

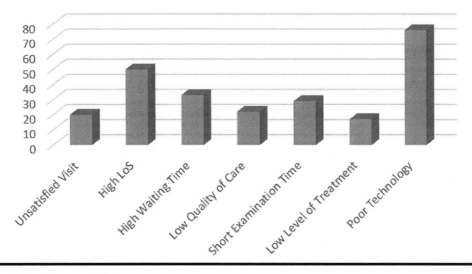

Figure 5.1   Survey statistics.

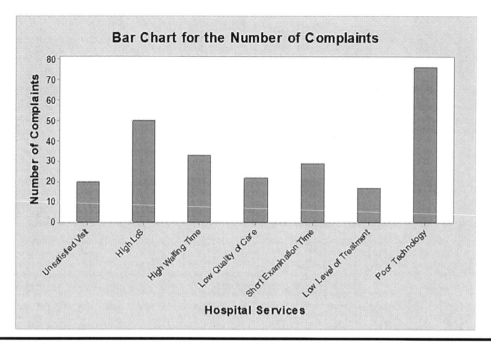

Figure 5.2 Bar chart.

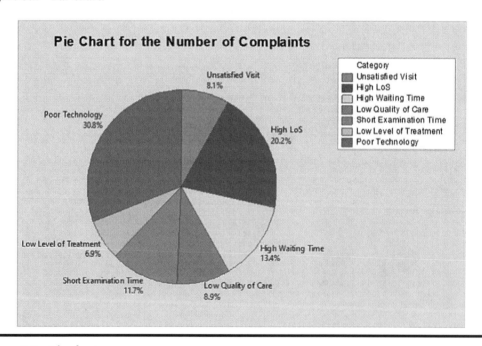

Figure 5.3 Pie chart.

seen of low importance. In other words, technology, high LoS, and high waiting time constitute the vital few while the others constitute the trivial many.

After identifying services causing 80% of the problems, the raw data need to be examined to understand if the gathered data is retrieved from a normal distribution or not. Normal distribution is a statistical distribution that has bell-shaped density curves with a single peak. The purpose

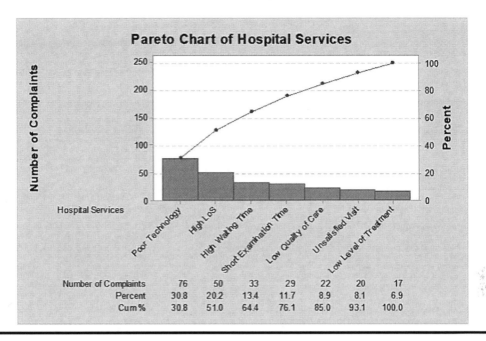

Figure 5.4   Pareto chart.

of conducting a normality test is to check if the data is derived from normal distribution. The test results confirm either that the hypothesis should be rejected or failed as there are chances that non-normal data may produce misleading results. The high LoS data values are used for study using the Kolmogrov Smirnov (KS) test. Figure 5.5 shows a p-value equal to 0.027 which is less than 0.05 and therefore means that the data gathered is not retrieved from a normal distribution. This result means that the variance in waiting times is high and therefore is causing the problem.

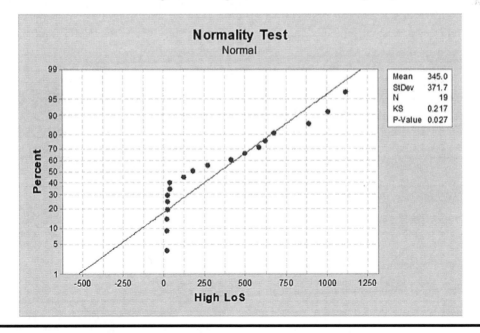

Figure 5.5   Normality test.

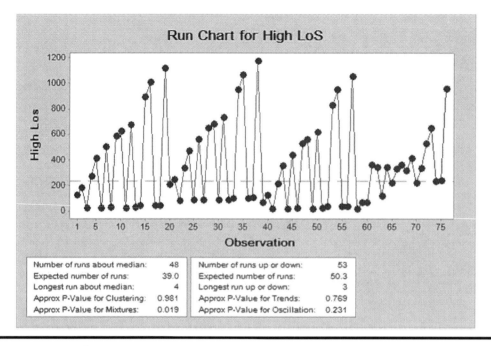

Figure 5.6   Run chart.

Knowing now that the data used is coming from a non-normal distribution, the variance that exists in this data should be studied. In order to display how process data changes with time, a run chart is used. This also reveals evidence of special cause variations. In distinguishing the reasons for variation in hospital services, the run chart presented in Figure 5.6 aids in analyzing the variations where high variations in the data are noticed.

Discussion: The main cause was defined as being the poor technology in the ED. This is a significant limitation and is being studied by decision-makers because of budget constraints, where new systems need to be implemented in order to improve the healthcare information system in the ED. Other causes referred to were high LoS and high queues waiting times. From interviews with medical staff, patients, and management, the main queue suffering from high waiting time and causing the bottleneck is the transporter queue, which in turn affects the system LoS. Therefore, it is decided to try adding extra resources to serve this bottleneck queue and study their effect on the system performance. This falls under improving the process stage. The maximum number of transporters allowed to be added as per the management decision is ten. Since the real-time system cannot be interrupted to perform this change, simulation with Arena is used and new results are achieved for high LoS data to be studied again. As a final stage of the DMAIC method, descriptive statistics are derived from the data and displayed in Table 5.1. The 6 σ level is calculated using capability analysis and found to be equal to 1.78.

Enhancement: The Six Sigma concept aimed to reduce defects by reducing the variations in processes. The 6 σ level is improved to 2.29. The descriptive statistics after changing the number

Table 5.1   Descriptive Statistics before Enhancement

Variable	Mean	SE Mean	Standard Deviation	Minimum	Median	Maximum
High LoS	345.1	37.8	329.3	11.2	237.1	1172.3

Table 5.2   Descriptive Statistics after Enhancement

Variable	Mean	SE Mean	Standard Deviation	Minimum	Median	Maximum
High LoS	112.86	5.74	59.38	15.61	129.87	219.43

Table 5.3   LoS Statistics

	Mean	SE Mean	Standard Deviation	6 σ level
Before Six Sigma	345	37.8	329.3	1.78
After Six Sigma	113	5.74	59.38	2.29

of transporters to ten and collecting the new data for LoS are presented in Table 5.2. The system LoS is reduced from 345 to 113 minutes which is a 67% enhancement to the system. Table 5.3 summarizes the statistical values before and after enhancement by applying Six Sigma.

5.1.3 Technology and Healthcare

Decision-makers and experts consider that introducing technology into the healthcare industry, such as electronic health records, computerized information technologies, and telemonitoring can transform the industry. Therefore, information management is necessary for healthcare delivery [Chassin et al. (1998)]. As per the literature, most information technologies were applied to the administrative and financial areas of the industry, although not taking the delivery of clinical care into consideration since healthcare systems are complex by nature [Audet et al. (2004)].

1. **Electronic Health Records**

    The studied ED suffers from a non-computerized system where everything is paper-based and needs to be saved in files for data collecting. Thus, patient information records, service time in each stage, diagnosis procedures, etc. are all collected by nurses and saved into the dedicated books/files. It is very obvious here that this will increase the waiting time of patients, the service time, and the staff utilization rates, not forgetting the medical errors that may arise from human/staff error. Therefore, information system technologies in the ED must be implemented to adhere to the best results. This also includes a computerized system for monitoring patients and delivering better healthcare levels. In order to adopt this technology, decision-makers should have a clear understanding of its application and effect on the overall industry. Thus, a review should be conducted on the benefits of applying such a technique on quality/efficiency and the extra costs that may arise. For implementing health information technology (HIT), first components need to be analyzed for building the framework and then a study on the types and capabilities of the health information technology system should be studied [Tang et al. (2003)].

    The implementation of a multifunctional HIT system has five major effects [Chaudhry et al. (2006)]:
    - Delivery of care is increased, always adhering to the general protocols and guidelines of the hospital
    - Medication error rates are reduced
    - Time utilization rates are affected
    - Care utilization rates are decreased
    - Disease conditions and care delivery can be monitored

Every healthcare institute proposes some general guidelines and protocols for delivery of care. Therefore, the major effect of technology application is on the quality of care where adherence to these guidelines/protocols is essential. One advantage of using information technology is to save patient health records in databases to be used at any time in the future by physicians, doctors, and any medical resource when needed. For example, before writing a medication prescription, the medical resource can check in the system if the corresponding patient has a documented allergy to that medication, thus decreasing the possibility of any medical error occurring and improving patient safety. Patient health records may include patient tracking, ordering tests, and displaying prior visit notes, ECGs, laboratory and radiology results, along with diagnoses, hospitalizations, information on medications/allergies, etc. [Pallin et al. (2010)].

By applying information technology (IT), EDs can benefit from an electronic patient management system. This leads to easy access to patient information, improves clinical decision support, replaces electronic medication and test ordering to enhance the paper-based time-consuming systems. These changes applied to the system help in reducing the service time in some stages of the ED (such as waiting to see a doctor, waiting for test results, etc.) and may improve efficiency [Feied et al. (2004); Landman et al. (2010)].

A recent study was applied to a group of national EDs over a multi-year period where the percent of visits seen in an ED is increased from 25% in 2007 to 69% in 2010 with a basic health IT system and increased from 3% to 31% with advanced IT systems. The study proves the efficiency of adoption of health IT where the number of tests, images, and medications ordered is increased and waiting times are reduced. Some limitations may arise in cases where the hospital adopts other process changes at the same time as health IT is implemented [Selck and Decker (2016)]. The Health Information Technology for Economic and Clinical Health Act of 2009 and the Centers for Medicare and Medicaid Services have studied the importance of replacing a paper-based system with an electronic health IT system. The emergency department information system (EDIS) is an important and effective component affecting the workflow, communication, decision-making, quality of care, and patient safety. EDIS stores access to patient health records and previous visits. The aim of this study was to examine the benefits and potential disadvantages of choosing a particular EDIS to the quality and patient safety along with the implementation and optimization of such systems. Some potential threats are: wrong order, communication failure, alert fatigue, and poor data display. The authors suggested some recommendations while deploying the EDIS, such as ED providers should actively participate in the selection of the EDIS product and its implementation, optimization, and ongoing monitoring of the chosen system [Farley et al. (2013)].

Deploying health IT in emergency departments may increase access to care where physicians may communicate with patients using emails and other technological means of communication, thus overcoming distance. Nevertheless, installing health IT may raise new problems in cases where patient records contain false information along with some privacy and security concerns due to unauthorized access and corruption of patient data [Herrick et al. (2010)]. Introducing an electronic triage system at the time of registration may improve efficiency and flow of patients in the ED. Also, it helps the ED staff to immediately identify the arriving patient and access previous care plan information, which allows for more consistency during care delivery [Stokes-Buzzelli et al. (2010)].

2. **Internet of Things:** "The revolution in information and communication technologies, and the spread of IoT and smart city industrial systems, have fostered widespread use of smart

systems, including in healthcare sectors. As a complex, 24/7 service, healthcare requires efficient and reliable follow-up on daily operations, service, and resources" [Oueida et al. (2018d)]. Data sharing, patient information privacy, and connected systems have led to smart and unified healthcare that addresses health issues such as data collection and sharing, patient privacy, resource and service utilization and medical records analytics. Cloud computing has proven to be the optimal solution to better deliver services over the Internet, and edge computing has shown great potential for data processing at the edge of a network, near the source of the data. "Cloud and edge computing are essential for smart and efficient healthcare systems in smart cities. Emergency departments are real-time systems with complex dynamic behavior, and they require tailored techniques to model, simulate, and optimize system resources and service flow" [Oueida et al. (2018d)].. Meeting ED constraints is necessary for modeling problems, and a modeling framework that takes constraints into consideration is vital. ED issues are largely due to resource shortage and resource assignment efficiency. In this subsection, "the resource preservation net (RPN) framework defined earlier, integrated with custom cloud and edge computing suitable for ED systems, is proposed. The proposed framework is designed to model non-consumable resources, and is theoretically described and verified previously. RPN is applied to a real-life scenario, and it provides performance and robustness information. Key performance indicators such as patient length of stay (LoS), resource utilization rate, and average patient waiting time are modeled and optimized. As the system must be reliable, efficient, and secure, the use of cloud and edge computing is critical" [Oueida et al. (2018d)].

The optimization of resource efficiency and availability is very important to smart healthcare in smart cities. Traditional healthcare systems falter without technological help or integration of other sources, and services cannot meet many challenges, including efficient resource distribution, medical service provision, data collection and sharing, access and availability of medical records, and analysis and recommendation based on these data. During the past decade, the exponential increase in adults suffering from chronic diseases and needing ongoing healthcare provisioning has highlighted the need to find innovative, efficient, and affordable solutions for patients, anytime and anywhere. And over the past couple of years, researchers have demonstrated the importance of cloud and edge computing to improve the management and processing of healthcare data, as well as provide provisioning services [Aloqaily et al. (2016)]. Tuan et al. proved the importance of IoT and fog computing to provide better health services [Gia et al. (2015)]. Esposito et al. used the recent developments in sensors and mobile embedded devices to build a smart architecture that is user friendly and allows rapid personal health monitoring [Esposito et al. (2018)]. Experts believe that cloud and fog computing have the potential to improve healthcare services and resource utilization, leading to a smart healthcare system that will facilitate the provision of better healthcare in smart cities. "The opportunities and challenges of adopting new technologies are evaluated in Kuo (2011), and the benefits of migration from traditional healthcare central systems into distributed cloud-fog-based healthcare systems, and the corresponding need for resource allocation, direction, and strategy, are also discussed. Moreover, wireless body area networks can be enhanced with the support of mobile cloud computing before deployment for healthcare applications [Otoum et al. (2015)]" [Oueida et al. (2018d)].

Healthcare systems are dynamic, complex, and unpredictable, and they must manage services and resources efficiently. Resources are assets that industrial systems compete for [Zeng et al. (2012)], while the quality of the provided services is an integral part of building a robust

Quality of Experience (QoE) model [Aloqaily et al. (2016)]. "Currently, the healthcare sector is facing a great number of problems due to exponential increases in population and chronic diseases. As traditional health technology cannot solve these challenges, cloud computing was introduced to address the problems of data and resource utilization. Cloud computing is a recent technology in the IoT era, and it is the best approach to enhance medical services due to its multi-tenancy, flexibility, and remote delivery [Anjomshoa et al. (2017); Islam et al. (2015)]. A 2016 study by Dubey and Vishwakarma highlights the application of cloud computing in healthcare, and the key principles required to build a smart healthcare system in a smart city. This paper also discusses the common limitations and problems faced when adopting cloud computing for healthcare [Dubey and Vishwakarma (2016)]. Mobile cloud computing and wireless body area networks can also be enhanced by the deployment of smart healthcare applications [Otoum et al. (2015)]. A study by Wan et al. highlighted the methodologies required to transmit data to a cloud, perform cloud resource allocation, and apply data security mechanisms [Wan et al. (2013)]. Patient data collection in healthcare systems requires extensive resources to collect, input, share, and analyze information to be used for certain medical services. Traditionally, patient information management has been slow, error-prone, and unable to provide true real-time accessibility. A solution to this problem is to introduce cloud and edge computing to the healthcare system, thereby transforming the system to smart healthcare. This requires sharing clinical diagnoses information and patient monitoring. Rolim et al. (2010), suggested attaching sensors to medical devices to automate the process. Sensors are connected through wireless networks to external gateways, and the information is stored in the cloud and accessible to all medical staff. This proposal ensured a cost-effective, reliable cloud computing system that is integrated with medical devices [Rolim et al. (2010)]. Doukas et al. developed a mobile system that provides storage, updating, and retrieval of electronic healthcare data through cloud computing. The application greatly improves the management of patient health records and images [Doukas et al. (2010)].

Fog computing is an extended version of the cloud computing paradigm that enables new applications and services based on particular characteristics, such as low latency, location awareness, mobility, strong presence of streaming, and real-time applications. A study by Bonomi proved the importance of fog computing, and proposed that it is the appropriate application for smart healthcare services in smart cities [Bonomi et al. (2012)]. The use of cloud computing to manage and process healthcare data and resources is of significant importance, and edge technology will be a prime enabler of smart healthcare for smart cities. The provision of a smart city mainly relies on the integration of all smart systems including smart healthcare. The successful deployment of smart healthcare services depends on cloud and edge computing. The workflow and resource pools of the proposed smart healthcare system are defined in the cloud, where the process is executed and resources are assigned. Every resource has its own edge node that reports the completion of an assigned task. Then the resource is reassigned by the scheduling algorithm in the cloud. Research has shown that cloud computing is more reliable, more efficient, and faster than regular client–server computing [Tolosana-Calasanz et al. (2014); Armbrust et al. (2010); Shimrat (2009);Shi et al. (2016)]. Having workflows in the cloud ensures that the process is always sound, due to fault tolerance policies supported by the cloud [Gupta (2017)]. Figure 5.7 shows the high-level structure of a cloud-fog-based workflow system. The databases and workflow software are stored in the cloud, and task assignment and notification of accomplished processes are sent from the edge nodes to the cloud. Every resource has a smart device, such as a cell phone or tablet that works as an edge node. When the resource accomplishes the assigned

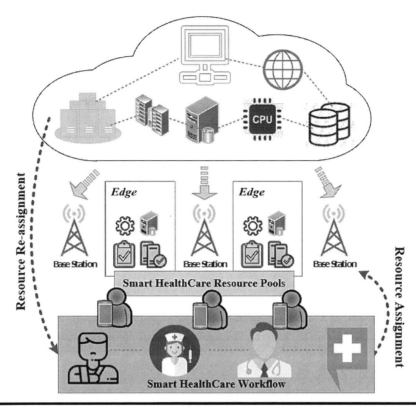

Figure 5.7 Edge-based smart healthcare framework [Oueida et al. (2018d)].

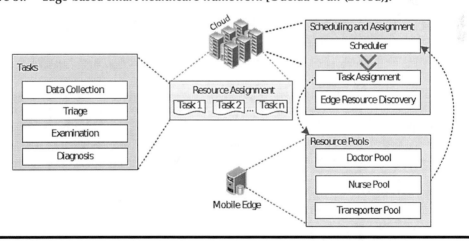

Figure 5.8 Overview of healthcare resource workflow [Oueida et al. (2018d)].

task, resource reports its status using the edge node to notify the cloud that the particular resource is available in the pool and ready to be reassigned. Figure 5.8 shows the two modes of the process: the cloud mode and the edge mode. Scheduling occurs in the cloud mode, and the assignment is sent to the edge. After the resource has completed the process, the edge mode notifies the cloud that the task is finished, and it is ready for a new task [Oueida et al. (2018d)].

"Smart healthcare depends on the cloud and edge computing. The workflow with its resource pools is defined in the cloud where the process is executed and resources are assigned. Every resource has its own edge node where it reports the finishing of the assigned task. Afterwards, the resource gets reassigned by the scheduling algorithm in cloud (refer to Figures 5.7 and 5.8).

A Smart HealthCare (SHC) is proposed here and validated mathematically.

$$SHC = (S, D, R, SR, DB, DA, E) \tag{5.1}$$

where *SHC* is a smart healthcare workflow, S is different workflow stages, D is a matrix that represents workflow dependencies, R is the set of workflow resources, S R is the stages resources, which is the cross product $S \times R$. DB is a database to store history of events and all required transactions. DA is data accessibility, a security module that assigns data visibility to stages, and finally E, the set of edge devices accessing data in an *SHC* system. In this section, we are using the same naming convention as the previous proposed workflow. In other words, S_j. S_k are different stages in S. $\bullet S_j$ is a set of input places to stage S_j. $S_j \bullet$ is the set of output places from stage S_j. S(i) is the first stage of the workflow. *S(o)* is the output stage of the workflow, and S_s is a sequence of stages in the workflow.

The model proposed is valid if the following conditions are met:

1. $\forall s \in S$, $\exists r \in R | (r, s) \in SR$. In other words, every stage requires some resources in order to accomplish required activities.
2. $\forall r \in R$, $\exists d \in DB | (r, d) \in DA$. In other words, the resources involved in a certain activity should be able to access the database.
3. $\forall e\, \exists E$, $\exists d \in DB | (d, e) \in DA$. In other words, at each specific stage, even each resource should have an edge device which in turn has accessibility of data belonging to that specific stage.
4. $\forall S_j, S_k \in S$, if $\exists (S_j, S_j) \in D$, then, $\exists e \in E | (S_j, e) \Rightarrow S_k$. In other words, if two stages S_j and S_K, are dependent then one stage needs an edge device in order to reach another stage.
5. $\forall r \in R$, $e \in E$, if $\exists (r, e)$, then $r \in DA$ and $e \in DA$. In other words, if a resource has the edge device, it should have the right to access the data as well.

Soundness of the SHC:

A healthcare workflow is a workflow such that $< S, R, e >$.

$S_j \bullet \equiv \bullet S_k \equiv e | e$ is a device that moves the resource from stage S_j to stage S_k.

Theorem 11 *A system SHC, S_{HC} is sound if and only if:*

1. *1- $\forall e \in E$, $\exists DA | S_j \bullet \neq \emptyset$ and $\bullet S_k \neq \emptyset$.*
2. $\forall S_j, S_k | S_j \Rightarrow S_k, \exists e \in S_j | S_j \neq \emptyset$.
3. $\exists S_s | S_s \in \left[S_i \right\rangle$ and $S_o \in \left[S_s \right\rangle$

Condition (1) states that for each edge device belonging to a set of edge devices E, there exists data accessibility such that the output of a certain stage S_j is never empty and the input of another stage S_k is never empty. This means, there is a movement from one stage to another, which can be done only if there is data accessibility for the edge device. Condition (2) refers to the topology of the workflow. If the patient moves from one stage to another with the resource, that means that an edge device at each stage exists. Condition (3) states that there is a sequence of stages S_s that exists, such that these stages belong to the reachability of the input stage S_i and the output stage S_o belongs to the reachability of the sequence of stages S_s. This means, patients are moving through the workflow from input to output and this can be possible in a smart healthcare workflow only if all the conditions listed here are met.

In other words, Theorem 11 guarantees that for a sound Smart HealthCare Workflow:

1. Each resource has an edge device
2. Each resource has the privilege to access the database based on its role and the stage it is serving
3. Each edge device can access the database pertaining to a certain stage
4. Input is reaching output after a sequence of stages

Proof 22

$\because \exists S_s | S_s \in [S_i\rangle \ and \ S_o \in [S_s\rangle$

$\therefore S(o) \ in \ [S(i)\rangle$

$\because \exists e \in E | e \in S_i \ and \ since \ e \in DA$

$\therefore \exists e \bullet | e\bullet = S_i \bullet,$

$\therefore \forall d \in DB, \ if \ d \in S_i, \ then \ eventually, \ d \in S_o.$

$\therefore$ *Therefore, the smart architecture* S_{HC}, *is sound"* [Oueida et al. (2018d)].

5.2 Elimination of Narrow Spaces

The NEDOCS score calculated earlier shows that the ED is severely overcrowded (overcrowding is Level 5). Therefore, optimization for the studied ED must be performed in order to eliminate bottlenecks; especially improving the bottleneck stage: the transporter queue. A new resource allocation is updated in the system and the model is simulated over another shift (6 hours) in order to enhance the system, such as increasing patient satisfaction (by decreasing the LoS), decreasing resource utilization rates and the number of patients waiting in the queues. The new resource allocation is deduced from the OptQuest tool-Variant 38 performed on the studied ED (refer to Table 5.5). The results of the optimization simulation are presented in Section 5.2.1.

5.2.1 One-Shift Simulation

The number of patients arriving into the ED during this shift (number in) along with the number of patients leaving the ED (number out) after applying optimization are depicted in Figure 5.9.

The waiting time in queues are presented in Figure 5.10. It is obvious from these results that the main bottleneck in the transporter queue is solved along with a zero-waiting time in almost all the queues.

From the resource detail summary represented in Figure 5.11, all resource utilization rates are less than 75% which implies a high resource satisfaction. All resources have a normal workload which reduces the percentage of medical errors that may occur in case of high resource utilization rates.

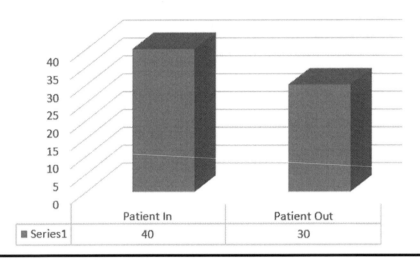

Figure 5.9   Number in/out after optimization during one shift.

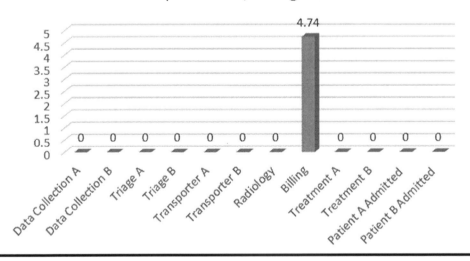

Figure 5.10   Queue waiting times after optimization during one shift.

The total time patients spend in the ED during this shift is represented by the LoS for ER A and ER B and is listed in Figure 5.12. Note that this value is reduced from 2 hours before optimization to 1.3 hours after optimization.

The number of patients waiting in the transporter queue for ER A and ER B is reduced to no patients waiting after optimization as presented in Figure 5.13. It is obvious that this is a huge enhancement of the system.

Resource Utilization Rates (%)
-after optimization, during one shift-

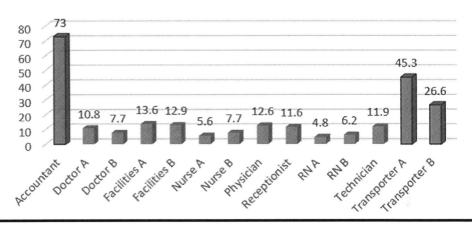

Figure 5.11   Resource utilization rates after optimization during one shift.

Patients LoS
-after optimization, during one shift-

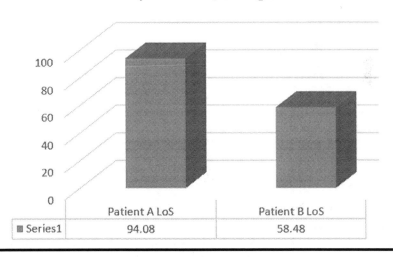

	Patient A LoS	Patient B LoS
▪ Series1	94.08	58.48

Figure 5.12   Patients LoS after optimization during one shift.

5.2.2 Measuring the ED NEDOCS after Optimization

Using the results of Section 5.2.1 and the web-based calculator, the NEDOCS score can be measured again. The numbers to be entered in the seven fields of the NEDOCS calculator are listed below and presented in Table 5.4:

1. Number of ED beds: equal to 9 for each ER, A and B, which leads to a total of 18 beds in the ED (refer to Table 5.5: resource type facilities)

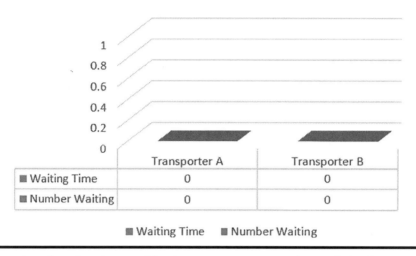

Figure 5.13   Number of patients waiting in transporter queue after optimization.

Table 5.4   NEDOCS Calculator Fields after Optimization

Calculator Fields	Numbers
Number of ED beds	18
Number of hospital beds	215
Total patients in the ED	0
Number of ED patients on ventilator	0
Number of admits in the ED	40
Waiting time of longest admitted patient (in hours)	1.3
Waiting time of longest waiting room patient (in hours)	0

2. Number of hospital beds: in total there are 207 beds + 8 beds added after optimization as facilities (for ER A and ER B)
3. Total patients in the ED: number of patients waiting in the transporter queue is equal to zero (which is the bottleneck stage under study) (refer to Figure 5.13)
4. Number of ED patients on ventilator: no patient is on ventilator during the measure
5. Number of admits in the ED: total number of patients arriving into the ED (refer to Figure 5.9)
6. Waiting time of longest admitted patient (in hours): the total visit time (refer to Figure 5.12)
7. Waiting time of longest waiting room patient (in hours): waiting time in the transporter queue being under study, which is reduced to zero after optimization

By entering these numbers into the NEDOCS calculator, the score is found to be 93, which is determined to be a Level 3 as per the score interpretation presented in Figure 5.14. This means that

Table 5.5 Best Resource Distribution-Variant 38

Resource Type	Best Capacity	Monthly Salary ($)
Accountant	6	1000
Doctor A	5	2000
Doctor B	5	2000
Facilities A	9	800
Facilities B	9	800
Nurse A	10	850
Nurse B	9	850
Physician	5	1200
Receptionist	5	500
RN A	5	1100
RN B	3	1100
Technician	5	800
Transporter A	10	650
Transporter B	10	650

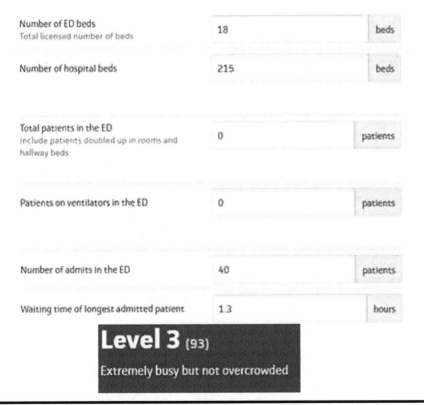

Number of ED beds Total licensed number of beds	18	beds
Number of hospital beds	215	beds
Total patients in the ED Include patients doubled up in rooms and hallway beds	0	patients
Patients on ventilators in the ED	0	patients
Number of admits in the ED	40	patients
Waiting time of longest admitted patient	13	hours

Level 3 (93)
Extremely busy but not overcrowded

Figure 5.14 NEDOCS web-calculator after optimization.

the ED is extremely busy but not overcrowded and thus a huge enhancement is noticed where the overcrowding is decreased from Level 5 to Level 3. Therefore, this optimization variant suggested by the OptQuest tool should be considered by decision-makers as an efficient and reliable solution but cannot be an optimal scenario where more scenarios can be suggested, always balancing between budget constraints, hospital revenue, patient satisfaction, and resource satisfaction.

5.3 Optimizing System Parameters

As a phase of experimentation, where different variants are simulated in order to find the most efficient one, OptQuest tool is used in order to find the optimal solution for a specific objective set: maximizing system out; always taking into consideration a constant level of care, a standard resource utilization rate and a decrease in patient LoS.

5.3.1 OptQuest during Normal Flow

The objectives set for this optimization simulation during normal flow are presented in Figure 5.15.

"To begin with the OptQuest, a control list is defined and all human resources are chosen. These controls are chosen in order to see the effect of resource changes on patient waiting time and system output. Then, responses are chosen, which reflect the decisions for improvement. The chosen responses are: Transporter A and B Utilization, Receptionist Utilization, Patient A and B LoS, System Number Out, Transporter A and B Queues Waiting time, Patient A and B Admitted to Hosp Queues Waiting time, Billing Queue Waiting Time, Tnow A and Tnow B, and finally patient number out. After defining the needed controls and responses, the replication number was set to 3 in order to get more accurate results and variation for each combination of controls. For each replication, a maximum of 300 simulations are chosen with an automatic stop option. The automatic stop option means that OptQuest would stop looking for solutions when it has not seen significant improvement for 100 different scenarios in a row. In this objective, the purpose is to reach the best or maximum number of patients exiting the system, taking into consideration all the responses defined earlier. The result from all simulations shows that the best solution is Simulation 38 (refer to Figure 5.16) with an objective value of 140 (system number out)" [Oueida et al. (2017e)].

The best combination of resources resulted from this optimal variant is depicted in the Table 5.5 along with their monthly corresponding salaries. This new suggested solution helps the hospital management to improve operations guaranteeing patient satisfaction by seeing more patients and increasing revenue in some cases (hospital satisfaction). Variant 38 suggests adding in total for both ERs: 15 nurses, 8 doctors, 4 receptionists, 18 transporters, 6 RNs, 2 technicians, 4 physicians, 8 facilities, and removing 2 accountants. The extra cost of this resource distribution change is $59,850 per month. The system is now serving 137 patients instead of 60 which means

Objectives Summary

	Included	Name	Type	Goal	Description	Expression
	☐	Objective 1	NonLinear	Minimize	Minimize Waiting Time A	[Patient A LoS]
	☐	Objective 2	NonLinear	Minimize	Minimize Waiting Time B	[Patient B LoS]
	☑	Objective 3	NonLinear	Maximize	Maximize Patient Out	[System.NumberOut]

Figure 5.15 Optimization objectives for normal flow.

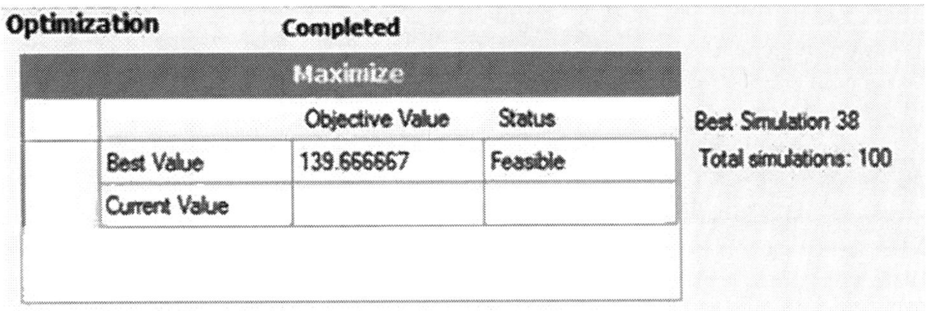

Figure 5.16 Best variant 38.

an extra revenue of 77 consultation fees. Each consultation fee is worth $35 which leads to a profit of almost $80,850 monthly. The net profit will be $21,000 monthly. This is almost $252,000 per year, which is an acceptable yearly profit that a hospital can add based on the huge enhancement of performance measures like decreasing the patient LoS and thus guaranteeing patient satisfaction. This may lead to a good reputation of the hospital and thus attracting more patients in the future. This cost analysis shows the importance of this optimization simulation and that this optimal solution suggested (Variant 38) should be considered by decision-makers and implemented into the real running system.

Running the Model with the New Resource Distribution:

Running the model again after changing all the resource capacities as per Table 5.5, other parameters should also be highlighted as an efficient result from Simulation 38 since a noticeable change occurs on these performance measures if this suggested solution is applied. These performance measures' improvements are depicted in Table 5.6 along with a comparison with the original scenario values.

This comparison shows that the output values are very efficient and the new distribution of resources suggested being the optimal solution is highly reliable; where, number of system out and

Table 5.6 Comparison between Original Scenario and Variant 38

Performance Measures	Original Scenario	Variant 38
Patient A Admitted to Hosp Queue Waiting Time	38.3	2.79
Patient B Admitted to Hosp Queue Waiting Time	36.6	2.91
Transporter A Queue Waiting Time	536	0
Transporter B Queue Waiting Time	660	0.05
Transporter A Utilization	99%	36%
Transporter B Utilization	99%	37%
Patient A LoS	345.04	91.37
Patient B LoS	368.21	88.65
System Number Out	60	140

revenue are increased and patient LoS is minimized along with a noticeable improvement in the transporter waiting queue.

This is based on four measurement metrics:

■ Number of System Out
■ Patient LoS
■ Resource Utilization Rates
■ Hospital Revenue/Net profit

5.3.2 OptQuest during Catastrophic Events

The OptQuest tool of Arena is used again in order to find the best and optimal solution for the problems faced by the studied ED during catastrophic events, where the system number out is maximized regardless of any other factor and considered as the main objective. New allocation of resources is suggested and stated in Table 5.7. The best solution is found to be Simulation 129. Results of the OptQuest simulation are depicted in Figure 5.17 where 3 replications and 300 simulations are chosen as settings.

The optimization was stopped at Simulation 293 because of the auto stop option added in the settings. The objective value is found to be 6,639 patients exiting the system and depicted in Figure 5.18. This is the maximum number of victims/patients receiving care and leaving the ED after being served.

Table 5.7 Best Resource Allocation

Resource Type	Capacity (Best Solution 129)
Doctor A	9
Doctor B	10
Accountant	10
Facilities A	20
Facilities B	20
Nurse A	10
Nurse B	10
Receptionist	10
Physician	10
RN A	9
RN B	7
Technician	10
Transporter A	10
Transporter B	9

Simulation	Objective Value	Accountant	Doctor A	Doctor B	Facilities A	Facilities B	Nurse A	Nurse B	Physician
129	6639	10	9	10	20	20	10	10	10
214	6613.66	10	9	10	20	20	10	10	10
138	6609	10	9	9	20	20	10	10	10
274	6582.66	10	10	10	20	20	10	10	10
99	6580.33	10	9	9	20	20	10	10	10
46	6575.33	10	9	9	20	20	10	10	10
5	6574.33	10	10	10	20	20	10	10	10
52	6569.33	10	9	9	20	20	10	10	10
196	6632	10	9	10	20	20	10	10	8
254	6578.33	10	9	10	19	20	10	10	8
211	6575.33	10	9	10	20	20	10	10	8

Simulation	Objective Value	Receptionist	RN A	RN B	Technician	Transporter A	Transporter B
129	6639	10	9	7	10	10	9
214	6613.66	10	9	7	10	10	9
138	6609	10	10	8	10	10	10
274	6582.66	10	8	9	10	10	8
99	6580.33	10	9	7	10	10	9
46	6575.33	10	9	7	10	10	9
5	6574.33	10	8	7	9	10	9
52	6569.33	9	8	7	10	10	9
196	6632	10	9	6	10	10	9
254	6578.33	9	9	7	10	9	8
211	6575.33	10	9	7	10	10	8

Figure 5.17   Best solutions.

1. Running the Model with the Optimal Solution:

   The best allocation of resources is updated in the model (refer to Figure 5.19). The model was simulated again and new results are collected to be studied. The system number out is increased from 489 to 6,631 patients leaving the ED as per Figure 5.20. This is a huge enhancement to the system objective: maximize the system number out. Patient LoS is decreased from 4,779.66 to 1,173.19 and from 4,605.46 to 1,025.59 respectively for ER A and ER B. As per the queues detail summary presented in Figure 5.21, the waiting times in the queues are highly decreased for most of the stages except the transporter queue waiting time. This can be for the reason that transporters are the only one responsible for transferring the patient from one unit to another and therefore all patients coming from all other stages (such as data collections, triage, examination, etc.) should use the transporter in order to reach the extra facility units (radiology and billing) or any other unit of the hospital. The resource utilization rates presented in Figure 5.22 are not enhanced during this optimization simulation and this is normal because of the catastrophic situation of the ED, where resources should be highly utilized in order to serve this surge of patients. Moreover, resource utilization rates are not set as an objective during simulation.

Optimization		Completed Stopped due to the Auto Stop option.		
	Maximize			
		Objective Value	Status	Best Simulation 129
	Best Value	6639.000000	Feasible	Total simulations: 293
	Current Value			

Figure 5.18 Optimization: Best objective value.

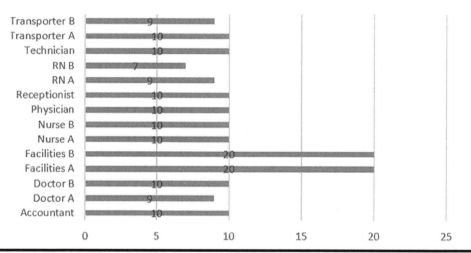

Number Scheduled

Figure 5.19 New resource allocation.

ED in Catastrophe

Time Units   Minutes

Key Performance Indicators

System   Average
Number Out   6,631

Figure 5.20 System number out.

2. Discussion:
   The comparison presented in Table 5.8 shows that the output values are very efficient and the new distribution of resources suggested, being the optimal solution, is highly reliable based on the three important measurement metrics.

Transporters (responsible for transferring patients to other units of the hospital) and nurses (responsible for data collection, preparing patients for examination/treatment, and monitoring patient throughout the care delivery process) will remain busy and with high utilization rates,

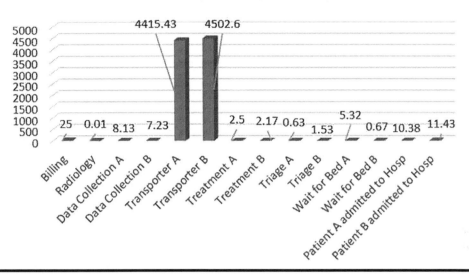

Figure 5.21 Queues detail summary.

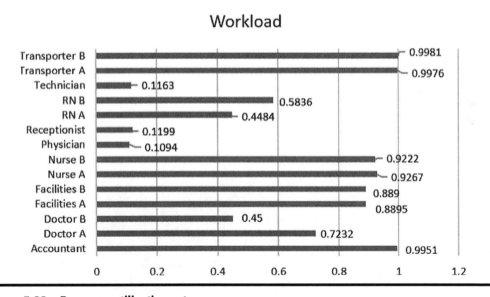

Figure 5.22 Resource utilization rates.

regardless of the slight improvement in their utilization rates, because of the surge of patients and the multitasks assigned to them as a job description.

Also, the billing queue waiting time is increased in the new Variant 129 for the reason that the number of transporters is increased from one to ten and nine for ER A and ER B respectively and thus more patients are arriving into the billing queue now where before only one patient was arriving at a time. For the doctors in both ER A and ER B, the utilization rates are decreased to 72% and 65% respectively, which gives space for the doctor to help in other tasks and have enough time for diagnosis or emergency small surgeries that can be performed inside the ED. As for RN A and

Table 5.8 Comparison between Original Scenario and Variant 129

Metrics	Original Scenario	Variant 129
Billing Queue Waiting Time	0	25.09
Radiology Queue Waiting Time	0	0.01
Data Collection A	2843.2	8.13
Data Collection B	3205.6	7.23
Patient A Admitted to Hosp Queue Waiting Time	43.67	10.38
Patient B Admitted to Hosp Queue Waiting Time	48.05	11.43
Transporter A Queue Waiting Time	4608.85	4415.43
Transporter B Queue Waiting Time	4648.73	4502.80
Treatment A Queue Waiting Time	2587.07	2.5
Treatment B Queue Waiting Time	2419.75	2.17
Triage A Queue Waiting Time	1945.4	0.63
Triage B Queue Waiting Time	1513.39	1.53
Wait for Doctor A Queue	2562.74	2.29
Wait for Doctor B Queue	2434.06	2.23
Technician Utilization	5%	11%
Facilities A Utilization	65%	89%
Facilities B Utilization	66%	89%
Receptionist Utilization	15%	11%
RN A Utilization	99.98%	44.8%
RN B Utilization	99.99%	58.3%
Nurse A Utilization	99.98%	92.6%
Nurse B Utilization	99.93%	92.2%
Doctor A Utilization	99.8%	72%
Doctor B Utilization	99.9%	65%
Transporter A Utilization	99.8%	99.7%
Transporter B Utilization	99.6%	99.8%
Physician Utilization	14%	10.9%
Patient A LoS	4,779.66	1,173.19
Patient B LoS	4,605.46	1,025.59
Number of System Out	489	6,631

RN B, the workload is also decreased to 45% and 58% respectively which is a low utilization rate compared to other type of resources. It is important to mention here that RNs can also be utilized to help doctors in case of emergency surgeries inside the ED, and to help nurses during preparation and treatment not only during triage stage. Moreover, RNs can substitute a doctor and make some decisions or diagnosis and give prescriptions in case of minor medical cases and low-priority cases, especially during disaster events. This cooperation among medical resources can improve the flow of patients in the ED and balance the workload of resources when needed, always maintaining the same level of care to patients. Here, patients do not care of who is attending them as long as they are receiving the required care and are exiting the ED alive.

The utilization rate of Facilities in both ERs will definitely be increased respectively with the increase in the nurse, doctor, and RN numbers since no treatment, triage, or diagnosis can be done without the resource type Facilities. The increase in the accountant utilization rate is due to the increased number of patients leaving the system and thus the need for accountants to prepare the insurance and bills and to receive payments. As for the queue waiting times, Table 5.8 shows a huge improvement in the majority of the queues due to the addition of medical resources suggested by Variant 129, especially the busiest stages: Transporter A and B queues, Treatment A and B queues, Data Collection A and B queues, Triage A and B queues, and Wait for Doctor A and B queues. The average waiting time of patients in each ER (LoS) is highly decreased, thus leaving room for other patients to be treated. This will definitely maximize the system number out, which is enhanced to 6,631 instead of 489 patients. Here, patient satisfaction, along with management satisfaction (more revenue) is noticeably increased. All waiting times in queues and LoS are expressed in minutes.

Patient satisfaction is related to the revenue produced by this optimal scenario and the factors used to calculate this revenue are as follows:

System number out is increased by 6,142 patients where each consultation is worth $35. Thus, a profit of $214,970/week and a $859,880/month. Data in Table 5.9 is used in order to calculate the cost of the additional resources suggested by the optimal Variant 129: 7 technicians, 2 accountants, 17 transporters, 17 doctors, 30 facilities, 16 nurses, 9 physicians, 9 receptionists, 14 RNs are added to the current number of resources. By calculating the salaries of these additional resources, the cost will be equal to $120,950. The net profit = revenue = $738,930. This revenue will definitely attract decision-makers in the hospital in order to adopt this scenario as a solution to the overcrowding that may be caused by a disaster event, especially that a huge number of victims may be attended to but the same level of care may be maintained. Moreover, the remainder of unattended patients can be transferred to other hospitals and ambulance diversion may be applied here and can be studied in future work. The monthly salary of Facilities A and B can include the price of material needed along with the repair, maintenance, and replacement of equipment and medical devices when needed.

5.4 New Resource Allocation Algorithm

Optimization is necessary during the process of enhancing and maintaining an industrial system without the need to interrupt its real operation. In this section, a new generic reward system is defined in order to study the three satisfaction factors of any industrial concurrent system: customer, owner, and employee satisfaction factors during normal flow and catastrophic conditions. A new reward-based optimization algorithm is then proposed in order to allocate new resources as part of enhancement and studying again the system behavior. This algorithm is called Maximum

Table 5.9   Resources' Capacities and Monthly Payment

Resource Type	ED Original Capacity	Suggested Capacity	Monthly Salary ($)
Accountant	8	10	1000
Doctor A	1	9	2000
Doctor B	1	10	2000
Facilities A	5	20	800
Facilities B	5	20	800
Nurse A	2	10	850
Nurse B	2	10	850
Physician	1	10	1200
Receptionist	1	10	500
RN A	1	9	1100
RN B	1	7	1100
Technician	3	10	800
Transporter A	1	10	650
Transporter B	1	9	650

Reward Algorithm (MRA). The reward system and MRA are generic and can be applied to any industrial system with queueing theory such as healthcare.

5.4.1 Model Definition

"In any business industry, customer satisfaction reflects the quality of service delivered. A satisfied customer tends to prefer that company and therefore returns for additional services [Wilson et al. (2012)]. In complex systems, such as healthcare, patients express their praise and preference for medical services when well treated and when the service delivered by medical resources meets their expectations. This patient satisfaction level increases the service use and market share which implicitly increase owner's satisfaction [Saad Andaleeb (1998)]. Another satisfaction factor that may lead to a successful process is employee satisfaction. Delivering a service well, in a short time, is related to the level of satisfaction of the employee involved in the delivery stage and is affected by two dimensions: the pay and the utilization rate. A well-paid employee with an acceptable workload tends to deliver a better-quality service and therefore indirectly affects the customer's satisfaction level [Naidu (2009)]. Here, we address the problem of satisfaction and how a new proposed reward-based optimization algorithm can enhance any industrial system with queueing theory. Optimization stands for the fact of improving the operation flow of the system without the need to interrupt its actual process. The enhancement of complex industrial systems must be considered for the increase of satisfaction levels of three factors: customers, owners, and employees.

Industrial systems are usually composed of business processes that always compete for resources [Zeng et al. (2012)]. The complexity and dynamic behavior of these business processes, along with the unpredictability nature, require workflow systems to control the flow of work and guarantee an effective allocation of these resources. Healthcare, being complex systems, and emergency departments (ED), in particular, being a non-stop medical service where patients arrive without any prior notice, implies the need for simulation modeling in order to study the system and predict malfunctions. EDs are currently facing several problems that affect their daily medical service and operation. The main common issue is overcrowding, resulting in large waiting times, long length of stay (LoS), and therefore leading to patient dissatisfaction [Buckley et al. (2010)]. A possible solution to this problem can be by increasing the ED capacity and providing extra resources. Nevertheless, this is not always an achievable solution because of the huge extra costs and budget constraints [Soremekun et al. (2011)]. Nowadays, addressing the problems of ED relies upon improving the processes of the ED, always taking into consideration the extra costs, patient safety/satisfaction, and the LoS [Holden (2011)]. Therefore, the new reward system is defined in this work in order to highlight the three satisfaction factors: patient satisfaction, owner satisfaction, and resource satisfaction. Mathematical equations are presented in order to calculate the level of satisfaction and therefore propose through simulation new resource allocation levels in order to increase these levels" [Oueida et al. (2018a)].

Previous studies include normal flow and only a few have covered disaster conditions. ED simulations during catastrophic events are very limited. Xiao et al., in 2012a, presented a workflow optimization during a disaster event [Xiao et al. (2012b)]. Another study was presented during a terrorism case where different arrivals into the ED were analyzed using DES modeling [Joshi (2008b)]. Patvivatsiri studied the patient flow and resource utilization rates during a bioterrorist attack; an appropriate resource allocation was determined accordingly [Patvivatsiri (2006)]. Another study focused on examining the advantages and efficiency of suggesting different scenarios during the triage stage and evaluating their effects on saving lives during an earthquake disaster case [Cao and Huang (2012)]. The study of the ED operations during catastrophic conditions was also modeled using different other scenarios [Al-Kattan (2009b)].

"As per the literature, simulation modeling is proven to be more efficient in addressing complex problems [Kuo et al. (2012)]. ED simulation models have been addressed by many researchers in the past decades. One simulation differs from the other in terms of the characteristics and layout of the ED, such as number of units, number of resources, patient flow, and the real input data collected from that particular ED. An ED's performance is measured by looking at the major Key Performance Indicator (KPI) in literature, the length of stay (LoS)" [Oueida et al. (2018a)]. Recall that the LoS refers to the total period of time a patient spends in the ED [Samaha et al. (2003)]. Different ways of improving patient flow in this model are addressed using experimentation [Centeno et al. (2003); Duguay and Chetouane (2007)].

The new generic reward system to improve the system is now defined. A new optimization algorithm is also proposed for normal flow of operations and during catastrophic events. The reward system depends on generic weights. Those weights can be set by the decision-makers of the medical institution. According to the values they set, the mathematical model will behave and give recommendations for the optimal number of resources. Table 5.10 is dedicated to explaining the most-used notations in this section.

"The reward system is defined by:

$$\Re = \sum_{i=1}^{3} W_i F_i \qquad (5.2)$$

The weight of importance reflects which satisfaction factor is mostly affecting the reward system defined. The factor that has highest weight should be considered first while applying enhancement

Table 5.10 Notations Used in the Reward System

Notation	Description
R	Reward System
F_i	$F_1 + F_2 + F_3$
F_1	Customer satisfaction factor
F_2	Owner satisfaction factor
F_3	Employee satisfaction factor
W_i	$W_1 + W_2 + W_3$
$\sum_{i=1}^{3} W_i$	is equal to 1
W_1	Customer weight of importance
W_2	Owner weight of importance
W_3	Employee weight of importance
x	Average customer LoS in the system

Source: Oueida et al. (2018a).

Note: Table adapted from *Multimedia Tools and Applications*, p. 1.

using this reward system. Improvement of satisfaction factors can be achieved by proposing new resource allocation and addition of new resources. Customers arriving into the system and requesting a service need employees to assist them. Thus, in order to increase the revenue and guarantee owner satisfaction, the system number out should be increased. Customer satisfaction is a factor of waiting time and level of care received. Employee satisfaction is a factor of utilization rates and workload. Weights values are based on the observations and site visits. Exact values are calculated based on management decisions and hospital preferences" [Oueida et al. (2018a)].

5.4.2 RPN during Normal Flow

This subsection is dedicated to presenting the model definition for the proposed reward system during normal flow, where three satisfaction factors are studied: customer, owner, and employee satisfaction.

1. <u>Customer Satisfaction:</u>

   "The customer satisfaction, F_1, is a factor of the average waiting time the customer spends in the system along with the level of care received by employees. Customer satisfaction is represented by:

   $$F_1 = \eta_1 e^{-x} + \eta_2 F_3 \tag{5.3}$$

   Where,

   (a) $x = \dfrac{\left(\text{actual LoS} - \text{expected LoS}\right)}{\text{expected LoS}}$

   (b) η_2 is the customer–employee medical relationship

   (c) $\eta_1 + \eta_2 = 1$

(d) $\eta_2 = 1 - \eta_1$
(e) η_2 is affected by the culture and utilization rate of the employee. Some employees are negatively affected by their high workload and therefore badly affect the level of care they deliver to customers
(f) Actual LoS is the current customer's LoS
(g) Expected LoS is the maximum length of stay a customer spends in a normal system flow

2. Owner Satisfaction:

The owner satisfaction, F_2, is a factor of the profit and the revenue. Therefore, in order to experience an increase in the owner satisfaction, the net profit must be increased. F_2 is represented by:

$$F_2 = \frac{\text{profit}}{\text{revenue}} \tag{5.4}$$

Where,
(a) Revenue is system gain regardless of the cost paid
(b) Revenue = k * Payment
(c) Payment is the money customers spend in the system
(d) k = number of customers arriving to the system
(e) Profit is the net profit after paying all the expenses for human resources, equipment, material, etc.
(f) Profit = Revenue – Total Expenses
(g) Total Expenses represents salaries, material, equipment maintenance/replacement, etc.

The values needed in order to calculate customer satisfaction are retrieved from meetings with management. This new proposed reward system can be considered by decision-makers only if the net profit is attractive. Simulation outputs can be relied on for proposing enhancement to the real operating system during normal flow" [Oueida et al. (2018a)].

3. Employee Satisfaction:

"Employee satisfaction is a factor of the pay and workload. The employee monthly wage should be increased and the daily workload should be decreased in order to guarantee a high customer satisfaction level. Employee satisfaction, F_3, is represented by:

$$F_3 = \sum_{n=1}^{m} \frac{f_n}{m} = \frac{f_1 + f_2 + \cdots + f_n}{m} \tag{5.5}$$

Where, m is the number of different employee categories such as: receptionist, actual workers, transporters, etc. The satisfaction of each category is defined by f_n where f_n is defined by:

$$f_n = \frac{\sum_{i=1}^{k} X_i \Delta_n}{k}$$

Where,
1. Δ_n is a certain category of employees
2. k is the number of employees in a same category
3. X is the balance between pay and workload for an employee belonging to the same category Δ,
4. $X_i = (W_1 * \text{pay}) - (W_2 * \text{workload})$

5. $W_1 + W_2 = 1$

6. $\text{pay} = \dfrac{\text{actual pay}}{\text{maximum pay}}$

7. $\text{workload} = \dfrac{\text{actual workload}}{\text{maximum workload}}$

Since each category type can have several employees then,

$$f_1 = \frac{(X_1(\Delta_1) + X_2(\Delta_1) + \cdots + X_k(\Delta_1))}{k}$$

$$f_2 = \frac{(X_1(\Delta_2) + X_2(\Delta_2) + \cdots + X_k(\Delta_2))}{k}$$

$$\vdots$$

$$f_n = \frac{(X_1(\Delta_n) + X_2(\Delta_n) + \cdots + X_k(\Delta_n))}{k} \text{ "[Oueida et al. (2018a)]."}$$

5.4.3 *Application to Healthcare*

"As discussed previously, healthcare, is a very complex system suffering from a high number of bottlenecks and overcrowding, especially the emergency department. Therefore, ED flow must be studied carefully in order to suggest ways to improve the system without any interruption. Previous studies mentioned that a very effective and efficient way to enhance the ED operations is the reallocation of resources and the addition of new resources. Therefore, three main factors are studied by applying the reward system, R, suggested in the previous subsection: patient, owner, and human resource satisfaction. The studied ED consists of several types of human resources serving arriving patients. As for the non-human resources referred to as Facilities, they are indirectly considered during the optimization stage since the addition of a human resource in order to accomplish a certain task implicitly includes the need of material, medical equipment, etc.

The resource type Facilities is referred to as everything needed to deliver care to an arriving patient such as: beds with all their accessories, medication, medical devices, cotton, syringe, etc. Recall that human resources fall under eight different categories: Doctor, RN, Nurse, Transporter, Receptionist, Technician, Accountant, and Physician. Each category type includes a different number of resources allocated and are depicted in Table 5.11. Applying the reward system equations defined previously to the studied ED leads to the satisfaction level values presented in Table 5.12. The reward system for the studied ED is defined by: $\mathfrak{R}_{ED} = \sum_{i=1}^{3}(W_i F_i)$. From interviews with management and observations from site visits, the weight W_i of each F_i is found to be: $W_1 = 0.6$, $W_2 = 0.3$, $W_3 = 0.1$; where the highest weight refers to the patient satisfaction factor which is the priority concern of decision-makers. Then, profit should be considered by decreasing the cost as much as possible and eliminating waste. Finally, staff utilization rates should be decreased to ensure staff satisfaction. The weight may vary from one hospital to another based on culture, hospital needs, budget constraints, etc. This leads to: $R_{ED} = (0.6 * F_1) + (0.3 * F_2) + (0.1 * F_3)$.

1. Owner Satisfaction:

   In order to calculate owner satisfaction, total expenses and revenue should be calculated first. The consultation fee per patient is \$35. The number of system out, found through

Table 5.11   Actual Pay and Expected Pay

Resource Type	Actual Pay($)	Maximum Pay($)
Doctor RN	2000	2500
Nurse	1100	1500
Transporter	850	1000
	650	700
Accountant	1000	1100
Receptionist Physician Technician	500	550
	1200	1800
	800	850
Facilities	800	Not considered in the satisfaction measure since it is a non-human resource

Source: Oueida et al. (2018a).

Note: Table adapted from *Multimedia Tools and Applications,* p. 1.

simulation with Arena, is 60 patients. Recall that the simulation of the ED model was run for 24 hours. Then, Revenue = $6,300 per month on average. The Total Expenses include all nine resource costs: human and non-human. Using the values of Table 5.11 leads to the result of $31,000 per month. The non-human expenses, called Facility Expenses, include the cost of material needed while delivering a service, maintenance, or replacement of medical devices, beds, etc. The non-human resource is from a single category called Facilities. Facility Expenses = η * Expenses = 0.6 * Expenses = $18,600. The value of η varies from one hospital to another. The more medical resources are appointed for a service, the more facilities are needed to accomplish a certain task; thus, the correlation between the Expenses (resulting from human resources) and the Facility Expenses (resulting from the resource type Facilities). Then, Total Expenses = $49,600. Now the owner satisfaction can be calculated and found to be: $F_2 = 20\%$. This is a very low percentage for owner satisfaction and improvement must be considered in order to enhance the system throughput and thus increase F_2 accordingly.

2. Resource Satisfaction:

Since human resources are classified under eight different categories, the satisfaction factor needs to be calculated for each type of resource separately in order to figure out the resource satisfaction,$_3$. Note here that the ninth resource, Facilities, is a non-human resource and thus will not be taken into consideration for the satisfaction measure. The maximum utilization rate of a resource in the ED should not exceed 80% for a normal flow of system, which reflects the value of maximum workload. Actual load are values resulting from the simulation with Arena. The actual pay and maximum expected pay for each resource are presented in Table 5.11. The maximum pay is the average maximum wage each resource can expect. It is deduced from investigations and observations at the hospital. Thus, the calculation of the satisfaction factor for each type of resource is depicted in Table 5.12.

Having calculated the satisfaction factors of all resources in the system, the total resource satisfaction can be deduced: $F_3 = 48.19\%$.

Table 5.12 Resource Satisfaction Factors during Normal Flow

Resource Type	Satisfaction Factor(%)
Doctor	$f_1 = 43.6\%$
Registered (RN) Nurse	$f_2 = 44.17\%$
Nurse	$f_3 = 48.62\%$
Transporter	$f_4 = 27.874\%$
Accountant	$f_5 = 57.38\%$
Receptionist	$f_6 = 58.01\%$
Physician	$f_7 = 41.85\%$
Technician	$f_8 = 64\%$

Source: Oueida et al. (2018a).

Note: Table adapted from *Multimedia Tools and Applications Journal*, p. 10.

3. Patient Satisfaction:

Here, patient satisfaction, F_1, of the current ED is calculated before applying optimization in order to measure the corresponding satisfaction level. After several observations and interviews with medical resources in the ED, η_2 is found to be equal to 0.3 and thus η_1 is equal to 0.7. From Arena simulation results, the average length of patient stay in the system is found to be equal to 357 minutes. This value reflects the actual LoS. The expected value for a normal stay in the ED is, as per the literature, 270 minutes (around 4.5 hours). Having these values, F_1 is calculated and found to be: $F_1 = 65.17\%$.

As a conclusion, using the calculated satisfaction factors from the previous subsections, the reward system for normal flow of patients in the ED is equal to: $R_{ED} = 50.1\%$. This reward measure doesn't look very satisfying as per the hospital owner opinion and it falls under the threshold of satisfaction, which should reach 70% for a satisfied reward system and above 70% for a highly satisfied reward system. In order to increase the reward system of this studied ED, R_{ED}, optimization is required where a study of all the three factors that affect this system is necessary. The owner satisfaction factor, F_2, is found to be 20% which is a very low measure and needs to be highly considered always taking into consideration the balance between the three satisfaction factors, F_1, F_2 and F_3" [Oueida et al. (2018a)].

5.4.4 Optimization Algorithm: MRA for Normal Flow

"The Maximum Reward Algorithm (MRA) is a new reward-based optimization algorithm suggested in this work in order to enhance any industrial system. This algorithm is generic for any type of system with queuing behavior. MRA is applied to the studied ED in order to enhance the flow of operation and maximize the reward system, R, during normal flow. The MRA flowchart is represented in Figure 5.23 where all steps to be followed in order to reach the final result and the near-optimal solution are presented. Some variables used for the algorithm are:

1. The first type of resource to start the algorithm with is the one causing the bottleneck in the ED.
2. The next type of resource is the one with the least wage.

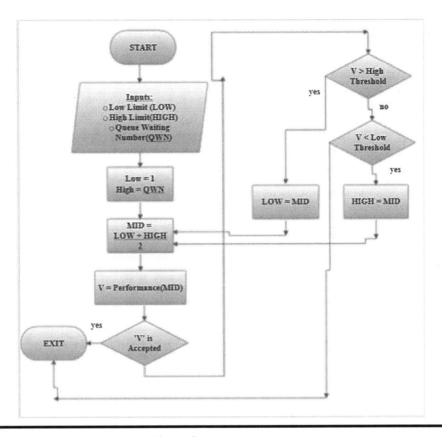

Figure 5.23   MRA flowchart [Oueida et al. (2018a)].

3. The threshold is the accepted value.
4. The algorithm is stopped when no more changes are occurring to the system.
5. The performance is the simulation results using the MID (Medium) value of a resource; it includes the performance of resource utilization rates, patients LoS, and Queue waiting numbers.
6. The threshold value is a range between two numbers. The optimal value should be lower than the high threshold and greater than the low threshold.
7. The threshold for patients LoS: LoS should be less than 2 hours and not exceed 4 hours.
8. The threshold for resource utilization: resource utilization rates should not be less than 20% in order to avoid wastes and not exceed 80%.
9. The threshold for queues waiting number (QWN): the waiting number in queues should not exceed 20 and cannot be 0 in order to avoid waste.
10. The threshold values, low and high, for each metric are represented in Table 5.13 and are based on ED observations and hospital's management decisions" [Oueida et al. (2018a)].

"From the simulation results during normal flow of operation, the ED system suffers from a bottleneck in the transportation queue (refer to Figure 5.24). Therefore, the proposed optimization algorithm, MRA, will start with the first type of resource: the transporter.

Looking at the simulation results, the number of patients waiting at the transporter queue is found to be on average 23 patients (refer to Figure 5.25). To start with the algorithm, the low and

Table 5.13   Threshold Details

Metrics	Low Threshold Value	High Threshold Value
Patient LoS	2 Hours	4 Hours
Resource Utilization Rate	20%	80%
Queue Waiting Number	0%	20%

Source: Oueida et al. (2018a).

Note: Table adapted from *Multimedia Tools and Applications Journal*, p. 12.

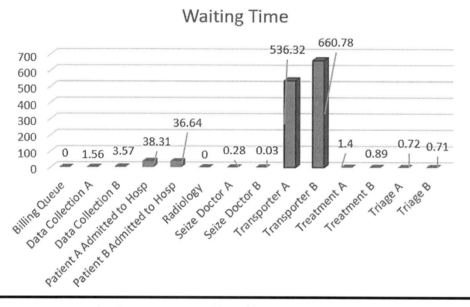

Figure 5.24   Queues details summary [Oueida et al. (2018a)].

high values for the resource should be identified. The low values are always 1. The high values are related to the performance. In case of bottleneck in more than one stage and available dependency among these stages, the values are calculated and the model is simulated using the new values of dependent bottleneck resources in parallel as one phase of the algorithm. For example, facilities depend on availability of doctors, nurses, and RNs; if both nurse and doctor stages are extremely busy then the algorithm is started by considering together: facilities, nurse, and doctor resources as a first phase" [Oueida et al. (2018a)].

"Three cases are studied for the transporter resource as per the following:

1. The HIGH value of transporter is equal to the number of patients waiting in the transporter queue which is 23. Thus, the value to be used in the next simulation is: MID = (LOW + HIGH) ÷ 2 = 12. The model is run again after changing the number of transporters to 12. The results show that the waiting time is decreased from, on average, 598.55 min to 0 min as per Figure 5.26 and almost no patients waiting in all queues as per Figure 5.27). Also, the LoS is decreased from 6 hours to almost 1.74 hours (refer to Figure 5.28). As for the resource utilization rates depicted in Figure 5.29, the workload of all the resources is very low where

Number Waiting

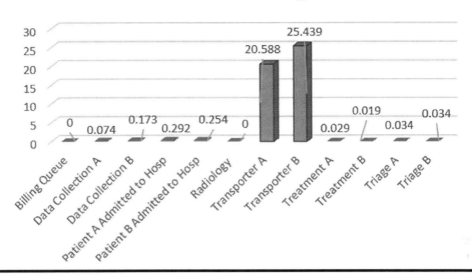

Figure 5.25 Queues waiting times [Oueida et al. (2018a)].

Waiting Time

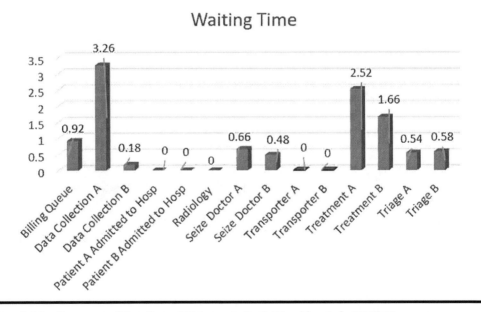

Figure 5.26 Queues waiting times (12 transporters) [Oueida et al. (2018a)].

the threshold of a resource utilization rate should be on average between the range of 20% to 80%. This means, in order to reduce this waste, the number of transporters should be decreased. Performance here is dependent on the QWN and utilization rates.

2. The new HIGH value = MID = 12, since the performance, V, is below the threshold. Thus, MID = (1 + 12) ÷ 2 = 6.5. The model will be run again with the number of transporters changed to 7.

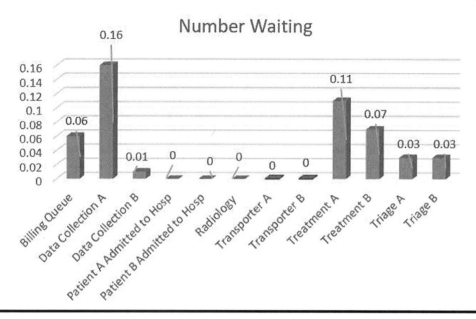

Figure 5.27 Queues number waiting (12 transporters [Oueida et al. (2018a)].

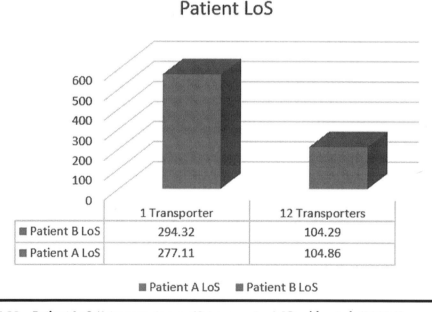

Figure 5.28 Patient LoS (1 transporter vs. 12 transporters) [Oueida et al. (2018a)].

The results of this simulation show a system LoS of 118.6 min in average which is equal to 2 hours as per Figure 5.30. As per the interviews with the hospital management, for a reliable optimization algorithm, the ED system LoS should be less than 2 hours. Therefore, a new value for the transporter resource should be calculated. Performance here is dependent on the LoS.

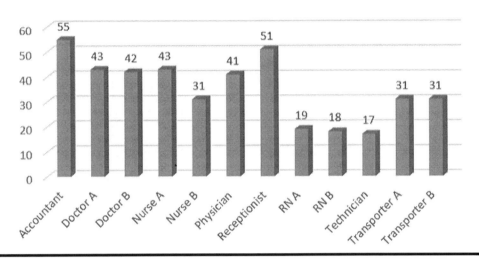

Figure 5.29   Resource details (12 transporters).

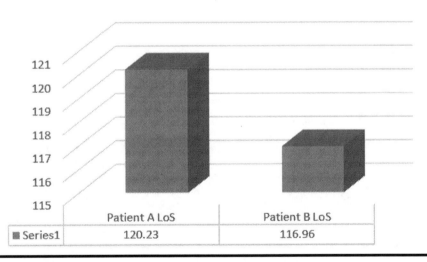

Figure 5.30   Patient LoS (7 transporters).

3. The new LOW value = MID = 7, since the performance, V, is greater than the threshold. Calculating the new value results in 9 transporters. Running the model again with the new value of transporters shows that the LoS is almost 1.7 hours as per Figure 5.31 which is below the lowest threshold and accepted by the hospital management. Looking also at all the resources utilization rates, all the workloads are accepted and below the hospital's high threshold and above low threshold as per Figure 5.32, always maintaining a low waiting time in the queues as per Figure 5.33. Note that the system number out is 134 for 137

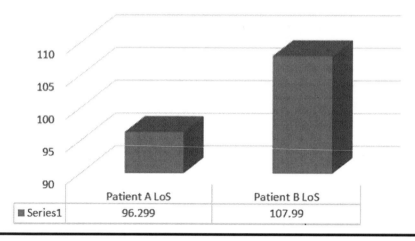

Figure 5.31 Patients LoS (9 transporters).

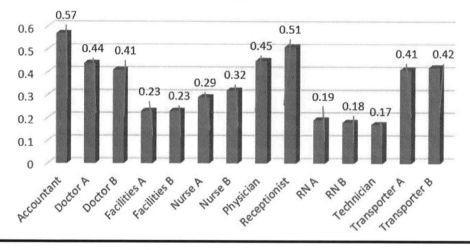

Figure 5.32 Resource details (9 transporters).

arriving patients as per Figure 5.34. Therefore, the performance, V, is accepted and MRA algorithm can be stopped here with a change in the transporter resource only from 1 to 9 transporters in each ER which is an addition of 16 transporters in total for the ED system. Recall that the ED consists of two emergency rooms: ER A and ER B.

As a conclusion, the optimal number of transporters in order to maintain a balance between the number of patients waiting in the bottleneck queue, the waiting time in the queues, resource

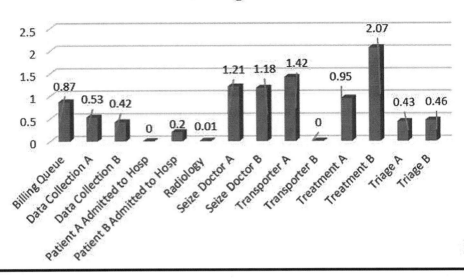

Figure 5.33   Queue waiting times (9 transporters) [Oueida et al. (2018a)].

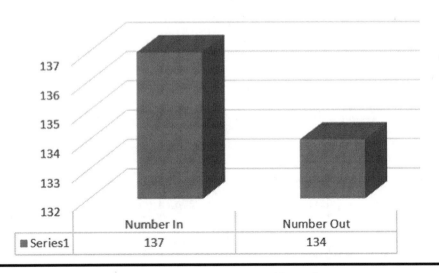

Figure 5.34   Number of system out (9 transporters) [Oueida et al. (2018a)].

utilization rates, and system LoS, always taking into consideration owner satisfaction resulting from a high number of patients exiting the ED, is equal to 9. Therefore, the system is totally optimized without the need to optimize other types of resources. The new allocation of resources is depicted in Table 5.14 for which the reward system will be calculated again after performing the optimization" [Oueida et al. (2018a)].

Table 5.14   MRA Resource Allocation

Resource Type	MRA Resource Allocation
Doctor	2
RN	2
Nurse	4
Transporter	18
Accountant	8
Receptionist	1
Physician	1
Technician	3
Facilities	10

Source: Oueida et al. (2018a).

Note: Table adapted from *Multimedia Tools and Applications Journal*, p. 17.

Table 5.15   Resource Satisfaction Factors after Optimization

Resource Type	Satisfaction Factor (%)
Doctor	$f_{1o} = 40.25$
RN	$f_{2o} = 44.37$
Nurse	$f_{3o} = 48.06$
Transporter	$f_{4o} = 49.33$
Accountant	$f_{5o} = 42.25$
Receptionist	$f_{6o} = 44.5$
Physician	$f_{7o} = 29.78$
Technician	$f_{8o} = 59.5$

Source: Oueida et al. (2018a).

Note: Table adapted from *Multimedia Tools and Applications Journal*, p. 18.

"Now that the number of resources is optimized, a new reward system, R_o, is calculated using the equations of previous sections:

1. The resource satisfaction is calculated after simulating the model with the new resource allocation (after the MRA algorithm is applied). Using the simulation results, the value of each resource satisfaction factor f_{io}, is depicted in Table 5.15.

   Having calculated the satisfaction factors of all resources in the system, the total resource satisfaction can be deduced to be: $F_{3o} = 44.75\%$.

2. In order to calculate patient satisfaction after applying the optimization algorithm, MRA, Arena simulation results are used. The average length of stay patients spend in the system is

found to be equal to 1.7 hours (102 min) (refer to Figure 5.31). This value reflects the actual LoS.

Expected LoS for an optimized system should not exceed 2 hours (120 min) as per the hospital's management. This leads to: $F_{1o} = 94.75\%$. This means that the patient satisfaction factor is very high and is a result of the system LoS that is decreased after applying the MRA. The patient satisfaction is increased from 65.17% to 94.75%.

3. In order to calculate owner satisfaction, F_{2o}, after applying the optimization algorithm, MRA, the new total expenses and revenue should be calculated. Arena simulation results show a system number out of 134 patients after optimization. Therefore, the new revenue is found to be equal to \$140,700 per month on average. Thus, $F_{2o} = 53\%$" [Oueida et al. (2018a)].

"As a conclusion, the owner satisfaction is increased from 20% before optimization to 53% after applying the MRA. This is normal since the bottleneck in the transporter queue is solved and thus more patients are exiting the system now and thus increasing the revenue.

Having all three satisfaction factors calculated, F_{1o}, F_{2o} and F_{3o}, the reward system for normal flow after optimization is: $R = 77.2\%$. This reward measure should look very satisfying for the hospital management since the threshold of satisfaction should reach a 70% for a satisfied reward system and above 70% for a high satisfied reward system. This increase in the value of R, from 50.1% to 77.2%, proves that the suggested reward system and the optimization algorithm, MRA, are reliable and efficient especially after applying them to a real-life problem: the emergency department of a healthcare system.

Table 5.16 summarizes all satisfaction factors and reward systems calculated in previous sections before and after MRA for normal flow along with the satisfactory level. From this table it is obvious that almost all satisfaction values are increased and therefore reward systems are increased except for F_3. It is due to the dependencies among resources. It is important to mention here that the resource satisfaction, F_3, is the lesser factor affecting the reward system, R. Therefore, slight changes can be neglected. It is also due to some limitations from the hospital management, where they granted additional resources for the bottleneck stages only. Therefore, accountants, receptionists, physicians, and technicians were not optimized and therefore future improvements can be done by applying the MRA to these resources as well. Nevertheless, the reward system was increased from 50.1% to 77.2%, thus proving the reliability and efficiency of the MRA and reward system proposed, R.

Through management perspectives, the satisfactory levels are measured as per the following:

- 0–20: Extremely Unsatisfied
- 21–40: Unsatisfied
- 41–80: Satisfied

Table 5.16 Satisfaction Factors and Reward System

Factors	Before MRA (%)	After MRA (%)	Satisfactory Level
F_1	65.17	94.75	Extremely Satisfied
F_2	20	53	Satisfied
F_3	48.19	44.755	Satisfied
R	50.1	77.2	Satisfied

Source: Oueida et al. (2018a).

Note: Table adapted from *Multimedia Tools and Applications Journal*, p. 18.

■ 81–95: Extremely Satisfied
■ 96–100: Optimal" [Oueida et al. (2018a)].

5.4.5 RPN during Catastrophic Conditions

This subsection is dedicated to presenting the model definition for the proposed reward system during catastrophic conditions, where the same three satisfaction factors are studied: customer, owner, and employee satisfaction. Catastrophic events are disaster conditions such as earthquake, an epidemic season, a terrorist attack, etc. As per Table 5.17, each resource category type includes different number of resources allocated. "From interviews with management, the weight W_{ic} of each F_{ic} during catastrophic events is found to be: $W_{1c} = 0.85$, $W_{2c} = 0.12$, $W_{3c} = 0.03$. This means that the main priority in catastrophic cases is to save as many lives as possible and make sure patients leave the system in order to leave room for other victims. Thus, the weight of patient satisfaction factor, W_{1c}, is 85%. Still owner satisfaction should be taken into consideration otherwise decision-makers will not be interested in enhancing their systems in order to cope with such disaster events. Thus, the weight of owner satisfaction factor, W_{2c}, is 12%. Which leads to a 3% for the weight of resource satisfaction, W_{3c}. Utilization rate of medical resources is definitely very high during such conditions due to the high patient surge, and decreasing their workload is not a priority here.

1. Patient Satisfaction:

    F_{1c} is a factor of system number out. Therefore, the system number out must be maximized in order to guarantee that the maximum number of patients are staying alive and exiting the system. The proposed equation for F_{1c} is:

$$F_{1c} = \frac{\text{rate of departure}}{\text{rate of arrival}}$$

Table 5.17 Maximum Resource Capacity

Resource Type	Maximum Capacity per ER
Doctor	10
RN	10
Nurse	10
Transporter	10
Accountant	8
Receptionist	1
Physician	1
Technician	3
Facilities	20

Source: Oueida et al. (2019a).

Note: Table adapted from *FAIMA Business and Management Journal*, p. 68.

where,

(a) $\text{rate of departure} = \dfrac{\text{number of patients leaving}}{\text{interval of time}}$

(b) $\text{rate of arrival} = \dfrac{\text{number of arriving patients}}{\text{interval of time}}$

(c) number of patients leaving = system number out

(d) number of arriving patients = system number in

Using the outputs resulted from Arena simulation of this studied ED during catastrophic events (refer to Table 5.18), patient satisfaction factor is found to be: $F_{1c} = 2.43\%$. This is a disaster measure for patient satisfaction and needs high consideration during optimization. Actually, the high surge of patients during catastrophic events explain this low satisfaction factor.

2. Owner Satisfaction:

In order to calculate the owner satisfaction factor, total expenses and revenue should be calculated:

(a) Total Expenses = Salary Expenses + Facilities Expenses

(b) Revenue = consultation fee * number of system out

(c) The value of η varies from a hospital to another. The number of Facilities proportionally increases with the number of medical resources; thus, the correlation between Expenses (resulting from human resources) and Facility Expenses (resulting from the resource type Facilities). After several observations and interviews with medical resources in the ED, $\eta_2 = 0.3$ and thus $\eta_1 = 0.7$.

(d) Consultation fees = \$35. As per Arena simulation, system number out before optimization is found to be 489 patients (refer to Table 5.18). Therefore, $F_{2c} = 32.37\%$. This is also a low satisfaction measure and need to be considered during future optimization.

3. Resource Satisfaction:

Actual load are values resulting from the simulation with Arena and are used to calculate the resource satisfaction factors of the eight different resources in the system during catastrophic conditions. The maximum workload is considered 80% as per interviews with the hospital's resources and management observations. The eight satisfaction factors are depicted in Table 5.19 using the equations defined previously.

After calculating the eight measures of the resource satisfaction factor, F_3, it is obvious that during catastrophic events, doctors, RNs, nurses, and transporters are the highest affected resources (very low satisfaction measures) and thus need to be enhanced accordingly for a better performance of the system. It is normal that physicians, technicians (responsible for the extra facilities, such as

Table 5.18   Arena Simulation Outputs before Optimization

Metric	Results
System Number In	20,097
System Number Out	489

Source: Oueida et al. (2019a).

Note: Table adapted from *FAIMA Business and Management Journal*, p. 68.

Table 5.19 Resource Satisfaction Factors during Catastrophic Conditions

Resource Type	Satisfaction Factor(%)
Doctor	$f_{1c} = 18.54$
RN	$f_{2c} = 13.81$
Nurse	$f_{3c} = 22.0$
Transporter	$f_{4c} = 27.56$
Accountant	$f_{5c} = 57.41$
Receptionist	$f_{6c} = 57.94$
Physician	$f_{7c} = 41.25$
Technician	$f_{8c} = 63.97$

Source: Oueida et al. (2019a).

Note: Table adapted from *FAIMA Business and Management Journal*, p. 69.

imaging), and receptionists and accountants (responsible for billing) are not highly affected, since patients are not reaching those stages and are stuck in previous stages such as triage, diagnosis, treatment, etc. Therefore, $F_{3c} = 37.81\%$. Also, F_{3c} is a low satisfaction measure and should be taken into consideration for future improvement. keeping in mind that the lowest satisfaction factor was F_{1c} and needs to be highly prioritized.

Using these calculated satisfaction factors, the reward system for a catastrophic case is equal to: $R_o = 7.08\%$. This result means that the reward system is highly unsatisfactory and needs urgent improvement. This is due to the surge of patients arriving into the ED during catastrophic events. The current ED system is extremely unprepared for such events. Therefore, a new optimization algorithm is suggested" [Oueida et al. (2019a)].

5.4.6 Optimization Algorithm MRA: Catastrophic Conditions

"The emergency department operations will definitely change in a dramatic way during disaster conditions; thus, new policies should be suggested, different from the normal flow periods. The optimization algorithm MRA defined in Section 5.4.4 is slightly updated during catastrophic events. When talking about disaster events, bottlenecks may occur at several stages of the system where high numbers of patients will be waiting in corresponding queues. Therefore, the high value here should be considered the maximum number of resources that can be added to the system as per management constraints. The performance, V, includes only the system number out since in a catastrophic case the most important part of a daily operation of the ED is to save as many lives as possible. If the performance of these bottlenecks and dependencies is not accepted then a further interview with management is needed to convince them to increase the high values. The updated optimization algorithm is presented in Figure 5.35" [Oueida et al. (2019a)].

"To start with the algorithm, three steps should be followed:

■ Define bottlenecks
■ Define dependencies
■ Conduct interviews with hospital management to realize the high values for resources

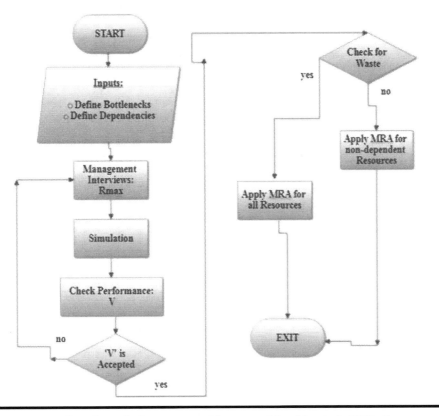

Figure 5.35 MRA flowchart during catastrophic events [Oueida et al. (2019a)].

Once the bottleneck stages are defined, dependencies among the corresponding resources are studied. The first simulation of the model starts with the highest values of these resources. As per Arena simulation, the bottlenecks occur in the transporter, nurse, RN, and doctor queues, where high number of patients are waiting to receive care. Note that nurses are responsible for data collection, RN responsible for triage, and doctors for treatment. Moreover, the resource type Facilities are a dependent resource among the four bottlenecks. Therefore, the model will be simulated after changing the number of doctors, nurses, RNs, and transporters to 20 and the number of Facilities to 20. Simulation results show that the system number out is equal to 6,222 which is an acceptable performance of the system. Also, the value of LoS is reduced from 78 hours to 15 hours. In case more improvement is needed and waste is available, then MRA (refer to Figure 5.23) should be applied to the rest of resources (Accountant, Receptionist, Technician, and Physician)" [Oueida et al. (2019a)].

"The new resources capacities in the model are depicted in Table 5.22 along with their actual pay. Since the number of resources is optimized, a new reward system, R_{oc}, can be calculated for the catastrophic case using the previously defined equations and the simulation outputs from Arena after applying the new resource allocation" [Oueida et al. (2019a)] (refer to Table 5.20). The resource satisfaction factors' values are presented in Table 5.21. "Patient, owner and resource satisfaction factors are found to be: $f_{1o} = 31\%$, $f_{2o} = 92.01\%$ and $f_{3o} = 30.89\%$ respectively. Note here that the satisfaction factors for the resources: Accountant, Physician, Technician, and Receptionist, are decreased after applying the optimization in a catastrophe. This is normal since decision-makers were concerned to add resources for the bottleneck stages only, which means the optimization stage

Table 5.20 Arena Simulation Outputs after Optimization

Metric	Results
System Number In	19,864
System Number Out	6,222

Source: Oueida et al. (2019a).

Note: Table adapted from *FAIMA Business and Management Journal,* p. 73.

Table 5.21 Resource Satisfaction Factors during Catastrophic Events

Resource Type	Satisfaction Factor(%)
Doctor	$f_{1o}=32.37$
Registered Nurse (RN)	$f_{2o}=36.5$
Nurse	$f_{3o}=25.75$
Transporter	$f_{4o}=27.46$
Accountant	$f_{5o}=26.5$
Receptionist	$f_{6o}=29.13$
Physician	$f_{7o}=15.16$
Technician	$f_{8o}=54.25$

Source: Oueida et al. (2019a).

Note: Table adapted from *FAIMA Business and Management Journal,* p. 73.

was limited and no additional resources are granted for these four types of resources. Therefore, future improvements can be achieved by applying the algorithm again, taking into consideration additional number of accountants, physicians, technicians, and receptionists.

Therefore, the reward system for catastrophe after optimization is: $R_{oc}=38.32\%$. This reward measure should look satisfying for hospital management since the satisfaction measure of the system is increased from 7.08% before optimization to 38.32% after applying MRA for catastrophe. This increase in the value of R proves that the suggested reward system, and the optimization algorithm, MRA, are reliable and efficient during catastrophic events.

Note that there is always room for additional improvement but limitations may arise based on budget constraints and management observations" [Oueida et al. (2019a)].

"All satisfaction factors and the reward system calculated in previous sections, before and after MRA, for disaster events, are depicted in Table 5.23. The satisfactory level is also presented. As per the results, all satisfaction values are increased leading to an increase in the reward system value except for F_{3o}. This is due to some limitations from hospital's management, where additional resources are granted for bottleneck stages only. Therefore, receptionists, technicians, accountants, and physicians were not optimized. Future improvements can be achieved by applying MRA to these resources as well. Nevertheless, R was increased from 7.08% to 38.32% for catastrophic events, thus proving the efficiency and reliability of the reward system and optimization algorithm suggested" [Oueida et al. (2019a)].

Table 5.22 MRA Resource Allocation for Catastrophes

Resource Type	Actual Pay($) per Resource	MRA Resource Allocation in the ED
Doctor	2000	20
Registered Nurse (RN)	1100	20
Nurse	850	20
Transporter	650	20
Accountant	1000	8
Receptionist	500	1
Physician	1200	1
Technician	800	3
Facilities	800	40

Source: Oueida et al. (2019a).

Note: Table adapted from *FAIMA Business and Management Journal*, p. 73.

Table 5.23 Satisfaction Factors and Reward System for Catastrophes

Factors	Before MRA (%)	After MRA (%)	Satisfactory Level
F1o	2.43	31	Satisfied
F2o	37.37	92.01	Extremely Satisfied
F3o	37.81	30.89	Satisfied
R	7.08	38.32	Satisfied

Source: Oueida et al. (2019a).

Note: Table adapted from *FAIMA Business and Management Journal*, p. 74.

The information in this chapter appears in the following journals, all authored by Soraia Oueida and reprinted by permission of the publisher.

- *International Journal of User-Driven Healthcare*, Copyright © 2017, IGI Global, [Oueida et al. (2017e)]
- *Multimedia Tools and Applications*, Copyright © 2019, Springer, [Oueida et al. (2018a)]
- *Sensors*, Copyright © 2018, MDPI, [Oueida et al. (2018d)]
- *FAIMA Business and Management Journal*, Copyright © 2019, Niculescu Publishing House, [Oueida et al. (2019a)]

Chapter 6

Building a Platform for ED Management and Its Socio-Economic Benefits

6.1 Platform Functions

In this chapter, a new platform is proposed in order to improve the daily operation of a healthcare system, specifically the emergency department of a hospital. The new platform is defined for hospital management and used to study the operational flow of one unit or more in the hospital along with calculating reward systems and performing optimization. The optimization phase suggests new resource allocations for better system performance, always guaranteeing a balance between patient, employee, and owner satisfaction. All the timings in the software are defined in minutes. To begin with, a new healthcare programming language is proposed for AMS platform in order to facilitate the way users enter the input data. Once data is fed to the platform, a user interface helps the user to choose what to perform on this data. The user needs to define the stages of workflow, dependencies among stages, resources needed per service (type and number referred to as pools). The user can simulate, compile, build a project, or choose to draw the graph corresponding to the system created in the input. It is a user-friendly platform where the user can easily integrate the stages of the system under study along with the pool of resources as statements written in English. Here, keywords are required to be available in the input statements, which will be described in detail in the next section. Another feature of this platform is the simulation paradigm. The language core is integrated with a Petri net simulator where all stages cooperate together and run concurrently in order to serve the patient. The simulator validates the model topology fed through the language core by making sure that the system is sound, all connections are valid, and siphons are controlled. The platform supports decision-making, priority, and concurrency. The results of simulation and statistics such as waiting times and total length of stay can be displayed. Finally, a very efficient and important advantage of the platform is providing optimization where the best resource allocation can be predicted for normal flow of patients or during catastrophic events. In the catastrophic mode, users can specify the type of event by loading into the program the number of patient arrivals. The optimization integrated with this platform offers the hospital

Table 6.1 Platform Objectives

Metrics	Advantages
Input Data	New language code based on English statements and keywords
Interface	User-friendly
Simulation	Simulation period can be defined. Soundness and critical sections-free are ensured. Study the system performance. Many experiments can be conducted.
Statistics and Outputs	Performance Measures: LoS, Utilization Rates, Service Times Spot and specify bottleneck areas
Optimization	Supports the MRA algorithm. Calculates satisfaction factors and reward system Suggests optimal allocation of resources

Source: Oueida et al. (2019b).

Note: Table adapted from *International Journal of Simulation Modelling*, p. 35.

an opportunity to better serve its patients, always taking into consideration patient satisfaction, employee satisfaction, and owner satisfaction. Recall here that patient satisfaction reflects decreasing the LoS, employee satisfaction reflects decreasing the staff workload, and owner satisfaction reflects increasing the revenue and decreasing potential wastes. The software developed is called AMS and is written in C-sharp (C#). C# is an object-oriented programming (OOP) language for Web development. As a result of the simulation, statistics are easily collected and saved as a text file if required by the user. The main objectives and advantages of this software are depicted in Table 6.1. The schematic view of the platform is presented in Figure 6.1.

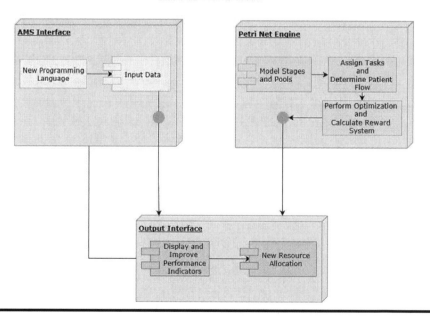

AMS Schematic View

Figure 6.1 AMS schematic view [Oueida et al. (2019b)].

Table 6.2 Other Medical Platforms

Platform Name	Description
ClearHealth	Hospital Management System. ClearHealth is a next-generation practice management and EMR. It supports Scheduling, Full Medical Billing, and Decision Support. It was released in 2003.
Capacity Planner	A predictive analytics tool for hospitals. It provides accurate forecasting of patient demand and optimizes resources. It was developed by Change Healthcare, LLC.
ClickSoftware	Resource capacity planning. It delivers the ability to optimize resource capacity. Once a resource capacity plan is made, ClickSoftware enables instantaneous changes to the resource allocation.
Business Analytics Software (BA)	It is a software tool for monitoring and predicting radiology throughput performance. It provides statistical analysis, forecasting, and predictive modelling.
Intermedix	TOPS: Tool for optimizing provider schedules. It employs the principle of granular data, statistical modeling and user-friendly visuals to provide medical directors with a solution tailored to meet their needs.
Priority Software	Priority Software provides enterprise resource planning and management for small, medium, and large enterprises.
Deltek Vision	Deltek Vision supports the management of resources. It is a project-based solution for professional services firms.
Meddbase	It is a web-based medical software package that allows resource scheduling and planning.

Some similar platforms are available on the market for scheduling, billing, and managing medical resources. The list is presented in Table 6.2 along with some short descriptions and applications.

6.2 Platform Presentation

This section is dedicated to the presentation of the proposed platform. The language primitives required to load the program responsible for the input data entry along with the system definition are described.

6.2.1 Language Primitives

The programming language proposed is a very simple and user-friendly interface. It is a new core language that is defined for any healthcare system. It is named AMS. In this section, the primitives of AMS are presented in order to explain to the user how to input the data to the platform interface by writing English statements only. Therefore, some important keywords and operators should be illustrated. The operators defined are: = and +. The logic operators are: >, <, ≥, ≤, ≠, %. The % operator is used in order to add comments. The keywords are presented in Appendix B. When the user writes the required statements in the platform interface, the program searches for the keywords in order to identify the number of stages, number of pools, along with all resource types referred to as tokens and connection types. Moreover, the mode can be specified to be during normal flow or catastrophic conditions, along with the simulation period of time. Having these details, the required system can be built and designed in order to start simulation. Before simulation and displaying the results and statistics, the system is verified and validated using the engine designed in the platform. When the system is ready and bottlenecks are defined, optimization can be applied to the model where new resource allocation can be predicted.

6.2.2 Defining the System

"Language preliminaries defined in the previous section are used in order to describe the system that needs to be studied and simulated. The steps needed to be added to the input data file are described in the following subsections.

6.2.2.1 Defining the Stages

Stages are referred to as each stop a patient makes in the ED during their journey in order to receive the required care. The steps to define the stages are:

- A name should be associated to each stage using the keyword NAME and the operator =.
- The Distribution should be set using the keyword DISTRIBUTION and the operator =. Here, it can be set to NONE in case the stage is not a process and does not follow any distribution type.
- The interval time should be set in order to define the delay. Here, it represents the time each stage takes in order to accomplish a task. The keywords to be used are INTERVAL FROM and INTERVAL TO.
- The stage should either support decision or not, which means a patient can be routed two different ways based on a certain percentage. If the stage supports decision then the keyword DECISION and the operator = should be used in order to set it to YES. Otherwise, DECISION should be set to NO. Once the stage is set to support decision, the percentage is set using the keywords PERCENTAGE TO or PERCENTAGE FROM and the operator =. For example, PERCENTAGE FROM = 0 and PERCENTAGE TO=40 means a percentage of 40.
- If two or more units cooperate together, the keyword ORING should be used followed by the operator = and set to YES in case the stage supports ORING. ORING means the stage may receive more than one type of patient coming from two different units or more. Therefore, receiving one type of patient only can fire the transition.
- A keyword WORKFLOW must be set to A or B using the operator =, if two different units are operating for example. WORKFLOW sets an attribute to patients coming from different units.
- Each line of the language code should end by a semi-colon (;).
- Each stage should end by END STAGE.

6.2.2.2 Defining the Pools

Pools are referred to as the resources needed in order to serve the arriving patients. The steps to define the pools are:

- A name should be associated to each pool using the keyword NAME and the operator =. The pool name usually refers to the type of resources associated with these pools.
- The type of resource residing in this pool should be set using the keyword TYPE and the operator =. The patient type refers to the token residing in the resource pool. Note that the input/output pools type is always "patient."
- The marking of each pool should be set using the keyword MARK and the operator =. Note that the input pool marking is the number of arriving patients to the system and the output pool marking should be always set to 0 at the beginning since no simulation is performed yet. The marking of pools represents the capacity of resources in the model.
- The salary that each medical resource receives should be entered using the keyword SALARY and the operator =. Salaries represent the actual salary of resources in the model.
- The maximum pay each resource is expecting should be entered using the keywords MAXIMUM SALARY and the operator =. The maximum pay is based on the expectation of salaries which resources wish to happen.
- A utilization rate threshold can be set using the keyworks MAXIMUM WORKLOAD and the operator =. This value represents a maximum workload that a resource can handle. A number higher than this value leads to employee dissatisfaction.
- Each line of the language code should end with a semi-colon (;).
- Each pool should end by END POOL.

6.2.2.3 Defining the Connections

Connections refer to the links between stages and pools. All siphons should be controlled, which means each resource returns to its corresponding pool after accomplishing a certain task. Connections are set as statements and the steps to define them are presented as follows:

- Use the keyword CONNECT as the first word in the statement in order to specify that the links are being defined.
- Use the pool name or stage name as the second word in the statement to specify the link from where the connection starts.
- Use the keyword TO as the third word in the statement.
- Use the pool name or stage name as the fourth word in the statement to specify the link where the connection ends.
- Use the keyword AS as the fifth word in the statement.
- Use the keyword INPUT or OUTPUT as the sixth word in the statement in order to specify the type of connection to be either input or output.
- Use the keyword PASS as the seventh word in the statement in order to pass the type of token inside the pool into the stage. The tokens can be either a patient moving across the stages or a certain type of resource serving this stage.
- Use the type of token as the last word in the statement. The token type can be either a patient, a doctor, a nurse, etc. These types refer to the type of token residing in the stage.
- Each statement should end with a semi-colon (;).

6.2.2.4 Defining and Setting Values

- In order to start the simulation phase a simulation time must be set. Here two keywords can be used: SIMULATE FOR and then the number can be specified followed by either MINUTES, HOURS, or WEEKS keywords. Of course, the statement should start by the keyword SET and end by a semi-colon (;).
- The input and output pools of the described system must be set by using the keyword SET as the first word in the statement. Then, the pool name can be added as the second word. The third word must be the keyword AS and finally the last word in the statement should be the direction either INPUT or OUTPUT. Here, two separate statements must be defined: one to set the input pool and another to set the output pool.
- The mode of simulation must be set by using the keyword SET as the first word in the statement. Then, the keyword MODE as the second word in the statement followed by the operator =. Finally, the last word in the statement must be either the keyword NORMAL or CATASTROPHIC depending on which simulation mode the user desires to run the system through.
- The number of iterations or simulation runs must be set using the keyword SET as the first word in the statement followed by the keyword MAXIMUM then NUMBER then OF then ITERATIONS and finally the operator = followed by the value and a semi-colon (;).
- The output results and statistics can be saved into a text file by adding to the program input data file the keywords OUTPUT followed by TO then FILE then specify the name of the file desired followed by a semi-colon (;).

6.2.2.5 Defining the Optimization Phase

The last part of the language code data input file is setting the needed factors for the optimization phase. During optimization, many factors need to be set in order to calculate the satisfaction factors: patient, owner, and employee satisfaction factors. These factors are then used in order to determine the optimization value which represents the reward system. To start with the optimization phase, the keyword OPTIMIZE must be added to the input data file followed by a semi-colon (;). Here, some values need to be set in order to apply the optimization algorithm defined in the software and calculate the optimization values. Once these values are set and simulation is started, the software will perform many iterations until the near-optimal solution is achieved. This solution suggests the best allocation of resources for a better performance of the system. The factors that need to be set are as follows:

- Setting the consultation fees using the keywords CONSULTATION FEES followed by the operator = then the value desired and ended by a semi-colon (;). The values are in US $.
- Setting the pay weight factor by using the keywords PAY WEIGHT followed by the operator = then the value desired and ended by a semi-colon (;). The values are in %.
- Setting the workload weight factor by using the keywords WORKLOAD WEIGHT followed by the operator = then the value desired and ended by a semi-colon (;). The values are in %.
- Setting the extra expenses factor by using the keywords OTHER EXPENSES followed by the operator = then the value desired and ended by a semi-colon (;). The values are in %.
- Setting the customer–resource relationship factor by using the keywords EMPLOYEE IMPACT followed by the operator = then the value desired and ended by a semi-colon (;). The values are in %.

- Setting the expected LoS by using the keywords EXPECTED LOS followed by the operator = then the value desired and ended by a semi-colon (;). The values are in minutes.
- Setting the employee weight factor by using the keywords EMPLOYEE WEIGHT followed by the operator = then the value desired and ended by a semi-colon (;). The values are in %.
- Setting the management weight factor by using the keywords MANAGEMENT WEIGHT followed by the operator = then the value desired and ended by a semi-colon (;). The values are in %.
- Setting the patient weight factor by using the keywords PATIENT WEIGHT followed by the operator = then the value desired and ended by a semi-colon (;). The values are in %.
- Setting the optimization threshold by using the keyword THRESHOLD followed by the operator = then the value desired and ended by a semi-colon (;). The values are in %" [Oueida et al. (2019b)].

6.3 Using the Platform

In this section the platform proposed is described in order to show the user how to deal with the interface and the output results statistics.

An example code is presented in order to help the user while using the platform.

6.3.1 Language Code Example

In this section, the user can benefit from a code example given to better use the input program tool. The user can use this code as a model to base their work on.

An example model is defined in Figure 6.2. This example is a very simple workflow that does not depict the real complex operation of a healthcare system and is presented in this section to help users get familiar with the new programming language designed and integrated for the AMS platform through a simple and straightforward graph. The system model, representing one medical unit, has two stages, S_1 and S_2, only; one input pool called IN containing a patient as a token type, one output pool called OUT also containing a patient as a token type; and two resource pools called DoctorPool and NursePool containing one doctor and one nurse respectively. The doctor

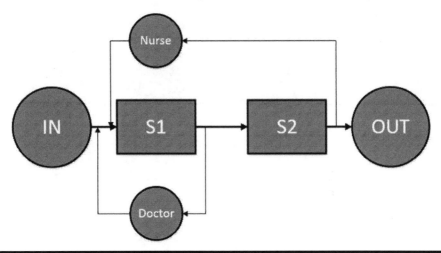

Figure 6.2   A system model example.

resource serves the patient in stage S_1 only where the nurse resource stays with the patient until stage S_2. The input pool IN has ten patients entering the system, which refers to the marking of this pool.

The marking of the OUT pool is zero initially since the system is not simulated yet. The maximum pay for a doctor is $1500 while the actual pay is $1200. The maximum pay for a nurse is $800 while the actual pay is $500. The actual pay refers to the salary of the corresponding resource. The maximum workload for both resources is equal to 85%. Note that stage S_1 follows a uniform distribution UNIF(1,5) and stage S_2 follows a uniform distribution UNIF(3,10). If a stage does not follow any type of distribution then the DISTRIBUTION field will be set to NONE. Neither stage supports decision. The simulation was run for 24 hours, during normal flow. Finally, the model is optimized in order to propose new resource allocations. During optimization, the employee, management, and patient weights satisfaction factors are set to be 20, 50, and 30 respectively. The consultation fee is $20. The pay weight is equal to 60% and the workload weight is equal to 40%. The extra expenses factor is equal to 70%. The expected LoS is equal to 250 minutes. The employee impact referred to as the customer–resource medical relationship factor is equal to 40%. Finally, the optimization threshold is 80%. These factors are predicted from management decisions and based on decision-makers' experience and may vary from country to country, culture to culture, and hospital to hospital.

Based on the data given, the input data file will be as follows; recall that % operator is used to add comments:

% Defining the stages along with the name, distribution type, time interval, type of decision and probability.

```
STAGE
NAME = S₁;
DISTRIBUTION = UNIFORM;
INTERVAL FROM 1;
INTERVAL TO 5;
DECISION = NO;
PERCENTAGE TO = 50;
PERCENTAGE FROM = 50;
END STAGE;

STAGE NAME = S₂;
DISTRIBUTION = UNIFORM;
INTERVAL FROM 3;
INTERVAL TO 10;
DECISION = NO;
PERCENTAGE TO = 50;
PERCENTAGE FROM = 50;
END STAGE;
```

% Defining the pools along with the name, type, marking, salary, maximum pay, and maximum workload

```
POOL
NAME = NursePool;
TYPE = Nurse;
MARK = 1;
SALARY = 500;
MAXIMUM SALARY = 800;
MAXIMUM WORKLOAD = 85;
END POOL;
```

```
POOL
NAME = DoctorPool;
TYPE = Doctor;
MARK = 1;
SALARY=1200;
MAXIMUM SALARY = 1500;
MAXIMUM WORKLOAD=85;
END POOL;

POOL NAME = IN;
TYPE = Patient;
MARK = 10;
END POOL;

POOL NAME = OUT;
TYPE = Patient;
MARK = 0;
END POOL;
```

% Setting the input and output pools.
```
SET IN AS INPUT;
SET OUT AS OUTPUT;
```

% Defining the links between nodes along with the directions and type of token passed.
```
CONNECT IN TO S₁ AS INPUT PASS PATIENT;
CONNECT S₁ TO S₂ AS INPUT PASS PATIENT;
CONNECT S₂ TO OUT AS INPUT PASS PATIENT;
CONNECT NursePool TO S₁ AS INPUT;
CONNECT NursePool TO S₁ AS OUTPUT;
CONNECT NursePool TO S₂ AS INPUT;
CONNECT NursePool TO S₂ AS OUTPUT;
CONNECT DoctorPool TO S₁ AS INPUT;
CONNECT DoctorPool TO S₁ AS OUTPUT;
```

% Specifying the simulation period of time.
```
SIMULATE FOR 24 HOURS;
```

% Performing optimization.
```
OPTIMIZE
```

% Setting the weight factors.
```
SET EMPLOYEE WEIGHT = 20;
SET MANAGEMENT WEIGHT = 50;
SET PATIENT WEIGHT = 30;
```

% Setting the threshold.
```
SET THRESHOLD = 80;
```

% setting the mode to be: normal flow.
```
SET MODE = NORMAL;
```

% Setting the consultation fees.
```
SET CONSULTATION FEES = $20;
```

% Setting the pay weight.
```
SET PAY WEIGHT = 60;
```

% Setting the workload weight.
```
SET WORKLOAD WEIGHT = 40;
```

% Setting the extra expenses factor.
```
SET OTHER EXPENSES = 70;
```

% Setting the expected LoS.
```
SET EXPECTED LOS = 250;
```

% Setting the employee impact factor.
```
SET EMPLOYEE IMPACT = 40;
```

6.3.2 Platform Interface

The platform interface is presented in this section where each feature is illustrated by some screenshots added as figures in order to become familiar with how to use it easily. The interface toolbar contains two buttons as depicted in Figure 6.3.

- File: used to input the data describing the system to be simulated
- Compile and Build: to compile the data and make sure the data entered is correct; then, build the data to be ready for simulation. As a start, the data should be fed by pressing the File button from the toolbar. One of the five options can be selected as per Figure 6.3.
- New: to create a new file where the data can be added
- Open: to open an existing data file
- Save: to save any changes performed on the data through the interface

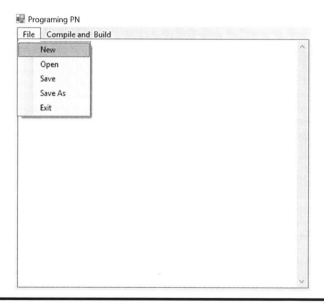

Figure 6.3   File options.

- Save As: to save changes under a new name
- Exit: to exit the interface

If the New option is selected, then data can be directly fed into the interface as shown in Figure 6.4.

The other option illustrated in Figure 6.5 is to open an existing data file describing the system to be studied. A part of the opened data file is shown in Figure 6.6.

Figure 6.7 illustrates the saving feature of a data file entry; either saving on the same file or as a new file under a different name. Once done with the data file and exiting the interface window is the target, the Exit option should be chosen. This option is presented in Figure 6.8.

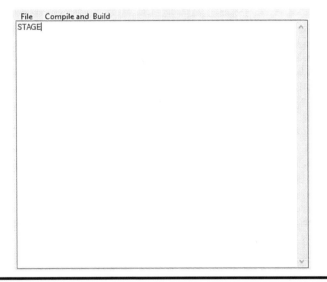

Figure 6.4   Data fed through the interface.

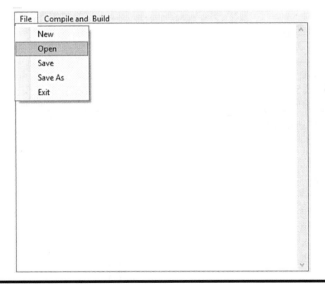

Figure 6.5   Opening an existing data file.

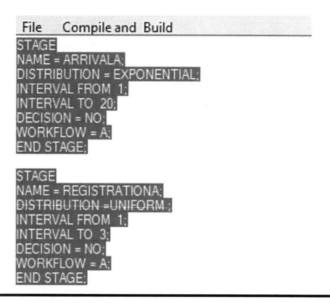

Figure 6.6   Data file sample.

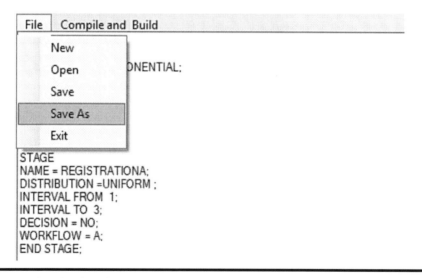

Figure 6.7   Saving the data file.

The next step, once done with data entry, is to compile the file to make sure that the data entered is correct; then, build the file where data is mapped into the engine in order to study the system described (refer to Figure 6.9). Building the file is necessary before starting the simulation as shown in Figures 6.10 and 6.11, where a message will appear on the screen when trying to simulate before building.

In the Simulate option, the data entered will be simulated based on an internal engine that maps all stages to transitions in the Petri net simulator, the pools into the resource pools, and connects both through directed links. More than one unit can be considered and can run in parallel since, as mentioned previously, the engine supports concurrency and scalability along

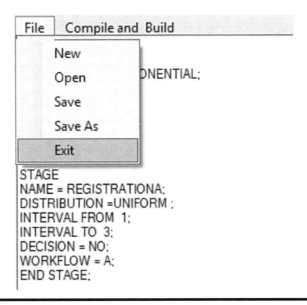

Figure 6.8   Exiting the interface.

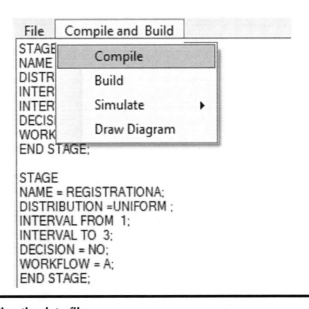

Figure 6.9   Compiling the data file.

with cooperation where two or more units can share resources with another unit. Two buttons are depicted in Figures 6.12 and 6.13 to start and end the simulation respectively.

Another feature of this interface is the Draw option. This option, presented in Figure 6.14, allows the user to draw the flowchart of the system described in the data input file. The stages are represented by rectangles and the pools by circles along with directed arcs referring to the links between both. This is a very useful feature where the user can get the system designed in seconds once the data input file is fed into the engine. It supports any size of systems and overcome the

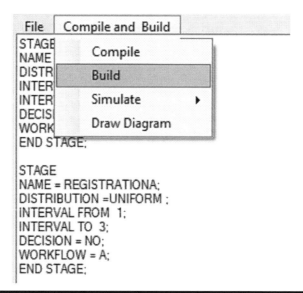

Figure 6.10   Building the data file.

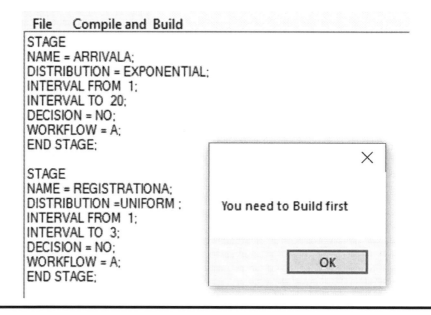

Figure 6.11   The must-build message.

hassle of representing complex industrial systems such as emergency departments. The drawing can be saved and used for any displaying purposes.

Once the Simulation button is pressed, the simulation starts. The progress bar shown in Figure 6.15 represents the status and the progress of the simulation. Once the simulation is over, the output window shows up as in Figure 6.16. The output window shows the various statistics needed to study the system described. From these statistics collected, a bottleneck can be highlighted and thus, in case of needed enhancements, the system can be run again by just requesting

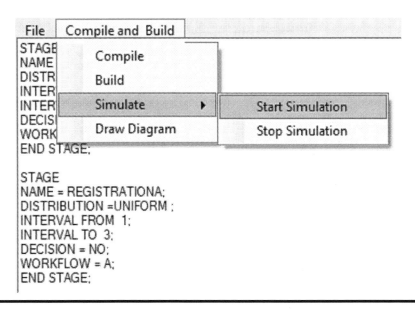

Figure 6.12   Starting the simulation.

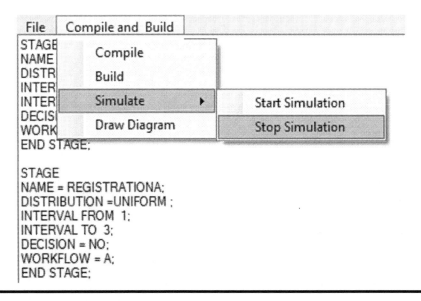

Figure 6.13   Stopping the simulation.

the optimizing feature, simply by adding the keyword OPTIMIZE in the data entry file and choosing the optimize button from the interface. During optimization, the engine looks for the optimal solution and displays the best resource allocation for which the system is guaranteed to better perform.

A sample of the output file is illustrated in Figure 6.17. The Output shows the system number out referring to the number of patients leaving the system, the bottleneck areas where optimization should be applied, the average patient LoS, and the initial marking of pools. In case of

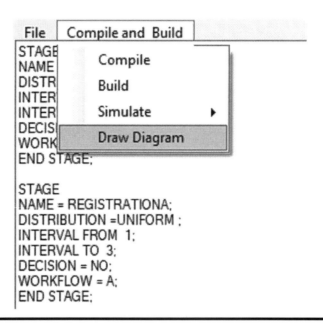

Figure 6.14 Drawing the system's flowchart.

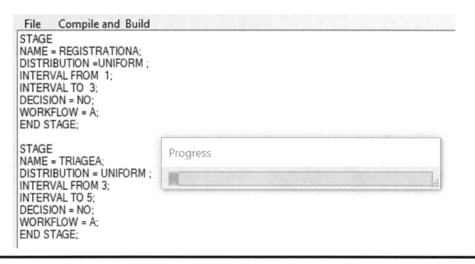

Figure 6.15 Simulation progress.

optimization applied, the output shows the new statistics along with the new optimal resource allocations advised for better performance of the system.

6.4 Platform Testing

In this section the platform proposed is applied to a real-life scenario where simulation of an ED is presented along with the study of system performance measures. The platform is verified and validated.

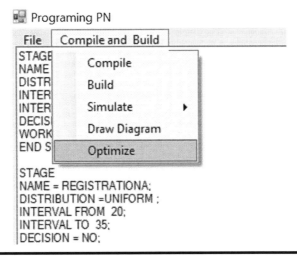

Figure 6.16   Optimization feature.

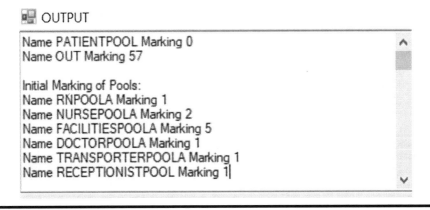

Figure 6.17   Output sample.

6.4.1 AMS Simulation, Statistics, and Results

"The studied ED is simulated using the developed software AMS during normal flow and compared with previous simulations using Arena software in order to prove the efficiency and reliability of this platform.

The ED is simulated for 24 hours during normal flow; therefore, the keyword NORMAL as the mode is fed into the input data file created to describe this system. The marking of the input pool is 140 arriving patients and the initial marking of the resource pools are as depicted in Figure 6.18. The output statistics collected are illustrated below.

Figure 6.19 shows the system number out after simulation where the marking of the patient pool is changed from the 140 initial value to 0, which means that all patients are being treated. The marking of the OUT pool, which represents the exit of the ED, is equal to 53. This value refers to the number of patients exiting the system from the two ERs (ER A and ER B).

Figure 6.20 shows the number of patients waiting in queues where the highest is 51 and refers to the transporter queue. The transporter is responsible for transferring the patient from the ED to

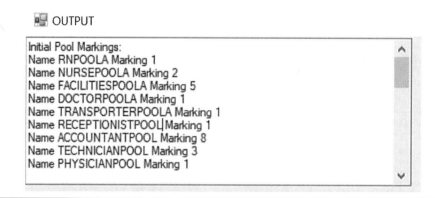

Figure 6.18   Initial pools marking [Oueida et al. (2019b)].

Figure 6.19   System number out [Oueida et al. (2019b)].

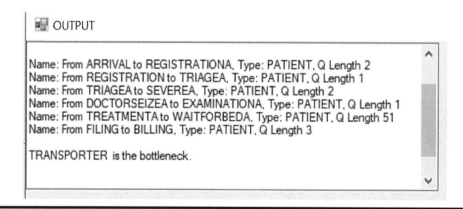

Figure 6.20   Number waiting in queues [Oueida et al. (2019b)].

the radiology unit in cases where a facility is requested or to admission in cases where admission to the hospital is needed (after waiting for bed availability). Therefore, it is noticed here that the transporter queue is suffering from bottleneck due to a shortage in the transporter pool, which thus needs to be optimized. The platform specifies the bottleneck area which is referred to here as the Transporter.

From Figure 6.21, it is noticed that the highest utilization rate corresponds to the transporter resource (99%). This is normal since the system possesses only one transporter to serve all incoming patients and therefore the bottleneck at this queue is justified.

The average patient LoS is equal to 395.09 minutes as per Figure 6.22, which is higher than the expected LoS which must be 270 minutes as a threshold for a satisfied patient. Therefore, the system must be optimized to decrease this value and thus increase patient satisfaction.

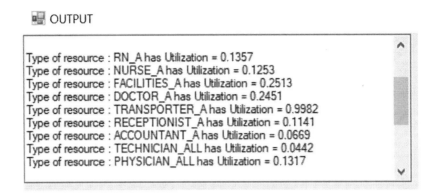

OUTPUT

Type of resource : RN_A has Utilization = 0.1357
Type of resource : NURSE_A has Utilization = 0.1253
Type of resource : FACILITIES_A has Utilization = 0.2513
Type of resource : DOCTOR_A has Utilization = 0.2451
Type of resource : TRANSPORTER_A has Utilization = 0.9982
Type of resource : RECEPTIONIST_A has Utilization = 0.1141
Type of resource : ACCOUNTANT_A has Utilization = 0.0669
Type of resource : TECHNICIAN_ALL has Utilization = 0.0442
Type of resource : PHYSICIAN_ALL has Utilization = 0.1317

Figure 6.21   Resource utilization rates [Oueida et al. (2019b)].

OUTPUT

Patient LoS = 395.094 minutes.

Optimization Threshold = 80.
Optimization Value = 81.

Figure 6.22   Patient LoS and optimization value [Oueida et al. (2019b)].

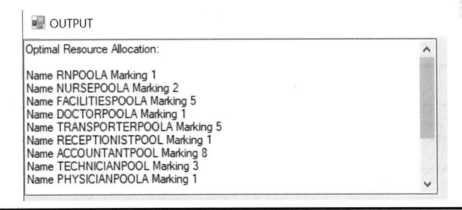

OUTPUT

Optimal Resource Allocation:

Name RNPOOLA Marking 1
Name NURSEPOOLA Marking 2
Name FACILITIESPOOLA Marking 5
Name DOCTORPOOLA Marking 1
Name TRANSPORTERPOOLA Marking 5
Name RECEPTIONISTPOOL Marking 1
Name ACCOUNTANTPOOL Marking 8
Name TECHNICIANPOOL Marking 3
Name PHYSICIANPOOLA Marking 1

Figure 6.23   New resource allocation [Oueida et al. (2019b)].

Moreover, the reward system which is represented by the optimization value is equal to 81. This value is higher than the optimization threshold and thus the new marking of resources is reliable for better performance of the overall system. The new resource allocation is depicted in Figure 6.23. Figure 6.24 shows the number of iterations where the simulation is stopped while reaching an optimization value higher than the threshold along with the three satisfaction measures. These values are depicted in Table 6.6.

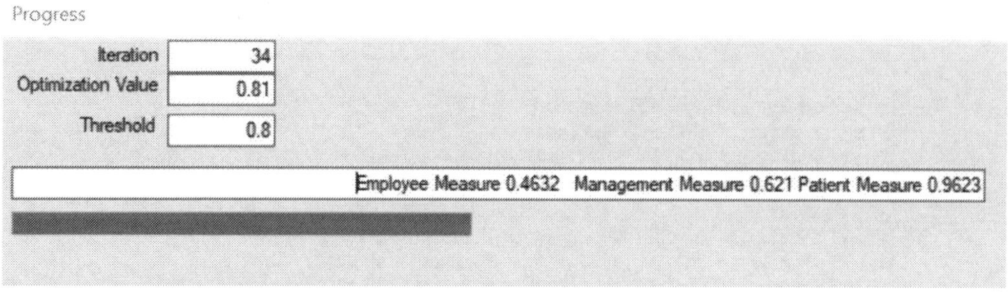

Figure 6.24 Best optimization iteration [Oueida et al. (2019b)].

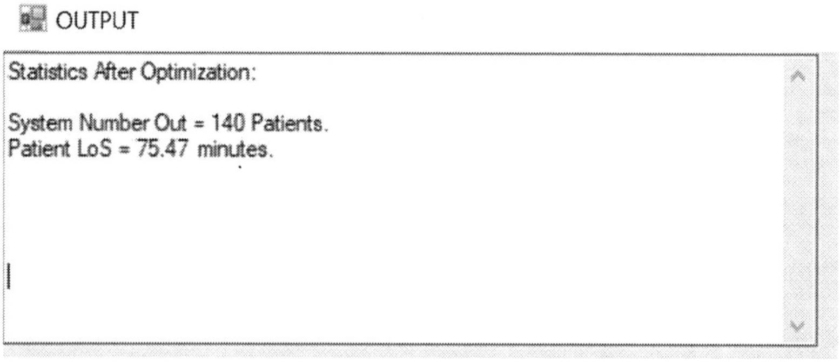

Figure 6.25 System number out and LoS after optimization [Oueida et al. (2019b)].

The system number out is increased from 53 to 140 patients after optimization as per Figure 6.25. This is a huge increase in the number of patients leaving the system, which means a higher revenue for the hospital's owner. The LoS after optimization is decreased from 395.09 to 75.47 minutes as per Figure 6.25; which means another attractive enhancement of the system. Recall here that the optimization algorithm takes into consideration the revenue which reflects the owner satisfaction while suggesting the optimal resource allocation" [Oueida et al. (2019b)].

6.4.2 Discussion and Platform Validation

The output results collected from the simulation of the studied ED show a bottleneck in the transporter queue and a high utilization rate with the transporter resource. The statistics collected are illustrated in Table 6.3. These values are compared to the values resulting from the Arena simulation performed in a previous chapter and are found to be very similar where a bottleneck is spotted in the transporter queue, thus the reliability of the software in studying the system flow of operation and defining the bottleneck areas. The user-friendly programming language used to feed the input data into the platform and the way statistical output results are collected make this new software a manageable platform for hospitals to rely on.

After applying optimization using AMS platform, which is based on the MRA algorithm defined previously, the values collected for the system out, patient LoS, and the reward system along with the three satisfaction factors, employee, owner, and patient, are very similar to those

Table 6.3 AMS vs. Arena before Optimization

Performance Measures	Arena Outputs	AMS Outputs
Number of System In	140	140
Number of System Out	60	53
Patient LoS	356.62	395.09
Transporter Workload	98.94	99.82
Accountant Workload	16.58	6.7
Receptionist Workload	14.99	11.41
Technician Workload	5.1	4.4
Physician Workload	12.66	13.17
Doctor Workload	33.05	24.5
Nurse Workload	28.97	12.5
Facilities Workload	20.27	25.13
RN Workload	19.37	13.57

Source: Oueida et al. (2019b).

Note: Table adapted from *International Journal of Simulation Modelling*, p. 43.

Table 6.4 Comparison after Optimization

Performance Measures	MRA Outputs	AMS Outputs
Reward System: R	77.2	81
System Number Out	138	140
Patient LoS	112.96	75.47

Source: Oueida et al. (2019b).

Note: Table adapted from *International Journal of Simulation Modelling*, p. 43.

calculated in previous sections. Moreover, the new resource allocation proposed by the AMS software is almost similar to the one resulting from the MRA algorithm, where only adding four extra transporters per unit enhanced the system number out along with a huge decrease in the patient average LoS. Thus, again, the proof of reliability of this platform and that the engine works exactly as intended. This comparison is presented in Tables 6.4 through 6.6.

As a conclusion, this similarity in outputs with the Arena simulation performed previously on the same ED proves the efficiency and reliability of this new proposed platform. Therefore, the software is ready for commercial use and the output statistics that can be collected are very useful for hospital management and system enhancement.

Table 6.5 New Resource Allocations

Resource Type	MRA New Resource Allocation	AMS New Resource Allocation
Doctor	1	1
RN	1	1
Nurse	2	2
Transporter	9	5
Accountant	8	8
Receptionist	1	1
Physician	1	1
Technician	3	3
Facilities	5	5

Source: Oueida et al. (2019b).

Note: Table adapted from *International Journal of Simulation Modelling,* p. 43.

Table 6.6 Reward System

Factors	Arena (%)	AMS (%)
F_1	94.75	96.23
F_2	53	62.1
F_3	44.755	46.32
R	77.2	81

Source: Oueida et al. (2019b).

Note: Table adapted from *International Journal of Simulation Modelling,* p. 43.

6.5 Social and Economic Benefits

"Economic and social benefits of the proposed platform AMS are presented in this section in order to highlight the advantage of using this software in emergency departments and why decision-makers should consider it during the potential system optimization phase. Moreover, the platform is tested in the studied emergency department and found to be reliable and efficient for hospital management. This study aims to improve benefit awareness and provide new empirical evidence on the socio-economic impact and lessons learnt from successful AMS implementation. The software proposes new resource allocations to better serve patients in an emergency department and to eliminate wastes. When the ED is well managed and system flow is improved, the number of patients being treated is increased. This is due to the advantage of this platform in decreasing the LoS and thus more patients are seen. As an outcome, the hospital's revenue is increased and thus there is an economic benefit to the AMS platform. This benefit affects all departments in the hospital since the ED is connected with the majority of the hospital units.

The most prominent benefits of AMS are efficiency and improved quality. Efficiency refers to improving productivity for treating patients such as lower waiting times, lower resources workload, and an increase in system revenue. The major patient gain here is the improved timeliness and quality of care. Gain also includes a reduced risk of errors since medical resources workloads are decreased" [Oueida et al. (2019b)]. AMS costs include the financial investment for the software, along with the cost of deploying additional resources proposed for optimal performance. Connected databases in order to transfer patient data among different units of the hospital improve the use of the software since healthcare data is needed to load the program input data file before studying the system.

"As part of the socio-economic evaluation, a cost-benefit analysis is performed showing a significant net benefit margin that can be achieved by applying the optimization proposed by AMS. Studying the net benefit of the software includes a measure of financial returns along with the value of all positive and negative effects including hospital revenue, patient satisfaction, and resource satisfaction. A well-satisfied system attracts patients and opens the door for more patients to come in the future leading to a good reputation of the hospital" [Oueida et al. (2019b)]. A patient stuck in a particular queue, such as waiting for a doctor, nurse, or bed to be available, increases the overall LoS and thus indirectly decreases the number of patients being cared for, since the system is overcrowded. This scenario will result in a potential loss of new arriving patients and therefore a loss in total revenue. The cost of adding new resources is high (for example adding a doctor in the studied ED will cost an extra $2000 per month). Nevertheless, the platform takes this metric into account. Proposing additional medical resources for system improvement while taking into account the extra costs vs. the hospital revenue, guaranteed by the platform AMS, highlights the main economic benefit of this platform. Future development of the platform allows potential future improvement and benefits of AMS. The platform is designed to be easily developed and new features can be easily integrated for future expansion.

The social benefit of this platform relies on the discussed satisfaction factors. A reward system balancing between the three satisfaction factors, of patient, owner, and resource, is integrated in this proposed platform. This reward system allows the software to better serve patients arriving into the emergency department, always taking into consideration the satisfaction of all parties. Moreover, when more patients are being served the risk to public health is minimized and infectious diseases, spread among waiting patients in the ED, are eliminated through decreasing system waiting times.

AMS is essential for healthcare organizations where process flow can be organized. The studied ED management considered the implementation of this platform to be a great opportunity for meeting the non-stop, increasing demand for medical care services. The services affected include all activities and in particular registration, admissions, transfers, laboratory, imaging, discharge, etc.

"In general, the implementation of this platform in the emergency department of a particular hospital needs some basic requirements such as medical and administrative IT applications (Patient Records Database and Departmental Level Information System). These databases and the link between different units are strictly needed in order to facilitate patient data retrieval and thus create the input data file that will be fed into the program. Electronic patient records, which include demographic and other administrative data, are essential to feed in to the administrative IT applications. AMS is built in a modular structure, which allows smooth expansions in scope for the future" [Oueida et al. (2019b)]. Analyzing the benefits resulting from AMS platform, the most prominent are improved quality of care and efficiency. While time savings and cost avoidance can be primarily assigned, patients mainly benefit from the improved timeliness and quality of care.

"Through interviews with many decision-makers and hospital managers, the numerous benefits and positive impacts of AMS are granted. The main benefit categories of AMS are summarized in Table 6.7" [Oueida et al. (2019b)]. This analysis of the benefits provides a better picture of the positive impact of implementing AMS platform in a healthcare system.

"The estimated price of the AMS framework is $20,000. It covers the software price including installation and person-hours for development. The fees are paid once. A CD is provided containing the software set up which any IT person can install easily" [Oueida et al. (2019b)]. As per the study performed in Chapter 5, the hospital's extra profit after applying optimization is $252,000 per year, considering a normal flow at the ED. By purchasing AMS, the profit remains attractive for decision-makers. A study on yearly ED profit is presented in Table 6.8.

In comparison with other popular similar simulation platforms, the cost of AMS remains attractive and feasible for purchasing when looking at its financial and technical benefits. Other similar simulation software costs range from $15,000 to $50,000 per year.

Table 6.7   AMS Socio-Economic Benefits

Benefits	Description
Efficiency	Coping with increased demand Low operating costs
Quality of Care	Patient Safety Reduce medical errors risk Better effectiveness of care Reduce resource workloads Faster discharge Better prediction and pre-preparation in case of an occurring transfer between units
Faster access	Reduce waiting times during visits
Satisfaction	Balancing between three satisfaction factors: patient, owner, medical resource

Source: Oueida et al. (2019b).

Note: Table adapted from *International Journal of Simulation Modelling*, p. 44.

Table 6.8   Yearly ED Profit Study after Purchasing AMS

	Year 1	Year 2 and Forward
AMS Purchasing Fees	$20,000	NONE
Extra Resources Salaries Expenses	$718,200	$718,200
Revenue from Extra Consultation Fees After Using AMS Simulation	$970,200	$970,200
Net Profit	$252,000	$252,000
Net Profit After Purchasing AMS	$232,000	$252,000

Source: Oueida et al. (2019b).
Note: Table adapted from *International Journal of Simulation Modelling*, p. 45.

"After purchasing and implementing AMS platform into the hospital's ED, decision-makers can perform as many simulations as needed. It takes around one hour for one simulation to be completed depending on the complexity of the system under study. After simulation, recommendations are given in order to enhance the system performance. The system starts gaining more profit as soon as decision-makers apply the recommendations given by the software. The cost increases or decreases based on the recommendations of the system, by either adding or removing resources to better serve the case. However, profit always increases based on the weights decision-makers specify in the software input data phase" [Oueida et al. (2019b)].

During catastrophic events, the simulation of the ED presented in Chapter 3 shows 20,097 arrival patients (refer to Figure 3.11). The recommendation as part of optimization performed in Chapter 5 is to change the resources distribution and add extra resources. When the system is simulated again using these recommendations, the LoS is decreased to an average of 1,099 minutes (refer to Table 5.8), which means the ED needs only around 18 hours to reorganize the flow of patients in the event of an unexpected disaster case.

The information in this chapter appears in the following journal, authored by Soraia Oueida and reprinted by permission of the publisher:

Chapter 7

Conclusion and Future Work

"Healthcare is a large, dynamic and complex system where different units, teams, resources, and patients interconnect in order to serve an activity. This interconnection of facilities requires multi-paradigm, flexible simulation modeling methodologies in order to capture this complexity and present a clear view on how to predict critical events and then reach optimal decision-making. The cascading effects of the various departments in the hospital and their direct link together are clearly presented in order to reach a future vision for the direction of this research. This link should be performed using a simulation platform. An emergency department (ED) is a medical treatment facility specializing in emergency medicine and the acute care of patients who present without prior appointment, either by their own means or by ambulance. Most problems affecting the healthcare system are derived from the ED, since patient flow is based on prediction without any prior appointment. This department is the biggest unit interacting with the whole hospital, which makes it the most complex system (as per the literature review) and thus the focus of this work" [Oueida et al. (2017b)].

7.1 Conclusion

The purpose of this work is to study the different problems affecting the ED as presented in Chapter 1 and implement a flexible effective platform to reduce these problems, and increase patient/owner satisfaction. After some investigations and based on previous work through the literature, Arena is found to be the best simulation platform that can act as multi-paradigm and perform the required analysis. A multi-facility platform is built to divide the complex system into simpler blocks. Each unit is represented as a block. All the blocks are then combined to form the overall ED system. A patient, modeled as an entity in the system, arrives into the ED where a registration desk handles all paper work and transfers them to the waiting room. The patient should wait their turn until a nurse calls their name and invites them in to the examination room. The designed model will differentiate here between high-acuity patients and patients requiring routine examination. The severe case patients will be transferred to a special unit where special treatment is required and a doctor will be responsible for diagnosis, laboratory tests/imaging requests; based on the results of both the requested tests and examination, admission or discharge will be performed. On the other hand, patients diagnosed with low-acuity illness will be treated in the triage room and then discharged from ED. This option can be a valuable solution for reducing overcrowding of ED, where patients with severe cases do not need to wait long in order to be called for care. Therefore, length of stay in the ED and waiting times will be reduced. The model supports normal flow and catastrophic events. Since arrival of patients is unpredicted and the majority suffer from the same medical issue, a predictive simulation modeling is needed in order to keep the ED prepared for such cases and thus prevent disaster conditions from happening (preparedness over patient surge). The main goal here is to study the needed resources, staff scheduling during peak times, increase staff utilization (preventing overtime), adding additional units/additional staff if needed. It has been well known for decades that increasing patient care and satisfaction is the main goal of any healthcare system; in this work another valuable goal is added: hospital revenue.

"Using Arena, the whole complex system representing the real system of the ED is built and then different scenarios are created in order to validate this model. Some changes can be imposed on the modeled system without affecting the real system in process and thus predictive analysis can be performed in order to evaluate the performance measures and find the optimal solution for any arising problem. Note that problems affecting the ED may be different depending on the region, season, patient age, patient mentality, etc. From these several scenario runs, the optimal solution can be chosen, taking into consideration patient satisfaction (by decreasing waiting times), increasing hospital revenue (by decreasing costs, increasing staff utilization, reducing hospital resources use). Therefore, the minimum number of resources required to serve the maximum demand should be predicted" [Oueida et al. (2017b)]. The main focus of this study is to solve the overcrowding of an ED (measuring different KPI's/factors causing this overcrowding and to propose solutions to these multi-problems using one platform). "The majority of the studies reviewed in literature did not focus on the financial effects of the scenarios tested and approached only the normal periods without considering epidemic and disaster times (availability of sufficient medical staff). Therefore, the proposed platform will aim to improve EDs, considering as well both cost and epidemic periods during performance measuring" [Oueida et al. (2017b)]. After building and validating the model, real input data is integrated into the model in order to build different scenarios and test any unpredictable changes and how the system should react to these changes in order to avoid any disaster conditions (case study).

Healthcare systems, being complex and hard to manage, need to be always followed up to improve its operations. One of the main reasons for ensuring patient satisfaction is to maintain a hospital's good reputation. From the study performed on the chosen ED and the survey suggested (refer to Chapter 2), analyzed responses and results showed that the main factor involved in patient satisfaction is the balance between the total length spent in the ED (LoS) and the level of care offered to the patient. Medical resources being overloaded may cause medial errors or negative attitudes of patients; therefore, staff workload is also considered.

A realistic ED model is built using Arena software (refer to Chapter 3). The ED consisted of two emergency rooms (ERs). Each ER possesses its own resources (material and human); they share only the radiology and billing departments. The first emergency room is called ER A and refers to the public emergency room and the second is called ER B and refers to the private emergency room. The continuous visits to these ERs and the interviews conducted with different staff levels and different departments interacting with the ED unit helped in recognizing the actual operation of the ED, so as to be able to model a system that is close to the real system. One of the main difficulties encountered while trying to model the system is the service time of each process during the whole patient journey through the ED. It is well known that the system cannot be 100% imitated but the main purpose while designing the model is to reach a queue average waiting time, a service time, a resource utilization, and a number of patients out similar, on average, to the real system. This will help identify bottlenecks and leave room for improvement suggestions.

The designed model is verified to be working properly and is then validated. All performance measures are compared with the real system's behavior and the model is found reliable. Then, experimentation is performed where improvement is suggested. The experiments focused on human resource levels, reducing the waiting time of patients in the system (LoS), and increasing the number of patients exiting the system (System Number Out). Using the Arena OptQuest tool, which is a stochastic program, simulation optimization is performed, where the optimal average LoS is analyzed as a function of staffing levels. Ten different best solutions are suggested where the optimal solution is based on an optimal staff distribution. Following this distribution, it is proven that decision-makers can efficiently enhance the system by getting a higher number of patients receiving care and a lower patient waiting time. Cost analysis is applied to all phases of experimentation in order to guarantee both patient and owner satisfaction. Adding resources will result in an additional cost which hospital management will not be able to accommodate due to budget constraints. Taking into consideration the Optimal Scenario Number 5 from the OptQuest optimization phase, patient and owner satisfaction will be guaranteed, where an additional 61 patients are receiving care, thus leading to an increase of $641,275 yearly revenue and the average waiting time in the system (LoS) reduced by almost three hours. Thus, LoS improvement can be generated by increasing the staffing budget. Therefore, this suggested solution should be considered by decision-makers when room for improvement is targeted.

In Chapter 3, a new extended type of Petri net is presented for all types of queuing system such as hospitals, restaurants, theaters, etc. This model is called RPN (Resource Preservation Net) where the main resources are human beings and are not consumable, siphons are controlled, and all resources return to their pools after accomplishing a certain task. The theory behind this suggested PN and the mathematical model is presented through some new theorems of soundness and some lemmas that can be applied to any organization. The model is proven to be sound for one or more cooperating or non-cooperating units through a theorem of scalability. An application of this RPN is applied to the ED studied in this work. Here, the RPN defines the operation and flow of the patient during a certain visit, from the time they arrive into the ER until they are discharged, always bearing in mind the cooperation of the two ERs. For example, if ER A is blocked then ER B can share some medical resources in order to alleviate the problem and vice versa. Moreover, sometimes patients can also be shared by the two ERs; so if an ER is overcrowded and the other ER has a free bed, the corresponding patient can be transferred to the other ER to receive the requested care and then return back to continue the flow in their original ER. The proposed Petri net model, RPN, is validated using discrete mathematics in Chapter 4. The validation is performed through proposing a theorem of soundness and a few lemmas. The model is validated for non-cooperative and cooperative systems.

Many techniques can be used to improve an ED system such as applying lean Six Sigma, simulation modelling, introducing technology such as health information technology (HIT), or introducing the Internet of Things (IoT) and medical telemonitoring (refer to Chapter 5). Telemonitoring is monitoring the patient status at distance. It includes the use of video, audio, and formation processing technologies. HIT plays also a critical role in patient management and system improvement. This suggestion is now under study by decision-makers in order to deploy a new software in the ED which will connect the ED system to other units of the hospital and make the transfer of patient information much easier and smoother. The same ED is studied using Six Sigma process improvement technique. The ED data is entered to the Minitab statistical tool in order to define bottlenecks, wastes and possible room for improvement. As a conclusion, the quality of care was enhanced using Six Sigma. All techniques used for enhancement prove that the studied ED suffers from a bottleneck in the transporter queue during normal flow of operation and thus this stage should be highly considered during the improvement process. In order to measure the level of crowding in the system and identify the bottleneck stages before starting the enhancement procedure, an indexing score called NEDOCS is used. This score, applied to the studied ED, shows a Level 5 of overcrowding, which indicates a severely overcrowded ED and thus much attention to improvement should be applied. This level is decreased after optimization to Level 3, which indicates only a busy ED.

When a model is simulated, output results should be analyzed in order to detect the bottleneck and to be able to propose enhancement procedures. The studied ED is simulated after adding a new type of resources, called Facilities. Facilities include any non-human resources such as beds, with all the needed accessories required to deliver patient care. The new modified model is simulated during normal flow of patients and catastrophic events where a high surge of patients occurs; this is presented in Chapter 3. Optimization of these two scenarios is performed later using OptQuest tool in Arena in order to propose new resource allocations and thus improve the system (refer to Chapter 5). The improvement reflects a decrease in patient LoS, a decrease in resource utilization rate, and an increase in revenue. Therefore, the optimization proposed increases patient, owner, and resource satisfaction.

Also in Chapter 5, as part of the optimization phase, a reward system is proposed that can be applied to any queueing system such as healthcare, theatre, etc. This generic algorithm emphasizes the balance between patient, owner, and resource satisfaction in order to guarantee efficient performance of the system. A new optimization algorithm is proposed, called Maximum Reward Algorithm (MRA), where the best allocation of resources can be achieved to enhance the system and is always balanced between the three factors of satisfaction: patient, owner, and resource. This algorithm is generic and is applied to the studied ED during normal flow and catastrophic events where efficient outputs result, thus proving the reliability of this approach. The reward system was increased from 50% to 77% and from 7% to 38% for normal flow and catastrophic events respectively.

Decision-makers are to study the proposed enhancement procedures to improve the system under study and decide the ability to apply those scenarios to the real system in order to improve the flow of operation and increase system satisfaction.

All of the work discussed above is integrated in a new platform called AMS and illustrated in Chapter 6. A new programming language for event-based simulation is presented. The language supports the modeling of any system as stages. The resources used are put in what the language calls pools. The language supports the description of topology of the system as connections between stages and pools. The language gives flexibility to choose the necessary distribution for every stage, the type of data passed from one stage to another, and, at the end of execution, the language provides statistics. One of the capabilities of the new proposed language is to perform multiple iterations of simulation to optimize resources needed in the system. This is done through the previously proposed reward system that balances between three satisfaction factors: those of patient, owner, and resource. Accordingly, new resource allocations are suggested for system enhancement. The compiler of the language takes an English-like text and converts it into a Petri net. The execution of the Petri net does not require any familiarity with the Petri net itself. Rather, the user describes the system in English-like statements and the compiler understands and converts the text into a Petri net structure. A case study is presented using this platform and optimization is applied in order to improve the main performance measures of the emergency department of the studied hospital located in the Middle East: patient length of stay (LoS), utilization rates, and queues waiting times. Finally, the socio-economic benefits of the newly proposed platform, AMS, are discussed in Chapter 6.

7.2 Future Work

As part of future work, there is a potential to integrate the platform with process learning capabilities through reading log files. Process learning consists of building a model of the process through reading a log of events. As a new feature of the proposed software, for every experiment, statistics will be saved as records for future comparisons with newly run experiments in order to find the optimization pattern. Other features will be integrated with the software AMS, such as adding the Draw option in order to visualize the system and represent it using a flowchart. More features can be integrated, such as allocating a unit in the hospital, calculating a service cost, collecting patient information, and enabling data security and information privacy by integrating databases. Moreover, transforming the software to a Mobile Application to be easily accessible by any decision-maker anywhere, anytime, is an option for future work.

Also as part of future work, new factors may be introduced to each of the satisfaction equations defining the reward system. For customer satisfaction, more focus will be on considering the quality of service produced by medical resources and considering the level of care and capabilities offered. For owner satisfaction, the short-term equations proposed may be improved to study the long-term investment in applying such equations. For employee satisfaction, a third factor affecting the satisfaction level of employees can be attributed to the working conditions.

7.3 Limitations

Some limitations were faced during this work and are illustrated as follows:

- A single ED was studied from a single country. Nevertheless, this emergency department is very complex since it includes two emergency rooms cooperating together and sharing resources. One ER is for public services and the other for private services.
- Some limitations were faced with the survey designed during the data collection phase. "It is related to the excluded patients: high-acuity cases, very old patients, or babies and patients not willing to participate.
- Measuring patient satisfaction is a very complex endeavor and there is no validated 100% instrument to do so. Thus, the measure of overall satisfaction may not fully capture the real situation. Nevertheless, the surveyed outcome measures resulted in responses and output statistics similar to previous studies" [Oueida et al. (2018b)].

The information in this chapter appears in the following journal/book chapter, all authored by Soraia Oueida and reprinted by permission of the publisher:

- *Handbook of Research on Data Science for Effective Healthcare Practice and Administration*, Copyright © 2017, IGI Global, [Oueida et al. (2017b)]
- *Stochastic Methods for Estimating and Problem Solving in Engineering*, Copyright © 2018, IGI Global, [Oueida et al. (2018b)]

Bibliography

A Van Duren. Patient warming plays a significant role in patient satisfaction, clinical outcomes. *Infect Control Today*, 12(6), 2008.

Adam B Landman, Steven L Bernstein, Allen L Hsiao, and Rani A Desai. Emergency department information system adoption in the United States. *Academic Emergency Medicine*, 17(5):536–544, 2010.

Aditi Naidu. Factors affecting patient satisfaction and healthcare quality. *International Journal of Health Care Quality Assurance*, 22(4):366–381, 2009.

Adrian Bagust, Michael Place, and John W Posnett. Dynamics of bed use in accommodating emergency admissions: stochastic simulation model. *British Medical Journal*, 319(7203):155–158, 1999.

Adriana M Alvarez and Martha A Centeno. Enhancing simulation models for emergency rooms using VBA. In *Simulation Conference Proceedings, 1999 Winter*, volume 2, pages 1685–1693. IEEE, 1999.

Akshay Venkitasubramanian, et al. Object-oriented framework for healthcare simulation. 2012.

Alan Wilson, Valarie A Zeithaml, Mary Jo Bitner, and Dwayne D Gremler. *Services Marketing: Integrating Customer Focus across the Firm*. McGraw Hill, 2012.

Albert Lee, Fei-lung Lau, Clarke B Hazlett, Chak-wah Kam, Patrick Wong, Tai-wai Wong, et al. Measuring the inappropriate utilization of accident and emergency services? *International Journal of Health Care Quality Assurance*, 12(7):287–292, 1999.

ALBK Abbas. Simulation models of emergency department in hospital. *Journal of Engineering and Development*, 18(2), 2014.

Alexander Komashie and Ali Mousavi. Modeling emergency departments using discrete event simulation techniques. In *Proceedings of the 37th Conference on Winter Simulation*, pages 2681–2685. Winter Simulation Conference, 2005.

Ali Azadeh, Fatemeh Rouhollah, Fatemeh Davoudpour, and Iraj Mohammadfam. Fuzzy modelling and simulation of an emergency department for improvement of nursing schedules with noisy and uncertain inputs. *International Journal of Services and Operations Management*, 15(1):58–77, 2013.

Alix JE Carter and Alecs H Chochinov. A systematic review of the impact of nurse practitioners on cost, quality of care, satisfaction and wait times in the emergency department. *Canadian Journal of Emergency Medicine*, 9(4):286–295, 2007.

Allan Wiinamaki and Rainer Dronzek. Emergency departments I: using simulation in the architectural concept phase of an emergency department design. In *Proceedings of the 35th Conference on Winter Simulation: Driving Innovation*, pages 1912–1916. Winter Simulation Conference, 2003.

Alon Halevy, Peter Norvig, and Fernando Pereira. The unreasonable effectiveness of data. *IEEE Intelligent Systems*, 24(2):8–12, 2009.

American Nurses Association, et al. *Analysis of American Nurses Association Staffing Survey*. Warwick, RI: Cornerstone Communications Group, 2001.

Amita J Joshi. *Study on the effect of different arrival patterns on an emergency department's capacity using discrete event simulation*. PhD thesis, Kansas State University, 2008.

Andrew M Hay, Edwin C Valentin, and Rienk A Bijlsma. Modeling emergency care in hospitals: a paradox-the patient should not drive the process. In *Simulation Conference, 2006. WSC 06. Proceedings of the Winter*, pages 439–445. IEEE, 2006.

Andrew M Thomas. Patient satisfaction: measuring the art of medicine. *JAMA*, 280(24):2127D–2127D, 1998.

Anne-Marie Audet, Michelle M Doty, Jordan Peugh, Jamil Shamasdin, Kinga Zapert, and Stephen Schoenbaum. Information technologies: when will they make it into physicians' black bags? *Medscape General Medicine*, 6(4), 2004.

Ashis Banerjee, David Mbamalu, and Geoff Hinchley. The impact of process re-engineering on patient throughput in emergency departments in the UK. *International Journal of Emergency Medicine*, 1(3):189–192, 2008.

Ashwin Belle, Raghuram Thiagarajan, SM Soroushmehr, Fatemeh Navidi, Daniel A Beard, and Kayvan Najarian. Big data analytics in healthcare. *BioMed Research International*, 2015, 2015.

Averill M Law. How to build valid and credible simulation models. In *Simulation Conference (WSC), Proceedings of the 2009 Winter*, pages 24–33. IEEE, 2009.

B Jerbi and H Kamoun. Using simulation and goal programming to reschedule emergency department doctors' shifts: case of a Tunisian hospital. *Journal of Simulation*, 3(4):211–219, 2009.

Babar T Shaikh. Quality of health care: an absolute necessity for patient satisfaction. *Journal of the Pakistan Medical Association*, 55(11):515–516, 2005.

Basit Chaudhry, Jerome Wang, Shinyi Wu, Margaret Maglione, Walter Mojica, Elizabeth Roth, et al. Systematic review: impact of health information technology on quality, efficiency, and costs of medical care. *Annals of Internal Medicine*, 144(10):742–752, 2006.

Benjamin C Sun, Renee Y Hsia, Robert E Weiss, David Zingmond, Li-Jung Liang, Weijuan Han, et al. Effect of emergency department crowding on outcomes of admitted patients. *Annals of Emergency Medicine*, 61(6):605–611, 2013.

BH Rowe, K Bond, MB Ospina, S Blitz, M Schull, G Innes, et al. Emergency department overcrowding in Canada: what are the issues and what can be done. *Technology Overview*, 21, 2006.

BM Richmond, P Vescuso, and S Peterson. iThink™ software manuals. *High Performance Systems*, 145, 1990.

Bradley C Strunk and Peter J Cunningham. Treading water: Americans' access to needed medical care, 1997–2001. *Tracking Report* (1):1–6, 2002.

Brigitte Jaumard, Frederic Semet, and Tsevi Vovor. A generalized linear programming model for nurse scheduling. *European Journal of Operational Research*, 107(1):1–18, 1998.

Bruce E Hillner, Thomas J Smith, and Christopher E Desch. Hospital and physician volume or specialization and outcomes in cancer treatment: importance in quality of cancer care. *Journal of Clinical Oncology*, 18(11):2327–2340, 2000.

Byron J Buckley, Edward M Castillo, James P Killeen, David A Guss, and Theodore C Chan. Impact of an express admit unit on emergency department length of stay. *Journal of Emergency Medicine*, 39(5):669–673, 2010.

C Carolyn Thiedke. What do we really know about patient satisfaction? *Family Practice Management*, 14(1):33, 2007.

C Doukas, T Pliakas, and I Maglogiannis. Mobile healthcare information management utilizing cloud computing and android OS. In *2010 Annual International Conference of the IEEE Engineering in Medicine and Biology*, pages 1037–1040, August 2010. doi: 10.1109/IEMBS.2010.5628061.

C Gómez-Vaquero, A Salazar Soler, A Juan Pastor, JR Perez Mas, J Jacob Rodriguez, and X Corbella Virós. Efficacy of a holding unit to reduce access block and attendance pressure in the emergency department. *Emergency Medicine Journal*, 26(8):571–572, 2009.

C Laroque, J Himmelspach, R Pasupathy, O Rose, and AM Uhrmacher. Simulation with data scarcity: developing a simulation model of a hospital emergency department. In *WSC'12 Proceedings of the Winter Simulation Conference*, 2012.

C Rieffe, P Oosterveld, D Wijkel, and C Wiefferink. Reasons why patients bypass their GP to visit a hospital emergency department. *Accident and Emergency Nursing*, 7(4):217–225, 1999.

Carl Anderson, C Butcher, and Amanda Moreno. *Emergency Department Patient Flow Simulation at Health Alliance*. Worcester, MA: Worcester Polytechnic Institute, 2010.

Charles E Saunders, Paul K Makens, and Larry J Leblanc. Modeling emergency department operations using advanced computer simulation systems. *Annals of Emergency Medicine*, 18(2):134–140, 1989.

Charles Johnson, Ram Shanmugam, Lance Roberts, Stephen Zinkgraf, Maria Young, Lana Cameron, et al. Linking lean healthcare to six sigma: an emergency department case study. In *IIE Annual Conference. Proceedings*, page 1. Institute of Industrial and Systems Engineers (IISE), 2004.

Chongsun Oh, April M Novotny, Pamela L Carter, Ray K Ready, Diane D Campbell, and Maureen C Leckie. Use of a simulation-based decision support tool to improve emergency department through-put. *Operations Research for Health Care*, 9:29–39, 2016.

Christine A Caligtan, Diane L Carroll, Ann C Hurley, Ronna Gersh-Zaremski, and Patricia C Dykes. Bedside information technology to support patient-centered care. *International Journal of Medical Informatics*, 81(7):442–451, 2012.

Christine Duguay and Fatah Chetouane. Modeling and improving emergency department systems using discrete event simulation. *Simulation*, 83(4):311–320, 2007.

CJT Van Uden, RAG Winkens, GJ Wesseling, HFJM Crebolder, and CP Van Schayck. Use of out of hours services: a comparison between two organisations. *Emergency Medicine Journal*, 20(2):184–187, 2003.

CO Rolim, FL Koch, CB Westphall, J Werner, A Fracalossi, and GS Salvador. A cloud computing solution for patient's data collection in health care institutions. In *2010 Second International Conference on eHealth, Telemedicine, and Social Medicine*, pages 95–99, February 2010. doi: 10.1109/eTELEMED.2010.19.

Committee on the Future of Emergency Care in the US Health System Institute of Medicine. The future of emergency care in the United States health system. *Annals of Emergency Medicine*, 48(2):115, 2006.

Craig F Feied, Mark S Smith, and Jonathan A Handler. Keynote address: medical informatics and emergency medicine. *Academic Emergency Medicine*, 11(11):1118–1126, 2004.

Cristian Mahulea, Liliana Mahulea, Juan-Manuel García-Soriano, and José-Manuel Colom. Petri nets with resources for modeling primary healthcare systems. In *System Theory, Control and Computing (ICSTCC), 2014 18th International Conference*, pages 639–644. IEEE, 2014.

D Miller. *Going Lean in Health Care*. IHI Innovation Series White Paper. Cambridge, MA: Institute for Healthcare Improvement, 2005.

Daniel J Pallin, Ashley F Sullivan, Rainu Kaushal, and Carlos A Camargo. Health information technology in us emergency departments. *International Journal of Emergency Medicine*, 3(3):181–185, 2010.

Dave R Eitel, Scott E Rudkin, M Albert Malvehy, James P Killeen, and Jesse M Pines. Improving service quality by understanding emergency department flow: a white paper and position statement prepared for the American academy of emergency medicine. *Journal of Emergency Medicine*, 38(1):70–79, 2010.

David C Lane, Camilla Monefeldt, and Johnathan V Rosenhead. Looking in the wrong place for healthcare improvements: a system dynamics study of an accident and emergency department. *Journal of the Operational Research Society*, 51(5):518–531, 2000.

David Morgareidge, CAI Hui, and JIA Jun. Performance-driven design with the support of digital tools: applying discrete event simulation and space syntax on the design of the emergency department. *Frontiers of Architectural Research*, 3(3):250–264, 2014.

David Sinreich and Ola Jabali. Staggered work shifts: a way to downsize and restructure an emergency department workforce yet maintain current operational performance. *Health Care Management Science*, 10(3):293–308, 2007.

David Sinreich and Yariv Marmor. Emergency department operations: the basis for developing a simulation tool. *IIE Transactions*, 37(3):233–245, 2005.

Deborah J Medeiros, Eric Swenson, and Christopher DeFlitch. Improving patient flow in a hospital emergency department. In *Proceedings of the 40th Conference on Winter Simulation*, pages 1526–1531. Winter Simulation Conference, 2008.

Devon M Herrick, Linda Gorman, and John C Goodman. *Health Information Technology: Benefits and Problems*. Dallas, TX: National Center for Policy Analysis, 2010.

Donald M Berwick and Andrew D Hackbarth. Eliminating waste in us health care. *JAMA*, 307(14):1513–1516, 2012.

Drew B Richardson. Increase in patient mortality at 10 days associated with emergency department over-crowding. *Medical Journal of Australia*, 184(5):213–216, 2006.

Edward L Hannan, Richard J Giglio, and Randall S Sadowski. A simulation analysis of a hospital emergency department. In *Proceedings of the 7th Conference on Winter Simulation*, volume 1, pages 379–388. ACM, 1974.

Eileen T Lake, Jingjing Shang, Susan Klaus, and Nancy E Dunton. Patient falls: association with hospital magnet status and nursing unit staffing. *Research in Nursing & Health*, 33(5):413–425, 2010.

Emilio Scotti and Filomena Pietrantonio. The hospital internal medicine specialist today: a literature review and strength, weaknesses, opportunity, threats (SWOT) analysis to develop a working proposal. *Italian Journal of Medicine*, 7(4):278–286, 2013.

Erik MW Kolb, Sebastian Schoening, Jordan Peck, and Taesik Lee. Reducing emergency department overcrowding: five patient buffer concepts in comparison. In *Proceedings of the 40th Conference on Winter Simulation*, pages 1516–1525. Winter Simulation Conference, 2008.

Eui H Park, Jinsuh Park, Celestine Ntuen, Daebeom Kim, and Kendall Johnson. Forecast driven simulation model for service quality improvement of the emergency department in the Moses H. Cone Memorial Hospital. *Asian Journal on Quality*, 9(3):1–14, 2008.

F Cowdell, B Lees, and M Wade. Discharge planning. Armchair fan. *The Health Service Journal*, 112(5807):28–29, 2002.

F Subash, F Dunn, B McNicholl, and J Marlow. Team triage improves emergency department efficiency. *Emergency Medicine Journal*, 21(5):542–544, 2004.

Farid Kadri, Fouzi Harrou, Sondès Chaabane, and Christian Tahon. Time series modelling and forecasting of emergency department overcrowding. *Journal of Medical Systems*, 38(9):107, 2014.

Fazel Anjomshoa, Moayad Aloqaily, Burak Kantarci, Melike Erol-Kantarci, and Stephanie Schuckers. Social behaviometrics for personalized devices in the internet of things era. *IEEE Access*, 5:12199–12213, 2017.

Felipe F Baesler, Hector E Jahnsen, and Mahal DaCosta. Emergency departments I: the use of simulation and design of experiments for estimating maximum capacity in an emergency room. In *Proceedings of the 35th Conference on Winter Simulation: Driving Innovation*, pages 1903–1906. Winter Simulation Conference, 2003.

Flavio Bonomi, Rodolfo Milito, Jiang Zhu, and Sateesh Addepalli. Fog computing and its role in the internet of things. In *Proceedings of the First Edition of the MCC Workshop on Mobile Cloud Computing, MCC'12*, pages 13–16. New York, NY, ACM, 2012. ISBN 978-1-4503-1519-7. doi: 10.1145/2342509.2342513. http://doi.acm.org/10.1145/2342509.2342513.

Florentino Rico, Ehsan Salari, and Grisselle Centeno. Emergency departments nurse allocation to face a pandemic influenza outbreak. In *Simulation Conference, 2007 Winter*, pages 1292–1298. IEEE, 2007.

Francis Diebold. A personal perspective on the origin (s) and development of 'big data': The phenomenon, the term, and the discipline, second version. *PIER Working Paper No. 13-003*, 2012.

Frederic W Selck and Sandra L Decker. Health information technology adoption in the emergency department. *Health Services Research*, 51(1):32–47, 2016.

Gabor D Kelen and James J Scheulen. Commentary: emergency department crowding as an ethical issue. *Academic Emergency Medicine*, 14(8):751–754, 2007.

Gary C Geelhoed and Nicholas H de Klerk. Emergency department overcrowding, mortality and the 4-hour rule in Western Australia. *Medical Journal of Australia*, 196(2):122–126, 2012.

Georges Weil, Kamel Heus, Patrice Francois, and Marc Poujade. Constraint programming for nurse scheduling. *IEEE Engineering in Medicine and Biology Magazine*, 14(4):417–422, 1995.

Ghazwan Toma, Wayne Triner, and Louise-Ann McNutt. Patient satisfaction as a function of emergency department previsit expectations. *Annals of Emergency Medicine*, 54(3):360–367, 2009.

Gillian Mould, John Bowers, Colin Dewar, and Elizabeth McGugan. Assessing the impact of systems modeling in the redesign of an emergency department. *Health Systems*, 2(1):3–10, 2013.

Hainan Guo, David Goldsman, Kwok-Leung Tsui, Yu Zhou, and Shui-Yee Wong. Using simulation and optimisation to characterise durations of emergency department service times with incomplete data. *International Journal of Production Research*, 54(21):6494–6511, 2016.

Hajo A Reijers. *Design and Control of Workflow Processes: Business Process Management for the Service Industry*. Springer-Verlag, 2003.

Hamidreza Eskandari, Mohammadali Riyahifard, Shahrzad Khosravi, and Christopher D Geiger. Improving the emergency department performance using simulation and MCDM methods. In *Proceedings of the Winter Simulation Conference*, pages 1211–1222. Winter Simulation Conference, 2011.

Heather L Farley, Kevin M Baumlin, Azita G Hamedani, Dickson S Cheung, Michael R Edwards, Drew C Fuller, et al. Quality and safety implications of emergency department information systems. *Annals of Emergency Medicine*, 62(4):399–407, 2013.

Huguette Beaulieu, Jacques A Ferland, Bernard Gendron, and Philippe Michelon. A mathematical programming approach for scheduling physicians in the emergency room. *Health Care Management Science*, 3(3):193–200, 2000.

Hui Cao and Simin Huang. Principles of scarce medical resource allocation in natural disaster relief: a simulation approach. *Medical Decision Making*, 32(3):470–476, 2012.

Iain Robertson-Steel. Evolution of triage systems. *Emergency Medicine Journal*, 23(2):154–155, 2006.

Ibrahim Al-Kattan. Disaster recovery plan development for the emergency department-case study. *Public Administration and Management*, 14(1):75, 2009.

Ilham Berrada. Planification d'horaires du personnel infirmier dans un etablissement hospitalier. 1996.

Ine Borghans, Sophia M Kleefstra, Rudolf B Kool, and Gert P Westert. Is the length of stay in hospital correlated with patient satisfaction? *International Journal for Quality in Health Care*, 24(5):443–451, 2012.

J Munro, S Mason, and J Nicholl. Effectiveness of measures to reduce emergency department waiting times: a natural experiment. *Emergency Medicine Journal*, 23(1):35–39, 2006.

J Wan, C Zou, S Ullah, CF Lai, M Zhou, and X Wang. Cloud-enabled wireless body area networks for pervasive healthcare. *IEEE Network*, 27(5):56, September 2013. ISSN 0890-8044. doi: 10.1109/MNET.2013.6616116.

James O Westgard and Sten A Westgard. Six sigma quality management system and design of risk-based statistical quality control. *Clinics in Laboratory Medicine*, 37(1):85–96, 2017.

James R Swisher, Sheldon H Jacobson, J Brian Jun, and Osman Balci. Modeling and analyzing a physician clinic environment using discrete-event (visual) simulation. *Computers & Operations Research*, 28(2):105–125, 2001.

Jay Devore, Nicholas Farnum, and Jimmy Doi. *Applied Statistics for Engineers and Scientists*. Nelson Education, 2013.

JG Cronin and J Wright. Breach avoidance facilitator–managing the A&E 4-hour target. *Accident and Emergency Nursing*, 14(1):43–48, 2006.

John C Moskop, David P Sklar, Joel M Geiderman, Raquel M Schears, and Kelly J Bookman. Emergency department crowding, part 2 – barriers to reform and strategies to overcome them. *Annals of Emergency Medicine*, 53(5):612–617, 2009.

John S O'Shea. *The Crisis in America's Emergency Rooms and What Can Be Done*. Washington, DC: Heritage Foundation, 2007.

Jomon Aliyas Paul and Govind Hariharan. Hospital capacity planning for efficient disaster mitigation during a bioterrorist attack. In *Proceedings of the 39th Conference on Winter Simulation: 40 Years! The Best Is Yet to Come*, pages 1139–1147. IEEE Press, 2007.

Jomon Aliyas Paul and Li Lin. Models for improving patient throughput and waiting at hospital emergency departments. *Journal of Emergency Medicine*, 43(6):1119–1126, 2012.

Jonghun Park. *Structural Analysis and Control of Resource Allocation Systems Using Petri Nets*. Georgia Institute of Technology, 2000.

José M Quintana, Nerea González, Amaia Bilbao, Felipe Aizpuru, Antonio Escobar, Cristóbal Esteban, et al. Predictors of patient satisfaction with hospital health care. *BMC Health Services Research*, 6(1):102, 2006.

JR Villamizar, FC Coelli, WCA Pereira, and RMVR Almeida. Discrete-event computer simulation methods in the optimisation of a physiotherapy clinic. *Physiotherapy*, 97(1):71–77, 2011.

Judy A Lowthian, Andrea J Curtis, Peter A Cameron, Johannes U Stoelwinder, Matthew W Cooke, and John J McNeil. Systematic review of trends in emergency department attendances: an Australian perspective. *Emergency Medicine Journal*, 28:373–377, 2011.

Junfei Huang, Boaz Carmeli, and Avishai Mandelbaum. Control of patient flow in emergency departments, or multiclass queues with deadlines and feedback. *Operations Research*, 63(4):892–908, 2015.

Katy Letham and Alasdair Gray. The four-hour target in the NHS emergency departments: a critical comment. *Emergencias*, 24(1): 69–72, 2012.

Kimberly D Johnson and Chris Winkelman. The effect of emergency department crowding on patient outcomes: a literature review. *Advanced Emergency Nursing Journal*, 33(1):39–54, 2011.

Kris Siddharthan, Walter J Jones, and James A Johnson. A priority queuing model to reduce waiting times in emergency care. *International Journal of Health Care Quality Assurance*, 9(5):10–16, 1996.

L Chia and WD Lin. Simulation study of patient arrivals and doctors scheduling in a children's emergency department. In *2016 IEEE International Conference on Industrial Engineering and Engineering Management (IEEM)*, pages 321–325. IEEE, 2016.

L Dunn. Four best practices for improving emergency department results. *The Studer Group Newsletter*, 2010.

Leigh Kinsman, Robert Champion, Geraldine Lee, Mary Martin, Kevin Masman, Elizabeth May, et al. Assessing the impact of streaming in a regional emergency department. *Emergency Medicine Australasia*, 20(3):221–227, 2008.

Lisa Patvivatsiri. A simulation model for bioterrorism preparedness in an emergency room. In *Proceedings of the 38th Conference on Winter Simulation*, pages 501–508. Winter Simulation Conference, 2006.

Lynne P Baldwin, Tillal Eldabi, and Ray J Paul. Simulation in healthcare management: a soft approach (MAPIU). *Simulation Modelling Practice and Theory*, 12(7–8):541–557, 2004.

M Aloqaily, B Kantarci, and HT Mouftah. Multiagent/multiobjective interaction game system for service provisioning in vehicular cloud. *IEEE Access*, 4:3153–3168, 2016. doi: 10.1109/ACCESS.2016.2575038.

M Dotoli, MP Fanti, G Iacobellis, L Martino, AM Moretti, and W Ukovich. Modeling and management of a hospital department via petri nets. In *2010 IEEE Workshop on Health Care Management (WHCM)*, pages 1–6. IEEE, 2010.

Manuel D Rossetti, Gregory F Trzcinski, and Scott A Syverud. Emergency department simulation and determination of optimal attending physician staffing schedules. In *Simulation Conference Proceedings, 1999 Winter*, volume 2, pages 1532–1540. IEEE, 1999.

Marelys L García, Martha A Centeno, Camille Rivera, and Nina DeCario. Reducing time in an emergency room via a fast-track. In *Proceedings of the 27th Conference on Winter Simulation*, pages 1048–1053. IEEE Computer Society, 1995.

Maria Pia Fanti, Agostino Marcello Mangini, Walter Ukovic, Jean-Jacques Lesage, and Kevin Viard. A petri net model of an integrated system for the health care at home management. In *2014 IEEE International Conference on Automation Science and Engineering (CASE)*, pages 582–587. IEEE, 2014.

Mark R Chassin and Robert W Galvin. The urgent need to improve health care quality: institute of medicine national roundtable on health care quality. *JAMA*, 280(11):1000–1005, 1998.

Martha A Centeno, Ronald Giachetti, Richard Linn, and Abdullah M Ismail. Emergency departments II: a simulation-ILP based tool for scheduling ER staff. In *Proceedings of the 35th Conference on Winter Simulation: Driving Innovation*, pages 1930–1938. Winter Simulation Conference, 2003.

Martijn Anneveld, Christien Van Der Linden, Diana Grootendorst, and Martha Galli-Leslie. Measuring emergency department crowding in an inner city hospital in the Netherlands. *International Journal of Emergency Medicine*, 6(1):21, 2013.

Martin J Miller, David M Ferrin, and Marcia G Messer. Fixing the emergency department: a transformational journey with EDSIM. In *Proceedings of the 36th Conference on Winter Simulation*, pages 1988–1993. Winter Simulation Conference, 2004.

Mary Martin, Robert Champion, Leigh Kinsman, and Kevin Masman. Mapping patient flow in a regional Australian emergency department: a model driven approach. *International Emergency Nursing*, 19(2):75–85, 2011.

Massimo Esposito, Aniello Minutolo, Rosario Megna, Manolo Forastiere, Mario Magliulo, and Giuseppe De Pietro. A smart mobile, self-configuring, context-aware architecture for personal health monitoring. *Engineering Applications of Artificial Intelligence*, 67:136–156, 2018. ISSN 0952-1976. doi: https://doi.org/10.1016/j.engappai.2017.09.019. http://www.sciencedirect.com/science/ article/pii/ S0952197617302336.

Matthew Cooke, Joanne D Fisher, Jeremy Dale, Eileen McLeod, Ala Szczepura, Paul Walley, et al. Reducing attendances and waits in emergency departments: a systematic review of present innovations. *Report to the National Co-ordinating Centre for NHS Service Delivery and Organisation R & D (NCCSDO)*, 2004.

ME Lim, A Worster, R Goeree, and JE Tarride. PRM28 physicians as pseudo-agents in a hospital emergency department discrete event simulation. *Value in Health*, 15(4):A163, 2012b.

Melissa L McCarthy, Dominik Aronsky, Ian D Jones, James R Miner, Roger A Band, Jill M Baren, et al. The emergency department occupancy rate: a simple measure of emergency department crowding? *Annals of Emergency Medicine*, 51(1):15–24, 2008.

MH Jansen-Vullers and HA Reijers. Business process redesign at a mental healthcare institute: a coloured petri net approach. In *Proceedings of the Sixth Workshop and Tutorial on Practical Use of Coloured Petri Nets and the CPN Tools (PB-576)*, pages 21–38, 2005.

Michael Armbrust, Armando Fox, Rean Griffith, Anthony D Joseph, Randy Katz, Andy Konwinski, et al. A view of cloud computing. *Communications of the ACM*, 53(4):50–58, 2010.

Michael J Bullard, Cristina Villa-Roel, Kenneth Bond, Michael Vester, Brian R Holroyd, and Brian H Rowe. Tracking emergency department overcrowding in a tertiary care academic institution. *Healthcare Quarterly*, 12(3): 99–106, 2009.

Michael J Schull, John-Paul Szalai, Brian Schwartz, and Donald A Redelmeier. Emergency department overcrowding following systematic hospital restructuring trends at twenty hospitals over ten years. *Academic Emergency Medicine*, 8(11):1037–1043, 2001.

Michael J Schull, Marian J Vermeulen, Therese A Stukel, Astrid Guttmann, Chad A Leaver, Brian H Rowe, et al. Evaluating the effect of clinical decision units on patient flow in seven Canadian emergency departments. *Academic Emergency Medicine*, 19(7):828–836, 2012.

Michael J Schull, Marian Vermeulen, Graham Slaughter, Laurie Morrison, and Paul Daly. Emergency department crowding and thrombolysis delays in acute myocardial infarction. *Annals of Emergency Medicine*, 44(6):577–585, 2004.

Michael Sipser. *Introduction to the Theory of Computation*. Boston, MA: Thomson Course Technology, 2006.

Michael W Carter and Sophie D Lapierre. Scheduling emergency room physicians. *Health Care Management Science*, 4(4):347–360, 2001.

Miguel A Ortiz Barrios and Heriberto Felizzola Jiménez. Use of six sigma methodology to reduce appointment lead-time in obstetrics outpatient department. *Journal of Medical Systems*, 40(10):220, 2016.

Miquel Àngel Piera, Mercedes Narciso, Antoni Guasch, and Daniel Riera. Optimization of logistic and manufacturing systems through simulation: a colored petri net-based methodology. *Simulation*, 80(3):121–129, 2004.

Mohamed A Ahmed and Talal M Alkhamis. Simulation optimization for an emergency department healthcare unit in Kuwait. *European Journal of Operational Research*, 198(3):936–942, 2009.

Mohammadreza Hojat, Daniel Z Louis, Fred W Markham, Richard Wender, Carol Rabinowitz, and Joseph S Gonnella. Physicians' empathy and clinical outcomes for diabetic patients. *Academic Medicine*, 86(3):359–364, 2011.

Morgan E Lim, Tim Nye, James M Bowen, Jerry Hurley, Ron Goeree, and Jean-Eric Tarride. Mathematical modeling: the case of emergency department waiting times. *International Journal of Technology Assessment in Health Care*, 28(2):93–109, 2012a.

Muhammet Gul and Ali Fuat Guneri. A comprehensive review of emergency department simulation applications for normal and disaster conditions. *Computers & Industrial Engineering*, 83:327–344, 2015.

Mu-Hsing Alex Kuo. Opportunities and challenges of cloud computing to improve health care services. *Journal of Medical Internet Research*, 13(3):e67, September 2011. doi: 10.2196/jmir.1867. http://www.jmir.org/2011/3/e67/.

Murat M Günal and Michael Pidd. Discrete event simulation for performance modelling in health care: a review of the literature. *Journal of Simulation*, 4(1):42–51, 2010.

Murat M Gunal and Michael Pidd. Understanding accident and emergency department performance using simulation. In *Proceedings of the 38th Conference on Winter Simulation*, pages 446–452. Winter Simulation Conference, 2006.

N Hellmich. Aging population making more visits to the doctor's. *USA Today*, 2008, Retrieved from http://www.usatoday.com/news/health/2008-08-06-er_N.htm. [Accessed 7 August 2008].

Nabeel Mandahawi, Mohammed Shurrab, Sameh Al-Shihabi, Abdallah A Abdallah, and Yousuf M Alfarah. Utilizing six sigma to improve the processing time: a simulation study at an emergency department. *Journal of Industrial and Production Engineering*, 34(7):495–503, 2017.

Namita Jayaprakash, Ronan O'Sullivan, Tareg Bey, Suleman S Ahmed, and Shahram Lotfipour. Crowding and delivery of healthcare in emergency departments: the European perspective. *Western Journal of Emergency Medicine*, 10(4):233, 2009.

Nan Xiao, Raj Sharman, HR Rao, and Sumant Dutta. A simulation-based study for managing hospital emergency department's capacity in extreme events. *International Journal of Business Excellence*, 5(1–2):140–154, 2012a.

Nathan R Hoot, Chuan Zhou, Ian Jones, and Dominik Aronsky. Measuring and forecasting emergency department crowding in real time. *Annals of Emergency Medicine*, 49(6):747–755, 2007.

Navid Izady and Dave Worthington. Setting staffing requirements for time dependent queueing networks: the case of accident and emergency departments. *European Journal of Operational Research*, 219(3):531–540, 2012.

Neha Dubey and Sangeeta Vishwakarma. Cloud computing in healthcare. *International Journal of Current Trends in Engineering and Research*, 2(5):211–216, 2016.

Nitin Gupta. How IoT can significantly improve healthcare in the context of smart city. Industrial Internet Consortium, 1–9, 2017.

Nomie Eriksson. Hospital management from a high reliability organizational change perspective: a Swedish case on lean and six sigma. *International Journal of Public Sector Management*, 30(1):67–84, 2017.

Nurul Fadly Habidin, Noor Zakiah Yahya, and Mohd Fahmi Shukur Ramli. Using LSS DMAIC in improving emergency department waiting time. *International Journal of Pharmaceutical Sciences Review and Research*, 35(2):151–155, 2015.

O Keegan, V McDarby, A Tansey, and H McGee. Community involvement in A/E satisfaction survey, 2003.

O Miro, M Sanchez, G Espinosa, B Coll-Vinent, E Bragulat, and J Milla. Analysis of patient flow in the emergency department and the effect of an extensive reorganisation. *Emergency Medicine Journal*, 20(2):143–148, 2003.

Ofer Shimrat. Cloud computing and healthcare. *San Diego Physician.org*, pages 26–29, 2009.

Olanrewaju A Soremekun, James K Takayesu, and Stephen J Bohan. Framework for analyzing wait times and other factors that impact patient satisfaction in the emergency department. *Journal of Emergency Medicine*, 41(6):686–692, 2011.

Omar Rado, Benedetta Lupia, Janny MY Leung, Yong-Hong Kuo, and Colin A Graham. Using simulation to analyze patient flows in a hospital emergency department in Hong Kong. In *Proceedings of the International Conference on Health Care Systems Engineering*, pages 289–301. Springer, 2014.

P Meredith and C Wood. The development of the royal college of surgeons of England's patient satisfaction audit service. *Journal of Quality in Clinical Practice*, 15(2):67–74, 1995.

PA Sommers, R Dropik, G Heilman, and T Vaughan. Patient satisfaction in 21st century medicine: revolution or evolution? *The Journal of Medical Practice Management*, 23(3):157–162, 2007.

Paul D Cleary and Barbara J McNeil. Patient satisfaction as an indicator of quality care. *Inquiry*, 25(1):25–36, 1988.

PC Tang, et al. *Key Capabilities of an Electronic Health Record System*. Washington, DC: Institute of Medicine of the National Academies, 2003.

Pengfei Yi, Santhosh K George, Jomon Aliyas Paul, and Li Lin. Hospital capacity planning for disaster emergency management. *Socio-Economic Planning Sciences*, 44(3):151–160, 2010.

Peter A Cameron. Hospital overcrowding: a threat to patient safety? *Medical Journal of Australia*, 184(5):203, 2006.

Peter S Satterthwaite and Carol J Atkinson. Using 'reverse triage' to create hospital surge capacity: Royal Darwin hospital's response to the Ashmore Reef disaster. *Emergency Medicine Journal*, 29(2):160–162, 2012.

Philip Yoon, Ivan Steiner, and Gilles Reinhardt. Analysis of factors influencing length of stay in the emergency department. *Canadian Journal of Emergency Medicine*, 5(3):155–161, 2003.

PJ Torcson. Patient satisfaction: the hospitalist's role. *The Hospitalist*, 23(4):25, 2005.

Rafael Tolosana-Calasanz, José Ángel Bañares, and José-Manuel Colom. Towards petri net-based economical analysis for streaming applications executed over cloud infrastructures. In Jörn Altmann,

Kurt Vanmechelen, and Omer F Rana, editors, *Economics of Grids, Clouds, Systems, and Services*, pages 189–205, Cham: Springer International Publishing, 2014. ISBN 978-3-319-14609-6.

Richard J Holden. Lean thinking in emergency departments: a critical review. *Annals of Emergency Medicine*, 57(3):265–278, 2011.

Riyad B Abu-Laban. The junkyard dogs find their teeth: addressing the crisis of admitted patients in Canadian emergency departments. *Canadian Journal of Emergency Medicine*, 8(6):388–391, 2006.

Robert A Berenson, Sylvia Kuo, and Jessica H May. Medical malpractice liability crisis meets markets: stress in unexpected places. *Issue Brief (Center for Studying Health System Change)*, 68:1–7, 2003.

Robert Shesser, Mark Smith, Sherry Adams, Ron Walls, and Mary Paxton. The effectiveness of an organized emergency department follow-up system. *Annals of Emergency Medicine*, 15(8):911–915, 1986.

Robert W Derlet and John R Richards. Overcrowding in the nation's emergency departments: complex causes and disturbing effects. *Annals of Emergency Medicine*, 35(1):63–68, 2000.

Robert W Derlet, John R Richards, and Richard L Kravitz. Frequent overcrowding in us emergency departments. *Academic Emergency Medicine*, 8(2):151–155, 2001.

Roberto Forero, Kenneth M Hillman, Sally McCarthy, Daniel M Fatovich, Anthony P Joseph, and Drew B Richardson. Access block and ED overcrowding. *Emergency Medicine Australasia*, 22(2):119–135, 2010.

Roger Bolus and Jennifer Pitts. Patient satisfaction: the indispensable outcome. *Managed Care (Langhorne, PA)*, 8(4):24–28, 1999.

Ruby E Blasak, Darrell W Starks, Wendy S Armel, and Mary C Hayduk. Healthcare process analysis: the use of simulation to evaluate hospital operations between the emergency department and a medical telemetry unit. In *Proceedings of the 35th Conference on Winter Simulation: Driving Innovation*, pages 1887–1893. Winter Simulation Conference, 2003.

Rudy Hung. Hospital nurse scheduling. *Journal of Nursing Administration*, 25(7–8):21–23, 1995.

Safa Otoum, Muayad Brenner, and Hussein T Mouftah. Sensor medium access control (smac)-based epilepsy patients monitoring system. In *2015 IEEE 28th Canadian Conference on Electrical and Computer Engineering (CCECE)*, pages 1109–1114. IEEE, 2015.

Sandra M Schneider, Michael E Gallery, Robert Schafermeyer, and Frank L Zwemer. Emergency department crowding: a point in time. *Annals of Emergency Medicine*, 42(2):167–172, 2003.

Shao-Jen Weng, Bing-Chuin Cheng, Shu Ting Kwong, Lee-Min Wang, and Chun-Yueh Chang. Simulation optimization for emergency department resources allocation. In *Proceedings of the Winter Simulation Conference*, pages 1231–1238. Winter Simulation Conference, 2011.

Sharoda A Paul, Madhu C Reddy, and Christopher J DeFlitch. A systematic review of simulation studies investigating emergency department overcrowding. *Simulation*, 86(8–9):559–571, 2010.

Sheldon H Jacobson, Shane N Hall, and James R Swisher. Discrete-event simulation of health care systems. In *Patient Flow: Reducing Delay in Healthcare Delivery*, pages 211–252. Springer, 2006.

Shirley McIver and Roy A Carr-Hill. *The NHS and Its Customers: A Survey of the Current Practice of Customer Relations. Booklet 1*. York, UK: Centre for Health Economics, University of York, 1989.

Shirley Y Coleman. Six sigma in healthcare. In *Statistical Methods in Healthcare*, pages 286–308, 2012.

Shreeranga Bhat, EV Gijo, and NA Jnanesh. Productivity and performance improvement in the medical records department of a hospital: an application of lean six sigma. *International Journal of Productivity and Performance Management*, 65(1):98–125, 2016.

Simon Samaha, Wendy S Armel, and Darrell W Starks. Emergency departments I: the use of simulation to reduce the length of stay in an emergency department. In *Proceedings of the 35th Conference on Winter Simulation: Driving Innovation*, pages 1907–1911. Winter Simulation Conference, 2003.

SM Riazul Islam, Daehan Kwak, MD Humaun Kabir, Mahmud Hossain, and Kyung-Sup Kwak. The internet of things for health care: a comprehensive survey. *IEEE Access*, 3:678–708, 2015.

Soraia Oueida and Sorin Ionescu. A resource aware extended workflow model for inconsumable resources: application to healthcare. In *International Conference on Management and Industrial Engineering, Number 8*, pages 377–389. Niculescu Publishing House, 2017.

Soraia Oueida, Moayad Aloqaily, and Sorin Ionescu. A smart healthcare reward model for resource allocation in smart city. *Multimedia Tools and Applications*, 1–22, 2018a.

Soraia Oueida, Pierre Abi Char, Seifeddine Kadry, and Sorin Ionescu. Simulation models for enhancing the health care systems. *FAIMA Business & Management Journal*, 4(4):5, 2016.

Soraia Oueida, Seifedine Kadry, and Pierre Abi Char. A recent systematic review on simulation modeling and emergency departments. *International Journal of Public Health Management and Ethics*, 2(1):40–68, 2017a.

Soraia Oueida, Seifedine Kadry, and Pierre Abichar. Emergency department proposed model: estimating KPIS. In *International Conference on Management and Industrial Engineering, Number 8*, pages 390–403. Niculescu Publishing House, 2017d.

Soraia Oueida, Seifedine Kadry, and Sorin Ionescu. Emergency department simulation: proposed model and optimization. *International Review on Computers and Software*, 12(4):172–184, 2017c.

Soraia Oueida, Seifedine Kadry, and Sorin Ionescu. Estimating key performance indicators of a new emergency department model. *International Journal of User-Driven Healthcare*, 7(2):1–16, 2017e.

Soraia Oueida, Seifedine Kadry, and Sorin Ionescu. Factors influencing patients' satisfaction. In *Stochastic Methods for Estimation and Problem Solving in Engineering*, pages 61–73. IGI Global, 2018b.

Soraia Oueida, Seifedine Kadry, Pierre Abichar, and Sorin Ionescu. The applications of simulation modeling in emergency departments. In *Handbook of Research on Data Science for Effective Healthcare Practice and Administration*, page 94. IGI Global, 2017b.

Soraia Oueida, Yehia Kotb, and Sorin Ionescu. Healthcare satisfaction in catastrophic conditions. *FAIMA Business & Management Journal*, 7(1):63–75, 2019a.

Soraia Oueida, Yehia Kotb, Moayad Aloqaily, Yaser Jararweh, and Thar Baker. An edge computing based smart healthcare framework for resource management. *Sensors*, 18(12), 2018d. doi: 10.3390/s18124307.

Soraia Oueida, Yehia Kotb, Seifedine Kadry, and Sorin Ionescu. Healthcare operation improvement based on simulation of cooperative resource preservation nets for none-consumable resources. *Complexity*, 2018c. doi: 10.1155/2018/4102968.

Soraia Oueida, Yehia Kotb, Sorin Ionescu, and G Militaru. AMS: a new platform for system design and simulation. *International Journal of Simulation Modelling*, 18(1), 2019b.

Spencer S Jones, Todd L Allen, Thomas J Flottemesch, and Shari J Welch. An independent evaluation of four quantitative emergency department crowding scales. *Academic Emergency Medicine*, 13(11):1204–1211, 2006.

SS Chan, NK Cheung, Colin A Graham, and Timothy H Rainer. Strategies and solutions to alleviate access block and overcrowding in emergency departments. *Hong Kong Medical Journal*, 21(4):345–352, 2015.

Stephanie Stokes-Buzzelli, Jennifer M Peltzer-Jones, Gerard B Martin, Maureen M Ford, and Andrew Weise. Use of health information technology to manage frequently presenting emergency department patients. *Western Journal of Emergency Medicine*, 11(4):348, 2010.

Steven J Weiss, Robert Derlet, Jeanine Arndahl, Amy A Ernst, John Richards, Madonna Fernández-Frankelton, et al. Estimating the degree of emergency department overcrowding in academic medical centers: results of the national ed overcrowding study (NEDOCS). *Academic Emergency Medicine*, 11(1):38–50, 2004.

Steven L Bernstein, Vinu Verghese, Winifred Leung, Anne T Lunney, and Ivelisse Perez. Development and validation of a new index to measure emergency department crowding. *Academic Emergency Medicine*, 10(9):938–942, 2003.

Stuart Brenner, Zhen Zeng, Yang Liu, Junwen Wang, Jingshan Li, and Patricia K Howard. Modeling and analysis of the emergency department at University of Kentucky Chandler hospital using simulations. *Journal of Emergency Nursing*, 36(4):303–310, 2010.

Stuart M Butler and Nina Owcharenko. Making health care affordable: Bush's bold health tax reform plan. *Health Care*, 2009.

Syed Saad Andaleeb. Determinants of customer satisfaction with hospitals: a managerial model. *International Journal of Health Care Quality Assurance*, 11(6):181–187, 1998.

Tao Wang, Alain Guinet, Aissam Belaidi, and Beatrix Besombes. Modelling and simulation of emergency services with ARIS and Arena. Case study: the emergency department of Saint Joseph and Saint Luc hospital. *Production Planning and Control*, 20(6):484–495, 2009.

Terry Young, Sally Brailsford, Con Connell, Ruth Davies, Paul Harper, and Jonathan H Klein. Using industrial processes to improve patient care. *British Medical Journal*, 328(7432):162, 2004.

Thomas Bodenheimer. High and rising health care costs. Part 1: seeking an explanation. *Annals of Internal Medicine*, 142(10):847–854, 2005.

Thomas Pyzdek and Paul A Keller. *The Six Sigma Handbook*, volume 4. New York: McGraw-Hill Education, 2014.

Timothy J Reeder and Herbert G Garrison. When the safety net is unsafe real-time assessment of the overcrowded emergency department. *Academic Emergency Medicine*, 8(11):1070–1074, 2001.

TN Gia, M Jiang, AM Rahmani, T Westerlund, P Liljeberg, and H Tenhunen. Fog computing in healthcare internet of things: a case study on ECG feature extraction. In *2015 IEEE International Conference on Computer and Information Technology; Ubiquitous Computing and Communications; Dependable, Autonomic and Secure Computing; Pervasive Intelligence and Computing*, pages 356–363, October 2015. doi: 10.1109/CIT/IUCC/DASC/PICOM.2015.51.

Toni Ruohonen, Pekka Neittaanmaki, and Jorma Teittinen. Simulation model for improving the operation of the emergency department of special health care. In *Simulation Conference, 2006. WSC 06. Proceedings of the Winter*, pages 453–458. IEEE, 2006.

TrendWatch Chartbook. *Trends Affecting Hospitals and Health Systems*. Chicago, IL: American Hospital Association, 2014.

V Augusto and X Xie. A modeling and simulation framework for health care systems. *IEEE Transactions on Systems, Man, and Cybernetics: Systems*, 44(1):30–46, January 2014. ISSN 2168-2216. doi: 10.1109/TSMC.2013.2239640.

Vittorio Miele, Chiara Andreoli, and Roberto Grassi. The management of emergency radiology: key facts. *European Journal of Radiology*, 59(3):311–314, 2006.

W David Kelton. *Simulation with ARENA*. McGraw-Hill, 2002.

W Shi, J Cao, Q Zhang, Y Li, and L Xu. Edge computing: vision and challenges. *IEEE Internet of Things Journal*, 3(5):637–646, October 2016. ISSN 2327-4662. doi: 10.1109/JIOT.2016.2579198.

Waleed Abo-Hamad and Amr Arisha. Simulation-based framework to improve patient experience in an emergency department. *European Journal of Operational Research*, 224(1):154–166, 2013.

Wil MP Van der Aalst. Challenges in business process management: verification of business processes using petri nets. *Bulletin of the EATCS*, 80(174–199):32, 2003.

Wil MP Van der Aalst. The application of petri nets to workflow management. *Journal of Circuits, Systems, and Computers*, 8(1):21–66, 1998.

Wil MP Van Der Aalst. Workflow verification: finding control-flow errors using petri-net-based techniques. In *Business Process Management*, pages 161–183. Springer, 2000.

William Boulding, Seth W Glickman, Matthew P Manary, Kevin A Schulman, and Richard Staelin. Relationship between patient satisfaction with inpatient care and hospital readmission within 30 days. *The American Journal of Managed Care*, 17(1):41–48, 2011.

Yariv Marmor. *Emergency-departments simulation in support of service-engineering: staffing, design and real-time tracking*. PhD thesis, Technion-Israel Institute of Technology, Faculty of Industrial and Management Engineering, 2010.

Yong-Hong Kuo, Janny MY Leung, and Colin A Graham. Simulation with data scarcity: developing a simulation model of a hospital emergency department. In *Proceedings of the Winter Simulation Conference*, page 87. Winter Simulation Conference, 2012.

Yong-Hong Kuo, Omar Rado, Benedetta Lupia, Janny MY Leung, and Colin A Graham. Improving the efficiency of a hospital emergency department: a simulation study with indirectly imputed service-time distributions. *Flexible Services and Manufacturing Journal*, 28(1–2):120–147, 2016.

YT Kotb and AS Baumgart. An extended petri net for modeling workflow with critical sections. In *IEEE International Conference on e-Business Engineering*, pages 134–141. IEEE, 2005.

Zhen Zeng, Xiaoji Ma, Yao Hu, Jingshan Li, and Deborah Bryant. A simulation study to improve quality of care in the emergency department of a community hospital. *Journal of Emergency Nursing*, 38(4):322–328, 2012.

Appendix A: Mathematical Notations

This appendix is dedicated to explaining the mathematical notations and symbols used in this work.

Table A.1   Mathematical Notations

Notation	Description
P	Set of places in the Petri net
T	Set of transitions in the Petri net
T_i	Transition with index i in the Petri net
P_i	Place with index i in the Petri net
i	Input place in Petri net
o	Output place in Petri net
F	Topology of the Petri net. The arcs between places and transitions
τ, t	Two different indices for time
M	Marking, distribution of tokens in places
$M(i)$	Marking of the input
$M(o)$	Marking of the output
M_τ	Marking at a time τ
M_0	Marking at initial time
M_p	Marking of place p
•P	Set of transitions input to place P
P•	Set of transitions output from place P
•T	Set of places input to transition T

(Continued)

Table A.1 (Continued)   Mathematical Notations

Notation	Description
T•	Set of places output from transition T
•*i*	Set of transitions proceeding the input place *i*. This set is always empty.
o•	Set of transitions following the output place *o*. This set is always empty.
a	Any token in a place
a_i	Token index *i* in a place
P_p	Set of pools
$[T_i\rangle$	Set of nodes reachable from transition T_i
$[P_i\rangle$	Set of nodes reachable from place P_i
Λ	Set of capabilities provided by resources and transitions
λ	Set of request for service
R	Set of resources in the Petri net
$\Theta(P_p, R)$	Mapping function that maps resources R to pools of resources P_p
RPN_θ	Any RPN, where $RPN_\theta \in \{RPN\}$

Source: Oueida et al. (2018c)

Note: Table adapted from *Complexity*, p. 13

The information in this appendix appears in the following journal, authored by Soraia Oueida and reprinted by permission of the publisher.

- *Complexity,* Copyright © 2018, Hindawi, [Oueida et al. (2018c)]

Appendix B: AMS Language Primitives

The purpose of this appendix is to explain the language primitives used in order to load the input data into the platform AMS.

Table B.1   Language Primitives

Keywords	Description
STAGE	Represents each stage in the system such as Triage, Registration, etc.
POOL	Represents each pool of resources such as DoctorPool, NursePool, etc.
END	Represents the end of each STAGE or POOL
SET	Used to set the input and output pools as well as the satisfaction weights, the threshold during optimization, the mode and the number of iterations
MARK	Represents the marking of each pool. The marking of pools is the number of resources available for each type.
CONNECT	Used to specify the link between two different nodes
INPUT/OUTPUT	Represents the direction of each link
AS	Used to specify the direction as input or output
PASS	Used with the link connection to pass the type of token such patient, transporter, etc.
INTERVAL	Represents the time interval of each stage to be executed
FROM	Used with the interval to specify the time interval from for each stage
TO	Used with the interval to specify the time interval to for each stage
NAME	Used to assign a name for each stage or pool
TYPE	Used to assign a type for each pool such as patient, nurse, etc.

(*Continued*)

Table B.1 (Continued)   Language Primitives

Keywords	Description
DECISION	Represents the availability of routing the resource to two different locations based on the decision probability
YES	Used to specify that the stage support decision
NO	Used to specify that the stage does not support decision
PERCENTAGE	Represents the probability percentage of a decision
DISTRIBUTION	Represents the distribution type followed by a stage
ORING	Used to specify if a stage may receive different inputs with different attributes
MODE	Represents the mode of simulation; whether during normal flow or catastrophic events
NORMAL	Represents the normal mode of simulation
CATASTROPHIC	Represents the catastrophic mode of simulation
WORKFLOW	Represents the type of the unit whether A or B or Common for all units
A, B, ALL	Used to set the specify the unit attribute. For example: A referring to unit A, B referring to unit B and ALL referring to a common unit
EMPLOYEE WEIGHT	Represents the weight of employee satisfaction factor
MANAGEMENT WEIGHT	Represents the weight of owner satisfaction factor
PATIENT WEIGHT	Represents the weight of patient satisfaction factor
OPTIMIZE	Used to apply model optimization
THRESHOLD	Represents the threshold of the optimization factor
SIMULATE, FOR	Two keywords used to specify the simulation period of time; such as for MINUTES, HOURS and WEEKS
WORKLOAD	Used to set the maximum workload of a resource pool; which reflects the threshold of a resource utilization rate
	Used with the WEIGHT keyword in order to set the workload weight factor
SALARY	Used to specify the pay amount of each resource pool
MAXIMUM	Used with SALARY and WORKLOAD to specify the maximum pay and maximum workload

(Continued)

Table B.1 (Continued)   Language Primitives

Keywords	Description
CONSULTATION, FEES	Two keywords to represent the consultation fees of each patient visiting the ED used during the optimization phase while calculating the hospital's revenue needed for the owner satisfaction calculation
WEIGHT	Represents the salary or workload weight factors used during the optimization phase while calculating the employee satisfaction factor for the reward system
OTHER, EXPENSES	Two keywords representing the extra expenses weight factor used during the optimization phase while calculating the owner satisfaction factor for the reward system
EMPLOYEE, IMPACT	Two keywords representing the customer–resource relationship used during the optimization phase while calculating the patient satisfaction factor for the reward system
EXPECTED, LOS	Two keywords representing the threshold or the expectation of the LoS in the system used during the optimization phase while calculating the patient satisfaction factor for the reward system
MAXIMUM	Used to describe the maximum of a value
NUMBER	Used to specify the number of a value
ITERATIONS	Used to set the number of iterations. Iterations reflect the number of simulation runs
FILE	Used to save the output statistics into a text file

Source: Oueida et al. (2019b).

Note: Table adapted from *International Journal of Simulation Modelling*, p. 37.

The information in this appendix appears in the following journal paper, authored by Soraia Oueida and reprinted by permission of the publisher:

■ *International Journal of Simulation Modelling*, Copyright © 2019, DAAAM Int., [Oueida et al. (2019b)]

Index